Joyously Free!

Stories & Tips to Live Your Truth As LGBTQ+ People, Parents and Allies

JOANIE LINDENMEYER

ELIZABETH ANN ATKINS

JOYOUSLY FREE: Stories & Tips to Live Your Truth as LGBTQ+ People, Parents and Allies

Copyright © 2024 **Elizabeth Ann Atkins & Joanie Lindenmeyer**

All Rights Reserved.

No part of this publication may be reproduced, stored in a retrieval system, or transmitted, in any form or by any means—electronic, mechanical, photocopying, recording, or otherwise—without prior written permission from the publisher, except for the inclusion of brief quotations in a review.

For information about this title or to order other books and/or electronic media, contact the publisher:

Two Sisters Writing & Publishing®

TwoSistersWriting.com

18530 Mack Avenue, Suite 166

Grosse Pointe Farms, MI 48236

ISBN-13: 978-1-956879-54-4 (Hardcover)

ISBN: 978-1-956879-55-1 (Paperback)

ISBN: 978-1-956879-56-8 (eBook)

Printed in the United States of America

All the stories in this work are true.

Cover and Graphic Design: Illumination Graphics.

Dedication

To all the trailblazers on whose shoulders

we now stand.

And to those who are seeking their truth today.

Love always wins!

Acknowledgements

From Elizabeth Ann Atkins

Thank you, God and my Spirit team, for providing the ideas, mental and physical stamina, resources, harmony, and skills that enabled us to create this beautiful book.

Immeasurable gratitude to **Joanie Lindenmeyer** for proposing that we collaborate to write this spirit-inspired book that can bless countless people everywhere. How fun and fascinating to work together to focus our topic, create the outline, and embellish our chapters with the help of our 32 phenomenal contributors from across America.

Teamwork makes the dream work, and it's an absolute honor and privilege to co-captain this literary team with you, Joanie. You are truly an earth angel, and it's been a divine gift to co-create this literary extravaganza that will, as a result, be a gift to people who need it most. May billions of blessings sparkle back on you for being such a blessing to me. Cheers to you, Joanie!

Here's a giant burst of immeasurable gratitude to the other superstars on our team:

Catherine M. Greenspan, co-founder and CFO of Two Sisters Writing & Publishing®. Expressing infinite gratitude and love for your brilliant guidance and editorial expertise throughout the creation, publication, and promotion of this book. You're the best!

Deborah Perdue, founder of Illumination Graphics. Expressing profuse thankfulness and adoration to you for creating the beautiful cover and interior design and formatting. We love how you work your Merlin Magic!

Our 32 contributors from across America. Showering you with billions of thank yous for courageously sharing your stories that can touch lives everywhere. Cheers to YOU!

Jessica Bonosoro, editor and project manager on the Two Sisters Writing & Publishing® team. Thanking you with ebullient joy and relief that you so concisely helped edit this book with great attention to details and deadlines. We appreciate you!

Cat Wilkes, executive assistant on the Two Sisters Writing & Publishing® team. Thanking you for so skillfully tracking and organizing the many moving parts of this project. You make the most beautiful spreadsheets ever, and your help has been a Godsend. Thank you!

Natalie Luterman and Emily Yarmack, publishing assistants on the Two Sisters Writing & Publishing® team. Expressing gratitude for your eagle-eyed editing and proofreading skills, as well as your speedy work, eagerness, and enthusiasm. Great job!

Sean Smith, SEO expert and founder of Ikusa. Giant gratitude for your continued support with TwoSistersWriting.com as well as your creative input. You rock!

And to you, **our readers**, a big burst of gratitude for picking up this book that we hope can help you shine your light from the inside out and cast sunshine into the shadows to illuminate the world with peace and love for all. Stay strong and celebrate!

From Joanie Lindenmeyer

Big, Big, Big thank yous from the top of my heart to each of you ... I couldn't have done it without you!
THANK YOU. I LOVE YOU!

Computer helpers: Diane Weir, Sally Roy, Jill Peroschi, Kennette Babb, Kameron McLean, and Terri Stewart.

Media helpers: Dan Perry Walkup, Cynthia Paulsen, Rebecca Bustamante, and Andrew Walkup.

Attorneys and legal advisors: Peter Spratt and Leah Halpert.

Organization/office: Carolyn House.

The Two Sisters Writing & Publishing® team: Cat and Jessica.

Book Cover font designs: Scott and Joyce Eason, and Steve Childs.

Book Cover Artists: Gail Baker and Deborah Perdue.

Spiritual team: (my unwavering prayer angels) Doris Westoby, Joyce Eason, Ruthie Murray, Maggie Kish, Dan Fowler, Janell Monk, Chloe Mc Crae, all of St. Tim's Episcopal Church Ministers, Bernie Lindley, Linda Lee, Cora Rose, and Marian Welch.

Supporters and encouragers: zillions of friends' and family texts, calls, and emails, The Brookings Bazaar Ladies, my Brookings Pickleball friends, and my "Lezzi" Tuesday Breakfast LGBTQ+ friends.

Book Launch and Southern Oregon Coast Pride Director Laura Erceg.

Oh golly, Here's a drum roll, please . . . to thank, really thank, and I mean really thank the stars of this book!

Our Contributing Writers

To each of you, let me look into your eyes so that you can see and feel the honor and the privilege it is for us to have YOU as a published author, alongside me and Elizabeth in this powerful, life-changing book. Your courage, your tenacity, your fortitude, your trust, and your *Joyously Free* truth overwhelm me. Thank you for exposing the real you, all in the name of helping others! This is a huge, momentous occasion for you and your beloved, that is a legacy all its own. Your unique story will lead to zillions of positive and influential ripple effects. THANK YOU SOOOOOO MUCH. I bless you with a life full of *Joyously Free* moments. **I LOVE YOU!**

My Spiritual Co-Authors:

Carol Tierheimer, my beloved angel who is leaping the mountains and singing her heart out in the heavenly choir. My best friend, confidant, and my lifetime lover who I miss so much!!!

But at the same time, you will always and forever be inside of me! I celebrate and live joyfully and *Joyously Free* each new day, week, month, and year since we met and since your passing on January 30, 2022. Your voice and spirit are alive in words and feelings in this book and beyond. Thank you, sweetie, for your profound love then and now! How fun!

Because of you, I have the courage and awe to live truthfully and *Joyously Free!* WOWIE! WOWZER! **I LOVE YOU, CAROL!**

Jesus, thank you for being the guts, the truth, and the way that burst of your love for me and Elizabeth in this book. You are our higher power!

YIPPEE, **I LOVE YOU, JESUS!**

Catherine Greenspan

Extra special praise and thanks to you, Catherine, for your loyalty and devotion as my friend, publisher, and editor! You are always truthful and joyful. Thank you! Your expert, kind guidance, honest and direct insights for improvements in my writing, and all the steps along the way were exactly what I needed when I most needed it. You kept me and Elizabeth on track!!

You are AMAZING! SHAZAM!

I LOVE YOU, CATHERINE!

Elizabeth Ann Atkins

OMG! How do I even begin to express the thankfulness and gratitude to you, Elizabeth, for co-authoring this book with me?

Bottom line, I wouldn't have done it without you!

From the beginning, you took a risk. This was an "us" book, not a me or a you book. Thank you immensely for your trust in Spirit, trust in me, and trust that we could collaborate, adventure, and make a burst of colors to circle the planet.

Elizabeth, you dreamed bigger, pushed longer and harder, discovered more *Joyously Free* truths, and poured out your brilliance in brain, heart, and expert writing!

You are the Princess Goddess, an earth angel, a visionary, and a dear friend.

Thank you, thank you, and thank you sooooooo soooooo much, Elizabeth, for accepting and celebrating the true me while hysterically laughing at my one-liner jokes and my off-the-wall, silly comments in my writing and with my "props" on podcasts.

Thank you for being patient, compassionate and empathetic, and crying with me as we lived our truths.

In my wildest dreams, I never imagined this moment of writing another book, let alone co-authoring one with a famous pro named Elizabeth Ann Atkins.

You really are the most incredible expert book coach, amazing publisher, and fabulous editor. It is an absolute HONOR AND DELIGHT to have my name and picture next to yours on this self-help book we call *Joyously Free! Stories and Tips to Live Your Truth as LGBGTQ+, People, Parents & Allies*.

YAHOO! Congratulations, Elizabeth!

I bless you and your sister, Catherine, and TwoSistersWriting.com for continued awesomeness!

I LOVE YOU, ELIZABETH!

Hugs and kisses to all, Joanie

Contents

Dedication iii
Acknowledgements v
Prelude xvi
Introduction 1

CHAPTER 1
Be *Joyously Free!*
Enjoy This Incredible Peace and Power 7

Let's Script Your LGBTQ+ Dream Life
Starring the Most Powerful, Peaceful YOU!
By Elizabeth 7

Free at Last: HOME, SWEET HOME with My Sweetie, Carol!
By Joanie 17

Contributors

    My Fierce Resolve to Live Authentically and Unapologetically
    By Anjua Maximo 23

    A Gay Man: Living My Truth & Loving Myself Just As I Am
    By Rodney Howell 26

Tips for Finding Peace and Power to Live Joyously Free! 29

CHAPTER 2
shOUT Loud and Proud!
Coming Out as LGBTQ+ 33

GO FOR IT!
My Coming Out Story
By Joanie 33

Coming Out is Your Choice. Go Within for Guidance
By Elizabeth 41

Contributors

    Coming Out: Grateful for My Journey
    by Charles Pugh 54

    Coming Out as a Bisexual Married Woman and Mom
    By Leah Halpert 59

    Not Ready to Come Out
    By "M"...62

Tips for Coming Out as LGBTQ+ 63

CHAPTER 3
You Got This, Sweetheart!
Courageously Living Your Truth..67

Speaking Our Truth—About a King-Size Bed!
By Joanie..67

Courageously Living My Truth
By Elizabeth... 71

<u>Contributors</u>
    Transgender: From Gray to Vibrant & Full of Life
    By Tay Ryan 77

    I Don't Have to Choose—On Being Bisexual and Loved Just
    As I Am
    By Frida.. 84

Tips for Courageously Living Your Truth 86

CHAPTER 4
KID POWER!
**Loving & Supporting Our LGBTQ+ Kids
as Parents, Guardians & Caring Adults**............................. 89

What If My Child is Gay?
By Elizabeth.. 89

Celebrating Parents Who Are LGBTQ+ & Sharing Unconditional Love
By Joanie..97

<u>Contributors</u>
    A Father's Story: Loving & Supporting My Gay Son
    By Scott Eason...107

    A Mother's Story: Wanting Love, Happiness, and Safety for
    My Gay Son
    By Joyce Eason 109

On Being the Mother of a Gay-Drag-Trans Adult: Stumbles,
Regrets & Love
By Markaye Simpson...112

Thank You for Being My Gay Son
by Janai "Grandma Boom" Mestrovich, M.S. 120

A High School Counselor's Support: No Room for Homophobia
By Sally Roy..126

Tips For Parents, Guardians & Adults Who Love & Support
LGBTQ+ Youth 129

CHAPTER 5
Be an Ally & Advocate:
Teamwork Makes the Dream Work...................................141

Allies and Advocates: Learn, Listen, and Lead
By Elizabeth..141

My Straight A's (Allies): Armored Friends & Family
By Joanie..148

Contributors

A Loving Ally & Joanie's #1 Fan: Her Big Sister
By Gail Baker...152

An Ally & Advocate Empowers a Teen's Transition
By Diane Weir with Bob Weir....................................156

Allies Committed to Changing Lives for the Better
By William Burse with Brittany Poe 157

My Adolescent Confession & Apology
By Kyle Clausen...159

Allyship: A Call to Action
By Pamela Ross McClain, Ph.D. 160

Tips for Being an Ally and/or Advocate 162

CHAPTER 6
How to Heal
Don't Listen to Naysayers.... 165

Stop Throwing Tomatoes!
They Only Bounce Off My Joan of Arc Armor
By Joanie.. 165

Find Power in Your Pain
By Elizabeth... 177

Contributors
    A Gay Man's Transformation Through Trauma
    By Anthony Martinez Beven................................... 194

    Trans Triumph: The Hurricane Is Finally Over & I Love Being
    a Man
    By Will Jaster.. 197

    A Bisexual Woman Navigating Life with Gaydar and Road
    Stand Signs
    By Jenny Leffler 208

    A Gay Man: Celebrating Love & Loss with My Forever Person
    By Michael Martin.. 214

Tips for Healing & Ignoring Naysayers................................216

Photo mosaic of contributors..220

CHAPTER 7
Gay Marriage
I DO, I DO! 223

You Are a Match Made in Heaven
By Joanie 223

I Only Have Enchanted Eyes for You
By Elizabeth.. 234

Contributors
    Lesbian Love of a Lifetime: The Magic of Marriage
    By Doris Beresford and Kathy Mullen 238

A Pastor's Perspective: Spiritual Awakenings That Opened
My World to LGBTQ+ Love
By Father Bernie Lindley...241

Tips for Gay Marriage...249

CHAPTER 8
Religion: Follow Your Own Path to God and Spirituality 257

How to Heal Religious Hurts
By Elizabeth.. 257

Pulpit Hate and Boxing
By Joanie...261

Contributors

The Grandson of Mary and Joseph . . . and the Purple Sofa
By Daniel Perry Walkup... 265

A Gay Man's Sister: The Hurt Never Seems To End
By Kennette Babb... 272

A Married Male Couple Hiding the Truth for Their Baby Godson's Baptism
By Derek.. 277

Questions About a Gay Man Officiating a Straight Wedding
By Skylar Windham 281

TIPS for Experiencing God & Spirit on Your Own Terms 283

CHAPTER 9
I've Got That JOY, JOY, JOY!
How to Create Your *Joyously Free* Life............................. 287

Fall in Love with the New You
By Elizabeth.. 287

How Carol and I Created a *Joyously Free* Life
By Joanie... 294

Contributors
    Lesbian for a Lifetime:
    Peace and Power, Living *Joyously Free!*
    By Eve DeRusha..303

    A Tearful Moment Unites Two LGBTQ+ Souls as Joy
    Takes Flight
    By Jeffrey Church 308

Tips to Create Your *Joyously Free* Life 311

CHAPTER 10
HOW FUN!
Rituals That Help You Live *Joyously Free* 315

Celebrating Yourself with Daily Rituals
By Elizabeth..315

About the Authors + Contact Info 329

Resources..335

Endnotes..337

Prelude

Something has brought you to this book.
You may be an LGBTQ+ person who seeks inspiration from others who have come out. You want to know how they did it, and what you can do to make your journey as smooth as possible.

You may be a parent, guardian, or supportive adult of an LGBTQ+ child, adolescent, teen, or young adult, and are seeking guidance on how to love and support your youth as they come out and create a life that they love.

You may be a sibling, relative, teacher, and/or a friend of an LGBTQ+ person, and you want to know how you can uplift them as an ally and/or advocate.

No matter where you are on your own journey or someone else's journey, this book is for you.

Welcome to this safe space to explore and learn.

Introduction

Consider this book an invitation to live *Joyously Free!* We teamed up to present this book as a valuable, heart-warming gift to YOU!

Enjoy our stories and tips, along with those from brave and diverse LGBTQ+ people, allies, and parents from across America who have contributed their stories.

Let this book inspire you to define what it feels like to live **YOUR truth** as a *Joyously Free* person, or to help a loved one do that.

You have the power to define what that means.

And since we love to share our life experiences and ideas in books, we ask that *you* select a title for your own story.

Call it something like, *Happy Me, Wild & Free.*

Or *Finally Sharing My True Self.*

Or *Opening My Closet Door.*

Or *It's OK to Cry, I'm Your Loving Ally.*

Or, *Smile, My Child, I Love & Support YOU
   Just as You Are.*

Have fun with it! Be creative. Because in each moment of your life, you are literally creating your story that can help those whose lives you touch. *You are awesome!*

Allow the abundance of stories and tips in this collection to inspire you to start a brand new, bold and beautiful chapter in your life. In each chapter, we share intimate insights and beliefs.

For Joanie, that includes her sacred relationship with Jesus and God, which is not limited to a religious setting or denomination. Please read her stories and tips with an open mind to see that Joanie's life mission is to show that you *can* be LGBTQ+, religious, and *Joyously Free* on *your terms,* the way *you* define your relationship with a Higher Power.

Likewise, Elizabeth's guidance for helping you define your LGBTQ+ identity and how to come out, as well as how to heal from any traumas, involves spiritually-inspired meditation and journaling exercises that are life-changing.

This collaboration aims to be **inclusive of all people**, no matter what your spiritual or religious beliefs and practices are, even if you are agnostic or atheist. We invite you to replace references to Jesus and God with Higher Self, which is the infinite power of the Universe that is within you.

We also decided that the best way to present this message would be to highlight and give voice to some of the many individuals who are living *Joyously Free* as LGBTQ+ people, parents, and allies. So we asked dozens of people we know to contribute their stories. What follows are deeply personal essays that can empower your journey. May their stories inspire you to keep searching for those moments when the truth bubbles up and the world responds.

Just like Elizabeth's "You are Goddess" moment that helped her bravely move from the depths of divorce to full empowerment, and Joanie's "Ho Hum Lane" turning point from behind-closed-doors secret love to being out in the world sharing a romantic lifetime with Carol, your moment will come. Believe it will!

If you're already living openly and freely . . . or supporting your children . . . or serving as an ally and/or advocate . . . KEEP IT GOING!

Introduction

We hope to encourage and motivate you to crank it up a notch or ten . . . to burst with joy and live even more out loud and proud.

In fact, **shOUT** about it!

So many people are still, for good and personal reasons, hiding in fear, and staying closeted. We support and encourage anyone who's currently living that story.

Everything happens in divine timing, and it's up to YOU to decide when, how, or *if* you come out or become an ally or advocate who proudly celebrates that your loved one is out.

Sharing your most intimate truths with the world can be scary and downright dangerous. That's why we encourage you to really know your ***why***. In knowing your why, you will figure out ***how*** to live *Joyously Free*.

So why does the world need this book?

Because, despite decades of turmoil, injustice, and inequality directed at LGBTQ+ people—along with racial and economic prejudices toward people of color—tremendous progress has and is happening . . . such as the U.S. Supreme Court legalizing same-sex marriage in 2015.

However, as this book goes to press, more than 100 pieces of anti-LGBTQ+ legislation are making their way through state legislatures. The state of Florida has the "don't say gay" law. Conservative parents, religious organizations, faith communities, and others are leading campaigns to ban queer books from libraries and school curriculums. Some people are so rabidly anti-LGBTQ+ that a fistfight erupted at a board of education meeting for one of the country's largest school districts.

In short, a chilling movement is afoot to reverse the freedoms and silence the voices of LGBTQ+ people, parents, allies, and advocates.

This book is a powerful antidote to that venomous reality.

Joyously Free

Yet, this book is not an angry rant against all of the above.

Our book is a symphony of stories that will make you want to get up and dance with happiness and liberation in the face of hatred, harm, and hurt! As you read and reflect, feel free to add your amazing ideas in the lines and spaces we provide for you throughout each chapter.

It's fuel for your heart and soul to dissolve the ominous thunderclouds of opposition with brilliant rays of sunshine. The only way to get rid of a shadow is to shine light on it.

So we—you!—are each a light. Shine bright into the shadows. Glow up into the person you truly want to become. And together our light will flood the world with positive change on a more progressive trajectory for LGBTQ+ rights and freedoms.

So, who are we—Joanie and Elizabeth—to present this information? How are we called, honored, and qualified to help lead this worldwide march?

First, Joanie is changing lives around the world through her 2023 memoir, *Nun Better: An Amazing Love Story* by Joanie Lindenmeyer with Carol Tierheimer. This unique book showcases the beautiful story of how love blossomed between two Catholic nuns and led to a 40-year romantic adventure for Joanie and Carol. Carol went to heaven in 2022, yet her magnificent spirit, wisdom and truths live on as her angel wings soar and swirl, while her soul dwells amongst us.

Both Joanie and Carol ultimately left religious-vowed life and the church, courageously creating their own LGBTQ+ community during the 1980s when LGBTQ+ singles and couples were enduring hate and deadly violence triggered by the HIV/AIDS epidemic. Also back then, today's freedoms, including legalized same-sex marriage, seemed like a distant, if not impossible, dream.

Now, the popularity and success of Joanie's best-selling book enables her to touch lives everywhere. At frequent in-person

Introduction

events across America, Joanie shines her loving light to create a safe sanctuary for people to reveal their authentic selves with her; this empowers them to speak—and *live*—their truths as LGBTQ+ people, parents, allies, and advocates.

And what qualifies Elizabeth to help guide this transformational journey for you? She is an LGBTQ+ ally!

As the best-selling author of dozens of books and co-founder of Two Sisters Writing & Publishing®, Elizabeth launched a podcast called The Goddess Power Show with Elizabeth Ann Atkins® to encourage people to create personalized "lovestyles" that free you to experience your greatest joy. This includes embracing your LGBTQ+ truths.

Elizabeth believes that all people should be embraced and lavished with love—exactly as our Creator made us. She believes that when our truths are suppressed, an internal maelstrom brews in ways that can hurt an individual's mind and body, and sometimes explode out in harm toward themselves and others.

When we cultivate a society where people are safe to live and love with healthy minds and hearts, then the world becomes a better place.

In addition, Elizabeth long ago became disillusioned by the traditional template that families, religion, and society instill in girls and women to conform to the oppressive standards of being a "good girl."

Elizabeth takes this mission to the next level with her book, *The Biss Tribe: Activating Your Goddess Power by Elizabeth Ann Atkins*. In it, she shares how verbal abuse during a terrible divorce awakened her GoddessPower and inspired her to create a joyous lifestyle and multimedia platform that shows people how to live and love bigger, better, and bolder to manifest their hearts' wildest desires.

Now, in *Joyously Free,* Elizabeth and Joanie share how to create happiness within the reality of pain, rejection, and grief. This journey can take you on a path that sparkles with stardust, blooms with fragrant flowers, flutters with butterflies and magical hummingbirds, radiates bright beams of colors, and glows under glorious rainbows.

We know that life's journeys can meander through a gloomy, treacherous forest where danger lurks in the shadows, like wolves lying in wait to attack your innermost being with fierce criticism, rejection, and loss of family, friends, and even your home, job, or career. You are not alone; we share many resources in this book to help you find the support you need.

We also present a teeter-totter of struggles and sorrows along with happiness and hope, to equip you with the emotional nourishment, soul inspiration, and practical tools to embark on a life that is *Joyously Free!!*

Let's do this, all of us, so that you wake up every morning with excitement, anticipation, and gratitude to experience the most extraordinary version of **you,** living and loving as your truest heart desires.

As Joanie says, LOVE ALWAYS WINS!

And as Elizabeth says, it's time to live bigger, better, and bolder to manifest your heart's wildest desires!

Sending you big hugs and lots of love,
Elizabeth Ann Atkins
Joanie Lindenmeyer

P.S.—Dear reader: Please use the blank spaces in this book to write and/or draw your unique vision of YOU, living *Joyously Free,* as inspired by each chapter.

Chapter 1

Joyously Free!

Enjoy This Incredible Peace and Power

Let's Script Your LGBTQ+ Dream Life & Love
Starring the Most Powerful, Peaceful YOU!

By Elizabeth

Joyously Free!

These two powerhouse words are splashed in big, bold letters amidst exploding rainbow clouds on the cover of this book for a reason: Liberating your mind, body, and spirit as an LGBTQ+ person to live and love as you truly desire opens the gateway to experience pure joy on every level.

You can also do this as a parent, ally, and/or advocate while helping others achieve peace and sovereignty over their lives.

Yes, it can be scary, difficult, and seemingly impossible.

And if it were easy, you and they would already be *Joyously Free*.

As with any goal, it helps to have a guide, and here we are. We want you to have fun . . . be creative . . . and never stop believing until you're living your dream in vibrant, 3-D reality.

Joyously Free

So, when you open this book, you're looking into a portal of infinite possibilities to unleash your wildest imagination and script your LGBTQ+ dream life and love, starring the most powerful, peaceful YOU!

You can even imagine that when you look at these pages, they become a high-definition video screen, streaming scenes from the life that you want to live.

No matter where you are right now, know that you are the writer, producer, and director of your life. You are not an "extra" on the set of somebody else's feature film, where they direct the dialogue and scenes for you to experience.

You are a superstar, and now's your time to take center stage and rock your role as the best **you** ever. This applies whether you are an LGBTQ+ person, parent, relative, ally, or advocate.

So, get ready to use the power of your pen to script the blockbuster story of your best life, and/or to help others do that. All you need are:

- An open mind and heart;

- A desire to step into your starring role;

- The imagination to dream bigger than ever;

- A willingness to use writing and/or the untapped power within yourself to boldly envision your best life;

- An openness to receive guidance from spiritual sources and/or your Higher Self;

- Belief in yourself that you *can* be and do anything; and

- Courage and confidence to lavish yourself and others with love.

Guess what!? If you feel that you're lacking any of the above, we're going to guide you every step of the way, while referring you to resources that can assist you and accelerate your journey.

So, before we begin, let me share why I'm so passionate about teaming up with Joanie to help you make this magic happen as an LGBTQ+ person, parent, ally, and/or advocate.

Sex is Taboo—So Liberating It Is the Ultimate Empowerment

Our intimate desires are the most taboo, secret, awkward, uncomfortable, potentially embarrassing, and private aspect of being a human being. These desires can be the scariest thing to acknowledge to ourselves, share with other people, and/or reveal publicly.

So, when you find the courage and confidence to showcase your most intimate truths for the world, not caring what anyone thinks because you are loving yourself and your life on your own terms, then you are *Joyously Free*.

Sadly, devastating and even deadly consequences can result. That's why so many metaphorical closets are hiding frightened LGBTQ+ individuals, while other people, rules, and fears are barricading the doors so they can't or won't come out.

So, please do as Joanie and her loving, lifetime partner and eventual spouse Carol did as a lesbian couple back during the dangerous 1980s: **always put safety first.**

We want you to be *Joyously Free*, but first and foremost, we want you to be safe and stable. So, even if you feel stuck and scared right now, you can create a solid strategy for independence, which may include moving to another city, earning a scholarship to college that pays for room and board, living with LGBTQ+ roommates, and exploring an endless list of possibilities.

Besides the obvious point of staying out of harm's way, safety includes maintaining financial support. If you are a teen, you must navigate your family dynamic. For example, too many trans teens suffer from disapproving parents who kick them out of the family home. For adults, losing a job can have devastating effects on a family. So please consider the consequences of how your coming out will affect your safety, well-being, and ability to support those who depend on you.

Next, let's acknowledge that it's really nobody's damn business what you do behind closed doors to share passion, pleasure, love, and commitment.

But we live in a world that *makes it* their business. Only 21 years ago, Texas and 13 other states had laws prohibiting "sodomy." Then in 2003, the U.S. Supreme Court nullified those laws in *Lawrence v. Texas 539 U.S. 558 (2003)*. This ruling made "all forms of private, consensual non-procreative sexual activities between two consenting individuals of either sex (especially of the same sex) legal in every U.S. state and territory," according to Wikipedia.

But while the laws have changed, other forces still flex their power to intimidate people into conforming to their discriminatory or prejudicial rules. For too many LGBTQ+ people, pleasure and power have been stolen by oppressive families, cultures, schools, religions, and traditions that have used fear, guilt, shame, and even violence to confine individuals to society's definition of what human sexuality "should" be.

It's time to take that power back. When we embrace and celebrate our birthright to enjoy our bodies and all the glory of our six senses, as well as every aspect of our lives, with whomever we desire as consenting adults, we reject society's conventions on the most intimate level, and that empowers us to create a life that sparkles with passion and purpose.

That makes us *Joyously Free!*

Unfortunately, until we reach that triumphant state, our daily realities aren't in sync with our deepest desires to truly enjoy how we feel about ourselves and how we experience other people and the world. So let's explore how to flip the switch inside ourselves to activate the energy that manifests the mind shifts, the people, and the experiences that we need to maximize our infinite potential as unique individuals.

Let Your Anger & Hope Inspire a Mission to Improve the World

You have the power to create innovative solutions that improve life for yourself, for LGBTQ+ people, and for the entire world.

I do this in many ways, as a journalist, as a best-selling author, and as a podcaster. In fact, I created and host The Goddess Power Show with Elizabeth Ann Atkins® to explore innovative ways that people are living and loving, with the hopes of finding an exciting, fulfilling lovestyle for myself and listeners/viewers. My podcast on YouTube, Spotify, and Apple Podcasts features interviews with trailblazers who exemplify my mission to activate the infinite energy within ourselves to live bigger, better, and bolder and manifest our hearts' wildest desires.

Past episodes include interviews with several bisexual women, as well as lesbians such as Mariah Hanson, founder of The Dinah, the world's most celebrated queer women/lesbian event. Every September, thousands of women from around the world enjoy a long, sun-splashed weekend of pool parties, DJs, dancing, and connecting in a safe, exciting space in Palm Springs, California.

In 1991, Mariah had a vision inspired by her desire to create fun, safe spaces for queer women to gather, meet, and celebrate. She took action, and this legendary event was born.

What can you do to create something that makes the world a better place for LGBTQ+ people? It starts with being true to yourself, and if you're called to innovate, you'll know and the Universe will respond with the resources you need to make it happen.

Joyously Free

My calling birthed The Goddess Power Show, and its mission applies to LGBTQ+ empowerment, as I wrote on TheGoddessPowerShow.com:

"Welcome to a fun, limitless realm, where you're free to explore traditionally taboo topics that help you fly fearlessly and fiercely forward into a whole new way of living, loving, and thriving, personally and professionally."

Liberating your LGBTQ+ truth is obviously personal, so what do I mean by professional? Well, once you free your mind and step boldly into your most authentic life, you'll be bursting with energy and ambition to devote your time and effort to work that helps you and others.

You may feel inspired to change your job or career by doing something as bodacious as opening a restaurant/bar, like the vibrant lesbian gathering place called Dana's on "The L Word," the Showtime series that aired from 2004 to 2009. The trailblazing show created by Ilene Chaiken was the first TV series featuring a cast of lesbians and bisexual women. The absolutely enthralling experience of watching this series, which is available to view online, continues to affirm and empower generations of queer women. And it all started with a vision by Ilene Chaiken to cast a lesbian rainbow over the starkly heterosexual landscape of television just 20 years ago.

Similarly, Vito Russo was disturbed by the media's sensational portrayal of HIV/AIDS during the 1980s, so he co-founded the media watchdog group GLAAD—the Gay and Lesbian Alliance Against Defamation, which has become a powerful resource.

And 23-year-old LGBTQ+ activist Jazz Jennings became an icon of trans activism and education through her TV show, books, social media, and her TransKids Purple Rainbow Foundation. After she told her parents—at age two—that she was a girl born in a male body, her mother and father supported her transition

Chapter 1 – Joyously Free

and shared their experiences with Barbara Walters on *20/20* in 2007, shining the first major media spotlight on a trans child.

You don't have to do anything as huge as starting a festival, a TV series, an organization, or a multimedia platform. But you can commit your time and energy to empowering LGBTQ+ people, parents, allies, and advocates in ways that resonate with your identity and passions.

For example, you could start an online or in-person support group for trans teens, or you could work *for* an established company or organization that is LGBTQ+ focused.

How exciting and fulfilling would it be to serve as the resource that *you* once needed when you began your journey, to help people who are embarking on their own rainbow path and desperately need a trusted guide?

It's Time for Your LGBTQ+ Glow-Up!

It's time to liberate your mind, body, and spirit from oppressive beliefs and behaviors that have kept us small, stuck, scared, and confined inside the conformist boxes that society tries to place us in as babies.

How do we escape those boxes?

By stepping through a portal of love and joy that activates our power to create the most sensational version of ourselves. This power can embolden you to take your LGBTQ+ living and loving to stratospheric levels that fill you with euphoria and awe every day, and help you weather life's storms with grace and peace.

That power is like a dormant starburst waiting for you to give it permission to explode inside you. This book is the spark, so you can glow from the inside out to illuminate the shadows within yourself, then light up the world in your own unique way.

So **how** do you activate this infinite power within yourself to live *Joyously Free?*

Joyously Free

The First Step to Being *Joyously Free* is to Know What You Want

You can't reach a destination if you don't know where you're going. And sometimes you don't know exactly where you want to go. You *do* know that you want to escape from your current reality into some faraway promised land where you feel happy in an environment you love. But destinations can be as varied as the dazzling lights and vibrant crowds of a big city, an intimate country inn, a plush resort on a tropical island, or a cozy Nordic cabin nestled in the snow and pine trees. Which best suits your fancy?

For now, start contemplating what living and loving *Joyously Free* looks like for you. Don't worry if you don't know all the details. It starts with a feeling, a revelation deep inside your heart and soul.

Now let's write about it. You can get started on the lines below, but please start a notebook, a journal, a computer file, an app, or notes on your phone, and write daily about your vision for your *Joyously Free* self and life.

Writing is one of the most powerful tools you can use to figure things out, all within the privacy of your pen and paper, or your keyboard and screen.

When you pour your feelings and ideas onto the page or screen, what you want will begin to crystalize into a clear vision of how your *Joyously Free* life looks and feels.

Start by describing a snapshot of your future self and life, or a scene that plays out like a filmstrip from the mental movie projector inside your head.

Allow the vision to unfold, unhindered by any critical eyes or voices or forces that have kept you from exploring your truth. Set the scene for this vision to materialize in a space where you are free! This may mean moving to a city with a large LGBTQ+ population where you can find your community and show your true colors.

Chapter 1 – Joyously Free

As you write, let your imagination run wild, because you are the screenwriter, director, and producer of your epic life. Describe how you as the star of this show thinks, talks, works, loves, dresses, and plays. What is the soundtrack? Blast it in Dolby stereo surround sound! Who is the supporting cast? What are the major plotlines? What are the conflicts and resolutions?

Don't worry if you think you're not a writer. You are!

Joanie—a former Catholic nun and retired physical education teacher—had never written a book, and she rocked it with *Nun Better: An Amazing Love Story,* which became a best seller! Plus, if you compose text messages, emails, and social media posts, you *are* a storyteller. So know that, because it's time to shine the spotlight on you as you take center stage.

The options are limitless and they're yours for the taking! Remember that this exercise is totally private. Nobody has to see it or revise it or tell you no. Your answer is Yesssssss!

So, as you write, know that **you have the right** to conceive and manifest your vision. It's *your* life, so be honest and creative and bold! Make it fabulous!

This writing exercise is totally optional. If you don't want to write and prefer to keep reading, please skip this section.

Describe your vision for your *Joyously Free* self and life:

_____

_____

_____

_____

_____

Do this exercise every day. Fill your journal or notebook or digital files with daily visions, ideas, and strategies. Let the story unfold, and believe that you can make it happen in reality.

If you don't like to write, use the audio or video app on your phone to talk out loud and record your vision. You can also do voice-to-text on your computer or tablet, so it will automatically type the words as you speak. You can also go "old school" and use a hand-held recorder.

We'll dive deeper into this manifestation process in the next chapter. But meanwhile, let the ideas burst in your mind and heart as brilliantly and brightly as the rainbow clouds that are exploding on the cover of this book.

In fact, look at the book cover for inspiration. Imagine those colorful clouds billowing inside you, clearing away hurts and fears and questions, to reveal a crystal-clear vision of the true you—stepping out into the world with courage, confidence, and pride.

You can do this, and the time is now!

Chapter 1 – Joyously Free

**Free at Last:
HOME, SWEET HOME with My Sweetie, Carol!**

By Joanie

Zillions of exhilarating moments sparkle like stars on my life's journey, and the extra-bright ones illustrate the thrill of discovering who I am. They also illuminate where, when, and why God was calling me to be more worldly and *Joyously Free* after years of uncertainty and secrecy.

I want you to experience this liberation, and that's why my heart and soul are inspired to share this particular story first. It's all about taking the first step into liberation.

On a glorious day in August 1986, Carol and I were officially embarking on a lifetime adventure of joy and freedom.

We sat in her gold four-door sedan, owned by the Sisters of St. Joseph, in the realtor's parking lot in the logging and fishing town of Aberdeen, Washington. We had scoured the classified ads in the local *World* newspaper, calling to inquire about every possibility of housing, with zero success.

Yet we beamed like sunshine, because we were taking the bold step of living together. No more sneaking in secrecy at the convent or cramming two women onto one twin bed.

Now we were making it official by courageously and confidently following our hearts and souls to create our own home, sweet home.

If you're seeing this through today's lens of LGBTQ+ freedoms, let me help you focus back on the harsh realities that we faced about 40 years ago.

First, we were Catholic nuns. I had just left the convent, thus liberated from the three vows of poverty, obedience, and

Joyously Free

chastity—known as the vow of celibacy—but Carol was still officially a religious sister.

Romantic love and sex were strictly prohibited!

And it was a very dangerous time to come out as gay or lesbian. The HIV/AIDS epidemic was triggering fear, rejection, hate, and deadly violence toward LGBTQ+ people. Today's freedoms—including the legalization of same-sex marriage—were only a distant and seemingly impossible dream.

Despite all of this, on that day, Carol's wide, contagious smile tickled me as I stared at her with my arm hairs perked up, facing the sun rays that were shooting through the gray clouds.

No wonder it's called Gray's Harbor.

Here I am, I thought, *FREE from my temporary religious vows, after serving five years as a nun.* I felt confident in this choice because I was following words that Jesus had shared with me:

"Joanie, leave the convent. I need you to be more worldly."

"OK, Jesus," I responded. "I will!"

I had heard my Higher Power's voice so clearly during my two intense years of discernment to decide yay or nay on whether to make final vows.

Now, my heart felt like it was doing backflips of bountiful joy because we—Sister Carol and I—were publicly starting our journey together as women in love.

She was still officially a Sister of St. Joseph, but her heart was telling her to leave her vows and her religious community, and live with me, her lover.

We exuded our incredible peace and power in knowing deep down that this would all be phenomenally fantastic. Together, we would make life work in our unique, beautiful ways. Our freedom and joy would be unlimited and shared with others. All we had was faith and love!

Chapter 1 – Joyously Free

Sure enough, the world affirmed us, starting with a serendipitous twist that we viewed as a "holy moment." It happened when the realtor told us that her mother-in-law had recently passed away and we could rent her now-vacant home.

Thrill of a lifetime! Shazam, yes!

"Here's the address, keys, and directions," the realtor told us. "Go check it out: 228 Ho Hum Lane."

The little note with the directions danced in my hands as I giddily bounced in the passenger seat while Carol drove the nun-mobile. Within seconds, we gasped at the sight before us. Carol spoke in a tone of wonder and exuberance: "Look!! Joanie, a rainbow!!"

Tears welled in my eyes. "I see it, sweetie!"

Oh, the colors were magnificent, brilliant, and bright. A spectrum of delight.

"It's for us. God is with us," Carol proclaimed in a higher-pitched, excited tone that sounded like music to me. "And look, it's exactly where we need to drive to."

"Yes, love," I said, "follow that rainbow!"

No written directions needed for this adventure!

Guess where the rainbow ended? Or should I say, guess where the arc of colors began?

Carol raced the car into the housing development marked with a large wooden sign at the entrance to Leisure Manor mobile home park.

Oh yes, that was so fitting for us—leisure, no worries. All is well with my soul.

Carol practically hydroplaned over speed bumps while I frolicked like a jumping bean in the passenger seat. This was our style: free and wild!

With the rainbow as our guide, the splashes of the colors affirmed being "OUT!" Out from the convent buildings and lifestyle that stymied, halted, and forbade our love. That was no longer our "call" or vision of life. God had changed our life completely!

Have you ever felt that joyously wild, erratic, passionate power of true freedom? It's absolutely AMAZING!

God's everlasting promises and joys were waiting for us at 228 Ho Hum Lane. We felt like we were in Noah's ark, spotting the dove carrying the olive branch and the rainbow turning to bright, golden, warm sunlight.

Oh my golly!

As soon as Carol parked, we jumped out of the car. I bounced up the four steps onto the metal porch. I felt nothing but sheer exhilaration. Carol turned the front door key in one simple movement and we were home!

Our prayers had been answered. Alleluia.

Nearly exploding with anticipation, we grabbed each other's hands, entwining our fingers in our special love hold and toured from room to room. Despite the gray day, sunbeams seemed to pour in from every direction, dancing on the walls, floors, and our faces.

Classic living and dining room furniture accentuated the homey feel of this grandma-style house. Together we envisioned the glass shelves within the built-in cabinetry displaying our simple, nun-like nick knacks of angels, crosses, stones, and shells.

This experience brings to mind Susan Boyle's song, "I Dreamed a Dream."

Because in those moments, we could feel and dream it all! The shag carpet would give us plenty of space to twist and shout. Never had we imagined we'd have our very own dance floor. We didn't fret that we had no beds. We knew everything would work out great! We could set up our sleeping bags on the floor or sofa cushions. That would do until we could buy our dream bed: a king-size waterbed.

Chapter 1 – Joyously Free

Our first home together was a treasure, a gift from above; a dead woman's house was now turned into a love nest for two grown women.

We had our abode. Our place to be us! A place to share meals, laughter, conversations, games, guitar playing, singing, prayers, and fun with friends. We'd make new friends in this place. Our old friends and family from afar would flock to us. They would be so excited to come visit, stay in our guest bedroom, and get to know the real us, Carol and Joanie.

Our first home signified so much. The rental on Ho Hum Lane provided a safe, private space for fun and intimacy. A place where our love could deepen and where we could be free to be our joyful selves. Oh, such freedom! No more hiding or holding back. Now we could have lip-locking smooches and passionate kisses as we twirled and swirled in love. Finally a place to intimately hold and caress each other and make passionate, sacred sexual love. We were in paradise as our convent bedroom secrets became a thing of the past.

As we settled in, our two heartbeats were now one heart, pumping and flowing. We were alive—joyful and peaceful as we lived everyday to the max with an attitude of gratitude.

Oh what a feeling. Yippee!

Contributors

You're about to meet dozens of brave, dynamic people across America, whom we invited to contribute their stories that can inform and inspire your LGBTQ+ journey.

Starting here and in each chapter, you'll meet these fascinating folks who are driven to persevere through pain, fear, and the shadowy unknown. They live by the promise of peace and love that awaits under the rainbow in the sparkling pot of gold that symbolizes a *Joyously Free* life.

May you glean golden nuggets from their stories that empower your path as an LGBTQ+ person, parent, ally, or advocate.

Love always wins!

Chapter 1 – Joyously Free

My Fierce Resolve to Live Authentically and Unapologetically

By Anjua Maximo

"When did you know?"
It's a question I've been asked countless times since publicly coming out, yet the answer eluded me until one fateful day in a super trendy restaurant in Union Square.

Picture it: the vibrant energy of New York City in the 1990s, pulsating house music floating through the air as I stood at my post, playing hostess to a sea of New York's most beautiful and fabulous diners. And then she walked in—exuding confidence and a hint of swagger, rocking baggy overalls and an oversized T-shirt like she owned the place.

In that moment, a whirlwind of emotions swept over me—fear, curiosity, and a strange sense of recognition that I couldn't quite put into words. For years, I'd stuck to society's script, never daring to question my desires or deviate from the norm. But there she was, stirring something inside me that I hadn't even realized was there—an attraction to another woman.

But fear gripped me tightly, shutting my newfound desires in a little box of uncertainty. What would this revelation mean for my identity, my relationships, my very sense of self?

What's crazy is that my family and friends would have accepted me. There may have been a few doubters and a few who didn't approve. My mom may have had a moment, but ultimately, she would have been fine and would've been ready to fight anyone who dared say anything negative against me. My dad would've been quick to learn all about being an ally and gone out of his way, if not a little over the top, to ensure I felt accepted.

And yet, despite my heart telling me this, the thought of traversing uncharted territory filled me with trepidation, leading me to bury my truth beneath layers of denial and self-doubt.

Years later, in my late twenties, I finally opened up to my husband at the time. His support was unwavering, but I struggled to accept myself. I didn't know what I wanted. Despite having someone willing to explore this journey with me, I hesitated, clinging to the safety of denial.

It would take nearly three decades for me to shed the weight of denial and embrace the full spectrum of my identity. Over this time, I discovered the power of personal development work, of understanding the importance of knowing what I valued over what I was taught to value, and to really begin to trust that my voice was my best tool for self-advocacy.

It was in these moments that I had to decide what felt too important to deny any longer about myself, about the life I wanted to lead and about the partner I wanted alongside me as I did. On this journey of self-actualization is where self-compassion and self-love were introduced to me.

Self-love and self-compassion formed my life raft when I risked drowning in a sea of guilt, because I was choosing to leave my marriage in order to honor my truth.

Through years of introspection and self-discovery, I came to realize that my queerness was not a flaw to be concealed or casually forgotten, but a vibrant thread woven into the tapestry of my being.

Gone are the days of regret and self-recrimination, replaced instead by a fierce resolve to live authentically and unapologetically. Life really is so damn short! Each day is a celebration of self-love and self-acceptance, a testament to the courage it takes to defy societal expectations and embrace one's truth.

So, when people ask, "When did you know?" I smile, knowing

Introduction

that it wasn't a single moment of clarity, but a lifetime of learning to love and accept myself. And as I step into this new chapter, I do so with gratitude and an unbound spirit—*Joyously Free* at last.

Anjua Maximo is a life and sensual movement coach, guiding women on a transformative journey towards self-discovery and empowerment. Specializing in overcoming personal development obstacles and embracing authentic sexual expression, Anjua's approach inspires women to reclaim their confidence and live life fully. Connect with her on TikTok and Instagram @mamagoddessqueenwoman.

Please watch Anjua Maximo's inspiring interview on the YouTube channel for The Goddess Power Show with Elizabeth Ann Atkins®.

Joyously Free

Living My Truth & Loving Myself Just As I Am

By Rodney Howell

Growing up as a gay man was very challenging, starting from childhood when I realized that something was different about me.

My first thought was, *Is there anyone else out there who's like me?* I always thought I was the only one. How scary is that as a child!

My second thought was, *What would my mother and father think if they found out? Would they still love me if they knew I'm different?* I never wanted to disappoint my parents.

You see, I grew up during an era—the 1970s—when it was not acceptable to be gay. That was something that you had to hide and leave in the closet under lock and key. Back then, you had to pretend to be something that you weren't, just to be accepted by others. Often, these same folks who would so quickly dish out disapproval were deeply wounded themselves and struggling with their own major life challenges.

Yes, everybody wears a mask. Everyone has issues, but it was clear that homosexuality had better not be one of them. I have always felt that everything else was accepted in life, except for being gay. As if horrified critics were wondering, "How could you possibly desire or be in love with someone of the same sex?"

When I was young, I prayed many days for God to take this desire away. So I decided to seek Christ and go to church. That's what you do when you're looking for deliverance or healing, or so I had been told.

I went to church, only to learn from the preacher's interpretation of religious teachings—which was echoed by his flock—that I was an abomination unto God, that I was a nasty pervert, a pedophile, and a disgusting person. And to top it off,

Chapter 1 – Joyously Free

that I was going straight to hell.

The Christian people even had names for people like us: faggots, sissies, queers, and a couple of hand gestures. That was horrifying to me!

I thought everyone was accepted by Christ. I didn't want to be the things that they said I was. I had a loving, kind heart and a true, gentle, and genuine spirit. I loved everyone, especially Jesus Christ. I felt His spirit dwelling inside me.

I couldn't understand why He made me like this, only to throw me away and cast me into the fiery pit of hell. What had I done to deserve this? I was only a kid. I had never had a sexual encounter, but I liked boys, and because of that, to the world and the church, I was just a horrible, disgusting faggot.

As I became an adult, I accepted Christ as my personal savior. Yes, I have a personal relationship with Him. I got to know Him for myself, and discovered that I am not the horrific person that the church had led me to believe that I was.

I am a strong believer of being true to thy own self. I've never been the man who tried to be something that I was not. I had too much self-respect and self-love. I am that guy who is comfortable with people being uncomfortable with who I am.

Being a same-gender loving person, there are many things we have to survive and overcome:

1. Disappointing our parents;

2. Being erased in our classes;

3. Being bullied;

4. Surviving HIV;

5. Being stigmatized by religion;

6. Fighting the government for our rights; and

Joyously Free

    7. Losing our jobs.

Some of us have chosen to die rather than to be who we are. And some of us choose to live secret lives.

I don't fully understand why I am the way I am. Some people call this "a choice," but have you ever asked yourself, "Did I choose my sexuality?"

The choice that I did make was to love myself.

Rodney Howell is an entrepreneur in Metro Detroit, Michigan. Please watch Rodney's inspiring interview on the Two Sisters Writing & Publishing® YouTube channel on the "White Party" playlist.

Tips for Finding Peace and Power to Live *Joyously Free!*

Attend Pride events and visit affirming community centers. Read books about queer struggles and learn how people find their peace and power. Perhaps their blueprints for personal happiness can provide ideas about how to create your best life.

Draw courage and strength from your grandparents and ancestors. Know your family's history and glean courage from their lives, even if they weren't queer. Your parents, grandparents, and ancestors survived, and may have even risked their lives for the greater good. Whether they fought in or survived wars, marched for civil rights and women's rights, lived through the Great Depression, triumphed over health crises, immigrated to America with no money and hearts full of hope, or blazed new trails in business and the nonprofit world, the people who preceded us passed down their DNA for us to survive and thrive through the toughest circumstances. Tap into that genetic strength to activate your courage to live *Joyously Free.*

Know that haters are out there. Practice safety first. Be aware of your surroundings. Respond with kindness rather than anything that fuels their fires or that could cause you or your loved ones harm. Contact the appropriate authorities, when it is safe to do so, if you feel threatened at school, work, home, or in public.

Hang on to each other! Cherish your LGBTQ+ friends and family. You never know when you'll need them or they'll need you. You can find your tribe at meet-ups and events, as well as in online forums. Hang out with positive, open-minded people. Let them know that you're available 24/7 if they need to talk, and hopefully they will extend that same offer to you.

Be thankful for the smallest of things about the people in your inner circle. Say "I love you" multiple times a day—to yourself and to whomever you value in your life. Smile big with a genuinely happy face. Say "please" and "thank you" and mean it. Treat your tribe with love and respect and they will shower it back on you.

Believe in miracles. When life gets tough, know that you are loved by a Higher Power. Make time to get quiet, rest your mind and heart, and pray for inner peace and world peace. Believe that when you pray and have faith, even the most difficult circumstances can resolve in ways that feel miraculous.

Trust your gut—and your heart. When you trust your gut, you are honoring your intuition. Scientific research shows an actual biological connection between your brain and your gut, so when you get that sudden "hunch" out of the blue, listen to it and act accordingly. Your intuition is your superpower. It is your Higher Self speaking your truth and what's best for you.

Sometimes a fear voice inside of us can sound like intuition. How can you discern between the two? Ask your heart. Literally. Put your hand on your heart, and in your mind, ask your heart the question that is causing confusion.

The answer that comes faster than you can think is the truth. This answer may come so fast, that it doesn't

Chapter 1 – Joyously Free

have time to form words. It's simply a feeling or a knowing. Write it down immediately, while it's fresh and before fear thoughts can dismantle it.

Respect the journey. In many ways, this is a solo trip; only you know what peace and power feel like for you as as an LGBTQ+ person, parent, ally, or advocate. If you're not sure, then get quiet and still, then meditate or journal about how to cultivate peace and power in your life.

You can get great clarity by thinking about how you feel power-*less* and the opposite of peaceful. What circumstances need to change to turn those situations around? What can you do to make that happen? How can you find your freedom, the most spectacular burst of fireworks of your authentic hopes and dreams? Have fun and celebrate it!

Chapter 2

shOUT Loud and Proud!

Coming Out as LGBTQ+

GO FOR IT!
My Coming Out Story

By Joanie

I knew I was "different" in first grade. I wore shorts under my blue-green plaid uniform skirt at Saint John the Evangelist School. I was enamored with my teachers: the beautiful, mysterious, happy, kind Catholic nuns and sisters, as we called them.

In elementary school, my friendship attractions were all female. Yet I couldn't put words to it at that young, naive age. I was a boney kid, hence my nickname, "Bones." My siblings still call me that endearing name and it makes us all giggle.

Greggie was my best, brother-like friend in class, in play, and as a neighbor five houses up the street. Back then, in the 1960s and 1970s, the culture was heterosexual-dominant, and I was never around gay people. Or so I thought.

During puberty, I heard two labels way too often: hetero and homo. Even then, I despised those words. It was the tonnage,

Joyously Free

the attitude, the stigma of hate, the division they created, and a box that I and others felt pushed into.

At the time, something bigger was changing in my mind and heart. I was learning and having feelings about prejudice on a personal level regarding my sexual orientation and sexual identity. Later, words formed around these feelings: straight and gay.

Either way, I was coming out to myself, knowing I was different and beautiful and riding a rollercoaster of teen hormonal emotions.

Little did I know that at this young age, I was growing in strength and character and would have another name, a label, a stereotype attached to me in the future: a lesbian. In my gut, it felt terrible, hurtful, and wrong when I heard people say it by stressing the *les* in lesbian, placing hard, negative emphasis on the first syllable. People did the same with homosexual, stressing the *homo*.

Yet at the same time, this was my first time coming out . . . TO MYSELF!

I played with Greggie until eighth grade, but I liked a "something special feeling" with Susan.

During my pre-teen and teen years, my girl friends began wanting to hold hands with boys. I thought, *Oh, yuck!* In my heart, I wanted to hold hands with Susan and Terry and Kathy—all girls.

I kept that secret to myself, hugging and kissing my large stuffed tiger, Henry, night after night, thanking Jesus in my silent prayers for making me, me. I knew down deep that I was OK, wonderfully made, and that Jesus would always take care of me.

Meanwhile, I loved the intensity of playing fast and hard outdoors, especially running, skipping, and climbing. By the end of the day, when it was too dark to see the tree branches or the kickball, I was sweaty and dirty and stained purple from the

Chapter 2 –ShOUT Loud & Proud!

berries I'd snacked on from the trees in our yard. Neighborhood games on the New Jersey Street asphalt and in my friends' backyards delighted my soul.

Dad and Mom gifted us with a basketball hoop attached to our garage roof next to the 20-foot-tall purple-blooming bougainvillea tree. I loved climbing that tree to retrieve balls that got stuck on the garage roof.

Jumping made me feel like *The Flying Nun*, my favorite TV show that aired from 1967 until 1970 on ABC, starring Sally Field as Sister Bertrille. This inspired my secret dream and bedtime pillow chat with Jesus. I felt called to be a nun, too.

I witnessed my friends struggle with heavy-duty drama in their boyfriend-and-girlfriend relationships. I didn't want that: I just wanted to play and have fun.

I kept my dirty blonde hair in a carefree bob cut tucked under my backwards-facing baseball helmet. My bowl cut was great for keeping my eyes open while swimming and boogie boarding in the warm Pacific Ocean at South Mission Beach. My shag hairstyle suited me well as the talented and team-oriented sports champ God made me to be. With a face full of kid freckles, I was a zealous "just watch me" kind of fireball.

I loved sports and Jesus so much that I always had a ball of some sort to shoot, throw, bump, chase, or kick. My all-time favorite portrait of Jesus today is what I call my "soccer Jesus." It looks like He's giving it His all with an extraordinary attitude, showcasing a messy athletic game, ending with sweat-soaked hair, big brown eyes, and skin that looks like the cells are plumped up from a cardio workout that leaves His neck sweaty, moist, and shiny. I can almost smell His body odor in that picture.

Like Jesus, I "gave it my all" in life. This was apparent when I handled my family responsibilities, which included household chores: setting and clearing the dinner table with my sister, Terri; washing and drying the dishes; and dusting the heirloom wooden buffet furniture from Grandma Ruby Irene from the floor to the ceiling.

I gave it my all, loving to ride my blue Schwinn bike, feeling the wind tickle my face, hearing the swish of fat tires speeding around corners, jumping up and down curbs, and closing my mouth to prevent bugs from flying into it.

I gave it my all while attending Catholic mass for the sole purpose of receiving Jesus in communion, eating the beige wafer bread host so He would be inside me for protection and unconditional love. I gave it my all in being extra thankful for my family and friends, trying my very best to be kind, helpful, and happy, and to say nice things rather than hurtful or sarcastic words.

As a young child, I sought from Mom and Dad extra hugs and kisses on my "little accidents" or bloody injuries. My "go for it" behavior often required Band-Aids to cover my bright red gushes. Thank goodness for the small bottle of merthiolate antiseptic medicine to prevent infections, along with my dear family's tender loving care. Plus, talking with Jesus and listening for His responses made it all better.

As life adventures continued with gusto, I earned a college degree and a California teaching credential. Then I joined the Catholic religious order of the Sisters of St. Joseph of Carondolet and was missioned to Lewiston, Idaho.

There, I received the greatest gift: a lifetime with Carol Tierheimer. I believe that God orchestrated for us to fall passionately, spiritually, and secretly in love. At the time, we were committing our entire lives to the Church. Yet upon meeting, our soul-deep connection was so strong, we were certain that our calling as nuns had been God's plan to place us each on life paths that would merge and take a new, glorious direction, together.

Chapter 2 –ShOUT Loud & Proud!

The song, "Do You Know Where You're Going To?" by Diana Ross and the Supremes beautifully expresses my feelings about how our life paths merged into our blessed union that began as a secret in a setting where romance and sex were strictly prohibited.

Carol and I didn't have it easy, but we did it anyway!

We each had to explore who our true selves really were. This was the ultimate "coming out!!" Yes, two adult women who were deeply in love—**COMING OUT AS LOVERS.**

We came out to ourselves first in 1982—when I was 23 years old and Carol was 38 years young. For the first time ever, all the stars in heaven aligned for us as individuals and we became an intimate couple! We felt accepted and celebrated by God.

So how did I actually come out to my family?

During this time, when I was in my twenties and absolutely knew my truth and future as a lesbian, I came out to my parents. I was pacing between the kitchen and dining room, the words spilling from my lips into the mouthpiece of the beige landline phone with the long black cord that attached to the wall. Each step I took led me closer to releasing something pure and beautiful.

"I'm gay, Mom and Dad."

What I confidently articulated to them that Saturday morning erased all my fears! It was a happy, happy freedom day for me and I felt like the elephant was finally off my back.

My parents reacted with calm yet excited voices that expressed their acceptance and affirmation.

"Joanie, we love you no matter what!" Mom said. "You are our daughter."

We are a family of unwavering support flashed in my brain as my pacing turned to gliding while looking out the window into a blue sky. Never underestimate the power of parents.

On that Coming Out Day, I was a young, independent adult, not needing my parents' understanding and support, but surely I wanted it. I wish I had had the courage to tell them sooner, but this was my grace-filled, appointed time. My mom already intrinsically knew I was gay, but I'm pretty sure she was keeping it secret in her heart, waiting patiently for me to share my deepest truth when I was ready. Parents are patient. I had just invited them into my new world.

Dad's caring voice chimed in: "We love you, Joanie."

He then sounded perturbed and hesitant as his voice lowered an octave, and he asked a question that has rattled and rallied me all of my life:

"Joanie, what do I say to people and who do I tell?"

What a phenomenal question! How do you answer?

This was an example of how my father's wisdom on parenting, together with Carol's father, Joe Tierheimer, enlarged our views of parenting.

So how did I answer this question that still arises? I told my father that answers can be simple, vague, or bold, depending on who's asking.

"I rely on feeling whether I trust someone or not, and I follow my gut instincts," I told Dad. "And first off, I really prefer to tell them the whole truth! Or I say: 'This is very personal and I don't feel like sharing that part of me today.'"

I also told my father that he can use these other responses that I use:

"It's really not for me to tell."

"It's none of your business."

"Someday I'll tell you all about it."

Or, "Not today."

Coming Out to Friends and Community

Next, it was scary to share that "I'm gay" during face-to-face meetings with my friends, yet I needed to get it off my chest. I wasn't going to keep it secret any longer.

Thankfully, I didn't always have to do it alone. The more Carol and I came out as a lesbian couple, the bigger and happier our love grew. We were blessed by growing up in loving, accepting families, which—along with our nonstop collaboration with God—laid the foundation for us to demand and expect the best out of life.

Thankfully, when we came out, we were 100 percent supported by dear family and friends who repeatedly assured us:

"It doesn't matter. We love you no matter what!"

We knew who we were and why we were this way. God doesn't make junk!

Shazam! Freedom!

It would be a process of time and place, how we declared "us" to our friends and family and then to our employers and community as the years clicked on. First off, we were seen and treated without labels or boxes. We were just us, Joanie and Carol.

Over the years, as societal acceptance gained momentum, we shared aloud with certain trusted friends and family our true commitment as a couple, revealing our sexual orientation status.

In September of 2012, we formalized a legal domestic partnership, providing us the legal right for Carol to be included on my employer-provided medical insurance. Eighteen years later, on August 5, 2020, we had the celebration of our lives with our sacramental marriage by Father Bernie Lindley of the Episcopal Church in our living room.

As beautiful as these events were, the real icing on the cake of coming out happened when Carol was diagnosed with cancer in 2012. Shortly thereafter, we dealt with her heart's atrial fibrillation, along with pacemaker challenges. Then in 2014, she suffered a massive brain bleed stroke. Amazingly, those very life-and-death scenarios deepened our trust and reliance upon everyone to whom we had come out in our community.

Carol's death on January 30, 2022, led to the writing and publishing of *Nun Better: An AMAZING Love Story* on March 19, 2023. I wrote our story with spiritual guidance from Angel Carol and Jesus.

If you haven't yet read the full story of my life and our 40-year love affair extravaganza, please order your copy at TwoSistersWriting.com. I poured out my heart and soul in that book and the feedback has been extraordinary.

In *Nun Better*, I exposed my deepest joys and pains about our love life. Our story is now circling the entire world and inspiring people everywhere. For everyone and anyone who wants to know about us, it's all there, in forever-black-typed print for you to read, learn, and feel encouraged.

Very importantly, Carol and I knew that our story was far bigger than ourselves. Coming out enabled us to provide a social and spiritual sanctuary for anyone and everyone who needed it. By dancing through life to the unique love songs in our souls, we showed others how to find the courage and confidence to come out, then live, love with joy and peace, and embody personal power.

If we could make this magic happen during a very difficult era, then so can you, today.

Chapter 2 –ShOUT Loud & Proud!

Coming Out is Your Choice. Go Within for Guidance.

By Elizabeth

What if you're ready to shOUT from the rooftops and mountaintops that you are Lesbian, Gay, Bisexual, Transgender, Queer, Questioning, Intersex, Asexual, Pansexual, Two-Spirit, Non-Binary, Trigender, Non-Gender Conforming, or another status for your gender identity and sexuality?

And what if you're *already* out and want to amplify your LGBTQ+ pride by founding a festival, leading protests, starting a podcast, blowing up your social media, writing a book, hitting the speakers circuit, and/or flaunting the flags everywhere you go?

Or—

What if you know where and how you live and love on the rainbow, but you *aren't ready* to step into the public spotlight?

What if you know that you're bisexual or pansexual, but you're in a monogamous hetero relationship or marriage?

What if you're just fine knowing your truth, and never want to publicly come out or even act on it in private?

Or what if you're loving your LGBTQ+ experiences behind closed doors only?

What if you justify staying in the closet because you don't want to disrupt or jeopardize your family, career, or reputation?

Whatever you decide to do is **your choice!**

Make peace with that.

You can always change your mind.

And you **can** live *Joyously Free* on your own terms.

It's **your** decision!

Your choice!

I have met many bisexual and pansexual women who have committed to hetero-monogamous relationships and marriages with men. These women are at peace with their decisions to not experience the passion and pleasure that they enjoy or crave with female lovers.

I know bisexual men who are married to women and have children, along with prominent careers and social status. These men enjoy their sexual preferences discreetly while maintaining the façade of a traditional lifestyle.

I have met bisexual women who are partnered and/or married to men, and who openly profess their attraction to women and engage in emotional and sexual relations—either solo or with their male partner/husband—in threesomes, foursomes, and at parties.

This fascinates me beyond measure! When I interview folks like this on my podcast, the journalist in me asks endless questions about their motivations, desires, and protocols for having sex that's way outside the restrictive lines that society draws for us.

Do you get jealous?

Does your partner/spouse feel threatened?

How do you find the courage to embark on this path?

What's your advice for anyone who wants to try it?

What I've learned from these adventurous people is that they are open, honest, and unapologetic about what they want and need in terms of socializing and having sex. We all owe that to ourselves, and that is the key to being *Joyously Free*.

We have to be honest with ourselves first, then find the courage to be truthful with lovers, partners, and spouses, so that we feel fulfilled.

Sadly, when people feel unfulfilled or unable to express their truths, they may sneak, lie, and deceive to satisfy their desires, unbeknownst to their partners. This deception may be rooted in

Chapter 2 –ShOUT Loud & Proud!

fear, shame, and guilt, which is only exacerbated by secret sex with people whom they truly desire.

This is a real phenomenon, as portrayed in the *New York Times* best-selling book, *Invisible Life: a Novel*, by my dear, departed friend E. Lynn Harris, an openly gay author. His blockbuster novel in 1994 first shined the spotlight on men who have sex with men while also dating and marrying women to hide that they are gay.

Deceit, sneakiness, and same-sex infidelity all shatter sacredness and trust in a relationship. And this points to the fact that we should never settle on a partner who does not vibe with what we truly want. We need partners who will be as mild or as wild as we want to be, and who align with our unique identities and desires. Everyone is on their own journey, and it's not our place to "out" or accuse or criticize their choices.

At the same time, settling for anything less than people who align with our truths is a betrayal of ourselves. It is self-inflicted deprivation of our ultimate fulfillment. And while that is tragic, it is so true for too many people.

That's why Joanie and I aim to be "way showers" for you to come out and play on the glorious playground of life, which you can design for yourself while recruiting like-minded playmates.

"How fun!" as Joanie always says.

So how can you liberate yourself and love yourself and your life to the max?

Know the Who, What, When, Where, Why, and How

As a journalist, I love exploring the 5Ws and H. That's the Who, What, When, Where, Why, and How. These comprise the foundation of every news story—and your story!

So, whether you're contemplating coming out or thinking about how to level up your LGBTQ+ personality, experiences,

Joyously Free

and lovestyle, consider exploring your own 5Ws and H.

Since this chapter is about coming out, let's start there. If you've already come out and want to shOUT about it more loudly and proudly, then that's your starting point. (Joanie conceived the clever "shOUT" which emphasizes the "out" and diminishes the symbolic "ssshhhh" of keeping a secret.)

With that in mind, let's write about it. This is totally optional. If you don't want to write, then please skip this section and keep reading. Describe the 5Ws and H of coming out and/or wanting to shOUT about it.

Who_____

What_____

When_____

Where_____

How_____

Why_____

You can do this exercise for many different subtopics, such as "telling my parents I'm queer" or "attending a Pride event/parade as my first public proclamation that I'm LGBTQ+" or "breaking up with my boyfriend because I want to openly date women" or "contemplating surgery to transition as trans" or "putting a photo of me and my husband on my desk at work where I've never shared that I'm gay."

What specific issue do you need to explore right now? Let's write about it.

Who_____

What_____

Chapter 2 –ShOUT Loud & Proud!

When_____

Where_____

How_____

Why_____

When you hit that last W, your Why, you will gain clarity on the reasons you're being called to take action on some aspect of your story. And as you proceed on your LGBTQ+ journey, continue asking yourself, "Why?" The answers will embolden you.

While you're at it, use your scripting powers to describe the best possible outcome for when you come out. You can do this by writing the words you want to say when you come out to specific people. These are the movie lines in the story of your life, so rehearse how you'll say them while playing the starring role. As you do this, see the best outcome in your mind and feel it in your heart. Practice in the mirror, and store up emotions that you'll use if challenged. Think about your why, and it will give you courage.

You can also write descriptions of these scenes where you are poised and standing tall, while the "characters" respond with love and acceptance. This may feel like a fantasy, but this writing exercise could be the first step to transforming an invisible thought or wish into physical reality. And even if the people in your "scenes" don't immediately respond the way you envision your best case scenario, your prayers and hope, plus your determination to stand by your words, can inspire change with time. Your dreams are alive and real! Keep believing!

You can write different scripts for different people. For example, the words you use for parents may be different from what you tell a friend or co-worker. You have the power to script a happy ending for the star of this show—you.

How Do You Describe Yourself?

Your coming out journey can take many twists and turns as you seek answers to understand how you feel and what you want. Be patient and gentle with yourself as you explore the many words that may describe you. You have the freedom and flexibility to choose one or more now, and others later, as you evolve and discover your authentic self.

These are the most common terms:

Lesbian—a woman who is romantically, emotionally, and/or sexually attracted to other women exclusively.

Gay—being romantically, emotionally, and/or sexually attracted to people who are the same sex as you. Women, men, and non-binary people use this term.

Bisexual—being romantically, emotionally, and/or sexually attracted to both men and women, or to more than one sex or gender.

Transgender—describing a person whose gender identity is different than the sex that they were assigned at birth.

Queer—an umbrella term for people whose gender or sexual identity is not straight and does not conform to mainstream views or traditional norms.

Intersex—describing a person who's born with reproductive or sexual anatomy that does not fit the classic definitions of male and female.

Asexual—having no sexual desires, feelings, or attraction to others.

Two-Spirit—describing a gay, lesbian, or transgender member of a North American Indian people.

Nonbinary—having a gender identity that is neither male or female, but embodying traits of both genders.

Questioning—describing someone who's exploring their gender and/or sexual identity.

Pansexual—romantically, emotionally, and/or sexually

attracted to people regardless of their gender or sexual identity.

Gender non-conforming—describing someone whose appearance and behavior do not conform to mainstream standards for how a person should look or act because of a certain gender.

Many acronyms include these terms, such as LGBTQ+, LGBTQIA+, LGBTQ2+, and LGBTQQIP2SA. The plus sign symbolizes the endless possibilities for queer individuals to self-define, and to indicate that the queer community embraces everyone who identifies as such.

By the way, conversations on gender identity often reference people who are "cisgender," which describes a person whose identity corresponds with the gender that they were assigned at birth.

The Human Rights Campaign provides an excellent glossary of terms on its website, HRC.org.

Choose Your Pronouns

Why do pronouns matter? Because they empower you want to identify yourself and how you want want others to identify you, and want others to do the same, personally and professionally. Here are the most common pronouns:[1]

> *Feminine: She, her, hers*
> *Masculine: He, him, his*
> *Gender Neutral: They, them, their*
> *Gender Neutral: Ze, zir, zirs*
> *Gender Neutral: Ze, hir, hirs*

After you choose your pronouns, you can announce them to people you know and meet, put them on your ID badge or nametag at work, and put them under your name on LinkedIn. Be prepared to receive questions from people who are curious about your pronouns. If someone is trying to respect your choice, and they accidentally call you another pronoun, gently correct them and give them grace for trying.

Also, please reciprocate. For example, if someone politely asks you to refer to her as a woman or a female—as opposed to "cisgender"—then it's fair to honor their preference, just as she is doing for you.

The Answers Are Inside You

Now let's take Chapter 1's writing exercise to the next level. It's time to tap into your supernatural power! Joanie and I do it every day, and it makes magic and miracles happen. People call us earth angels, because we love to spread joy, peace, and harmony.

Why else would serendipitous circumstances have evolved for Joanie's Godson Daniel Perry Walkup (a contributor in this book) to meet my sister Catherine Greenspan in Oregon, and then meet me to introduce us to Joanie just two short years ago, and now here we are, sprinkling rainbow sparkles on your road to being *Joyously Free?*!

Note: This path is not all butterflies and bonbons. We are very much aware of—and horrified by—the realities of trans suicide rates, hate and violence toward LGBTQ+ people, the 100+ pieces of anti-LGBTQ+ legislation pending in states across America, book bans, and the far-right's mission to reverse progress and freedoms. However, we choose to be beacons of hope and happiness to counter the despair and fear triggered by these grim realities.

"Returning hate for hate multiplies hate, adding deeper darkness to a night already devoid of stars," wrote Dr. Martin Luther King, Jr. in his famous sermon, "Loving Your Enemies."

"Darkness cannot drive out darkness," Dr. King said. "Only light can do that. Hate cannot drive out hate; only love can do that."

Chapter 2 –ShOUT Loud & Proud!

This pertains to how we treat ourselves, as well as how we operate in the world.

How to Get Supernatural Guidance on Your LGBTQ+ Journey

Meditation and journaling are two powerful tools that you can use for self-discovery, healing, and transformation. I'm going to teach you the *PowerJournal®* technique that I created and published in a workbook, after learning to meditate in 2010 and pairing it with my lifelong love of journaling. This process can help you figure things out and find answers within yourself and from your Higher Power. It has healed and empowered me, and it can do the same for you.

Stay tuned for the *PowerJournal to Live Joyously Free* workbook, coming in October 2024.

Meanwhile, you're about to learn how to use the potent manifestation tools of meditation and writing to transform yourself from the inside out and create the life of your dreams. You can also use this technique as a parent, relative, ally, or advocate.

I will guide you into meditation. You can either read the instructions on the coming pages or follow my voice on a video that will be provided shortly through a QR code. During meditation, you'll tap into your intuition or your Higher Self, which is attuned to the infinite energy of the Universe. What is your Higher Self?

"Unlike when sounds come from the outside world into our ears, spiritual messages come from within, through a voice that you can call your inner voice, your Higher Self, your intuition, your spirit, God, Source, Creator, the Universe, angels, or whatever loving entity you believe is helping you," I wrote in my best-selling memoir, *God's Answer is Know: Lessons From a Spiritual Life,* published in 2019 by Two Sisters Writing & Publishing®.

49

Joyously Free

"These divine beings deliver messages and ideas as immediate responses to prayers—or as unsolicited, spontaneous guidance, seemingly out of the blue."

Even if you are atheist, your Higher Self will speak your truth. You can also refer to this inner voice as your intuition. We all have it, but sadly, since birth, we're taught to value external, physical cues and other people's opinions and expectations over our own inner wisdom. Ignoring the calling of our inner voice often leads to misery misery, causing us to live and love based on what other people dictate for us.

Now is the time to connect with that inner voice, amplify it, listen to it, and follow its guidance to live and love *Joyously Free*. I won't ask if you're ready, because **you are!**

This voice is within you, possibly speaking through an imaginary microphone and speakers that are unplugged. Let's plug into this phenomenal power! This voice will speak loudly and clearly when we're in a meditative state that silences both the chaotic noise of the world and of our minds, where and our minds where our truths get tangled in worries, wounds, what other people think or have said and done, and a long list of "woulda, coulda, shouldas." Fear is usually somewhere in the mix, and it can be worse than hate.

Don't worry if you've never meditated or if you think you're not "good" at it. Just get silent and still and follow my lead. You may see, hear, or simply feel and know information that flashes with lightning speed into your mind and heart; this affirms that it's coming from your Higher Self or Spirit, because it comes faster than you can think, and it's probably something you never considered before. This is a magical process; trust it. Practice and be gentle with yourself.

Before you do the meditation, have a pen and paper or computer available to immediately write whatever guidance you

Chapter 2 –ShOUT Loud & Proud!

receive, while it's fresh in your mind. Writing is the first step to creating a physical manifestation of an idea or vision in your thoughts. Those words on the paper or screen are seeds that can sprout into the most mind-blowing people, places, things, and life experiences. If you don't want to meditate or write, then please skip this section.

Start by using this QR code to follow my guided meditation to go within and ask for the clearest vision of your most authentic self, living your best life.

Meditation

As you meditate, ask for guidance to embellish every possible detail in the scene of Future You: how you feel; how you present your physical appearance; how you dress; where you live, work and play; who your friends are; who your lover(s) is/are; whether you have a partner/spouse; how you're thinking; and how the world is receiving you.

Then when Spirit/your intuition/your Higher Self delivers your vision, write it all down—every detail!—like a scene from the future where you're about to step into the starring role.

_____

_____

_____

_____

_____

Now, while you're still in a very mellow, post-meditation state, do the following exercises. You can also repeat the meditation and set the intention to receive answers for each individual topic.

What's blocking me from becoming this best, most authentic version of myself, and living my dream life?

_____

_____

_____

_____

_____

Next, list the action steps you need to take to become the person with the life you see in your vision.

_____

_____

_____

_____

_____

Now here's some extra fuel for the internal engine propelling you to live *Joyously Free*. What are the **consequences** of never liberating the real you, or placing limits on yourself?

_____

_____

Chapter 2 –ShOUT Loud & Proud!

_____

_____

_____

How would you feel upon your dying breath—after a long life—with the realization that you never lived and loved with the wildest abandon that your heart desired, because you were scared of what other people would think or do?

_____

_____

_____

_____

When you live *Joyously Free*, what do you want to tell yourself as your final thoughts after a long, happy life?

_____

_____

_____

_____

_____

Coming Out: Grateful for My Journey

by Charles Pugh

Conversations don't get much harder than those about coming out. Whenever I would finally get the courage to try, the words would just stick to my tongue. I'd stutter and stammer and never finish. It would start as a grand idea and end in a heap of jumbled words that never "came out"—literally or figuratively.

These random episodes would begin as brave declarations in my head. However, I'd then think about the "enormity" of what I was about to do and would settle on the lie that I was straight. Lying was easiest. Safest. Most comfortable.

To help avoid this flaming hurdle, I just started blurting coded phrases to strangers and random co-workers:

"My boyfriend and I . . . "

"I don't date women"

"The guy I like..."

I was Black and male and "normal." What was more unusual about the prospect of coming out was that I was in the "public eye." I was a newscaster on TV and radio.

At the time, Ellen DeGeneres had come out. Rosie O'Donnell had come out. RuPaul never had to come out. But those were two white, female celebrities and a drag queen. So, in my head, they'd never have quite the same blowback I'd get as a Black male public figure living in a predominately African American city that pretty much has a church on every other corner.

I did it anyway! I took the final step in my coming out journey.

From start to finish, the whole process took more than a decade. The first person I told was my younger sister, after my first full sexual encounter with a guy in college. I was 18. After the talk with my sister went well—as I expected it to—I told one person at a time, based on how I thought they'd react.

Thank goodness, over the years, only one person I cared about rejected me. It was a straight friend and former roommate from college who told me he wasn't comfortable talking about guys I liked. Years later when he called me asking for money, I quickly reminded him of that conversation. I blurted out something along the lines of, "If you can't hear about my boyfriends, you don't deserve my money."

After I turned 30, I decided to stop giving a fuck about what other people thought of my sexuality. By that time, I had the full support of those I loved and admired, so I gave up worrying about what "haters" thought or what random strangers felt.

With my newfound freedom, I found a way to work my sexual orientation into practically every conversation. That got old fast because I quickly realized two things. First, that I had given myself the burden of constantly disclosing my sexuality—which straight people didn't have to do. Second, that being gay was only one small part of me. Therefore, it wasn't necessary to connect to every conversation.

I was finally comfortable in my skin and learned to only mention being gay when it was significant.

Coming out to friends, family, and coworkers was one challenge, but coming out publicly—in the newspaper, on TV and radio—was quite another gargantuan undertaking.

In 2002, I had decided to emcee a community-wide discussion about being gay in Detroit. To help promote the event, I agreed to be interviewed in the local LGBTQ newspaper about being gay.

When that article hit, there was a small pushback from my TV station's management because I agreed to an article without getting it cleared first. Even though I'd been interviewed on multiple occasions about other topics without having to approve it. I guess speaking openly about being gay crossed the line of "appropriate" subject matter.

Soon after that article, a well-known columnist and author reached out to ask me for an interview for her own article in one of Detroit's main daily newspapers.

The response to the second article in the mainstream media was immediate and overwhelming.

A normal response to a story that aired on our TV station was 50 to 75 emails. We got more than 2,000 emails on a news story that never even aired on our channel. It was quite significant.

The overwhelming part was the onslaught of angry, vicious, and threatening phone calls and voicemails, many of which said I should be fired, attacked, shot, and basically lynched publicly. People can be quite mean. And they were.

However, the majority of emails were encouraging—many thanking me for doing what they couldn't. While most of the emails gave me hope, the phone calls gave me anxiety.

As I expected, some well-known clergy reacted publicly. One pastor held up the article during a Sunday sermon and said, "Charles Pugh needs to be back in the closet. His spiritual closet and find Jesus!" As if gay people couldn't find love and be loved by Jesus.

Because I had talked about how cool it was to have other gay family members—though I mentioned no one by name—a cousin sent me a long, frank, hand-written letter admonishing me for "outing" other family members. Her message was borderline rude and definitely not a letter of support. Thank God, she was the only relative who took that tone.

Michigan law does not protect LGBTQ folks from being fired for their sexuality. So, I took a big risk coming out, but it was worth it. I felt so liberated—finally able to be my authentic self, and that meant way more to me than the threat of being terminated.

Soon after coming out, my boss at the radio station where I worked called me into his office and shared that many Program Directors from around the country told him they would fire me. However, he told me to be more of myself: bold and honest, while continuing to compliment my favorite celebs, and talk about dating and boyfriends—be me! I'm grateful to him for empowering me to have real conversations that others were afraid to have. He was a visionary and believed in me.

I also was pleasantly surprised at the reaction of most of my straight male friends. I never wanted any of them to feel uncomfortable around me, fearing I'd be attracted to them.

My friend Calvin was mad at me for not telling him for many, many years. But during college, after many late nights of debating and studying, we had fallen asleep in the same bed—like brothers. I never wanted him to worry that I would come on to him. I was afraid. So, when I finally told him a decade later that I was gay, he told me that our brotherhood was stronger than anything I could throw at him. That was the typical reaction from my straight male friends.

I'm sure everyone "knew" already. I wasn't the most masculine guy. In fact, I got called "fag" a lot in elementary and middle school. I didn't want to be a "girlie boy" anymore, so—by the time I got to high school—I went overboard with chasing girls, flirting, dating, and having sex with women.

For years, I pretended to be attracted to women, because I figured that's what "society" wanted of me. I was 28 years old before I got brave enough to stop dating women. I felt it was unfair to continue being disingenuous with women, just to give the appearance of being straight. It was not her fault that I wasn't brave enough to be fully honest and out. So, I stopped.

Joyously Free

When I ran for political office, my team and I over-prepared for a negative reaction about an out gay man being in the race. Many people told me I was crazy for even trying. We were pleasantly surprised that my orientation never became an issue during the campaign. In fact, on election day, I came in first place for both the primary and general elections. I am the first openly LGBTQ+ elected official in Detroit's history. I'm extremely proud of my city for electing me as I was: an out gay man.

There's only one part of coming out that I regret. I often aggressively and publicly criticized Black celebrities who "refused" to come out. I now realize how unfair that was. Everyone—celebrity or not—needs to come out at his or her own pace and comfort level. They should never be prodded or shamed for staying in the closet. I fully understand why people stay tucked away in the back of the closet with last year's Christmas tree.

I am, however, grateful for my journey in and out of the closet. I wouldn't change one thing. Especially the part about being out.

Charles Pugh is constantly evolving. His goal is to improve and grow until his last day on earth—and beyond. He enjoys reading, cooking, writing, loving, and being the world's greatest uncle (and nephew). One day he hopes to be an awesome husband as well.

Please watch Charles Pugh's powerful interview on the YouTube channel for The Goddess Power Show with Elizabeth Ann Atkins®.

Chapter 2 –ShOUT Loud & Proud!

Coming Out as a Bisexual Married Woman and Mom

By Leah Halpert

It was the middle of the night in March 2022, and I was doing what I normally do when I can't sleep—scrolling through social media.

But this particular night, my scrolling was different. I had recently been watching a lot more LGBTQ+ material and coming out stories on Instagram and TikTok, and specifically bisexual stories.

Ever since college (some 20 odd years ago), I'd always wondered if I was "different"—if I also was attracted to women the way I am attracted to men. I'd always pushed that down, though, never wanting to delve into it, due to a fear of rejection from all people rather than a fear of rejection from men only.

And by this point in my life, I am a woman who is in a very happy 20+ year relationship with my husband. We met early in college and that was pretty much it. We've been together ever since. That's not to say we never had any issues or problems (who doesn't), but we've grown together, and my husband is my best friend. Why would I ever question my sexuality when I don't have any desire to change my relationship? Would looking into this aspect even change our relationship? Did it have to?

As I was scrolling, I started looking up questions I couldn't bury anymore—am I bisexual? What does that even mean? How do I even know? When all I want in a relationship is what I have with my husband, how can I tell if I'm bisexual? I mean, I've never had experiences with women, non-binary, trans, or other queer folks, and don't plan to.

In my late-night "research," I found the wisest advice on

Reddit I'd ever seen. The original poster asked the same questions I had, and this amazing person responded that you are bisexual if you feel that you are. Experiences—whether real or desired—didn't matter.

WOW. I felt clarity. My experiences don't make me bisexual. I just AM bisexual. I had to sleep, but I knew then and there that I would come out to my family.

Coming out to my daughters was simple. Living in a small, very progressive town, I'd already been talking to them for years about different sexualities and gender identities. They are so accepting and loving of all people; they just took my announcement as another thing they just learned about Mommy and off they went to play and color (now in the bi-pride flag colors!).

Coming out to my husband, however, was much scarier. I didn't expect the racing heart, short breath, and sweating hands when I told him. He's always been so supportive of me in every endeavor, so, rationally he would be here, too.

But my irrational side feared he'd feel betrayed, as if I'd kept this secret from him for more than two decades. I feared he'd think I'd want to change our monogamous relationship. I feared he'd just somehow be crushed. Part of me hoped my kids would "out" me by just saying, "Mommy is bisexual!" with the same ease and nonchalance as they tell us about their days at school. But that didn't feel right either—he should hear this from me, not them.

I often tell my kids that they can be brave and do hard things, and I had to take that advice. We sat and I told him. He did wonder why I hadn't told him sooner (because I didn't know), and then he simply said, "Is this going to change our relationship?"

When I said, "Not at all. I love our family and you," he just went, "Great! I love knowing all of you."

And that was that. I now feel whole. I have clarity in who I am and who I've always been. I feel like a piece of me has fallen into place to complete the puzzle. I love showing my pride for my bisexuality, perhaps a bit too much, but after all, I need to make up for lost time in expressing who I am.

Leah Halpert is a trademark attorney at Halpert Trademark Law. She's a legal powerhouse who helps entrepreneurs and business owners safeguard their intellectual property. Leah is also a fun, devoted wife to her partner of 20+ years and a super creative mom for their two dynamic daughters.

Not Ready to Come Out

By "M"

Here is a message from a person whom we're identifying as "M" who texted Joanie about their coming out story. (This is printed with M's permission.)

M: Hello, I'm sorry to be texting so late, but it was really hard to find words to tell you that I don't think I'll be able to be a part of your book anymore.

As I was writing and trying to describe that part of my life, I realized I'm not ready for my mom and dad to read what I have to say. My thoughts and emotions through those years are too hard to face with my parents and thousands of others who will read it.

I'm so sorry to disappoint you, but I hope sometime I will be able to come to you and face my insecurities.

I appreciate you wanting me to be a part of your story and telling me about your life when we met. I'll never forget it; it changed what I wanted in life :).

Of course, please use my text and initial M. It's the least I can do!

Joanie: Oh, M! My heart aches for you! For our world that has stifled people's joys and freedoms.

I support and love YOU!

Your past, present and future.

You are not a disappointment to me, and never will be!!!

Your honesty is profound.

You are so beautiful inside and out.

Be in touch. Big hugs.

Thank you, brave one! Joanie

Tips for Coming Out as LGBTQ+

Come out to yourself. Coming out is a great self-revelation. It's also an act of self-love, because you're no longer hiding, feeling ashamed, or being secretive. When you're honest with yourself and get a clear understanding of who you are, it's easier to share that with others.

Come out your way. Follow your own timing. You get to decide when and how you will come out, and to which people first. Will it be in person? By phone, text, video call, or email? Rehearse with a trusted friend if you're nervous about telling your parents or anyone whom you believe may be disapproving. Think through how this may affect every aspect of your life.

Make a list of people you want to tell. Decide where, when, and how you will do it, and be flexible if circumstances are not right. This list can include your friends and family, as well as people at school, at work, in your business, in clubs and organizations, at your place of worship, on sports teams, and in your community.

Be honest. Flex your courage muscles. Every time you come out to someone, you build confidence and strength, making it easier to do with the next person. Deep secrets can be unhealthy. Truth is joyous and liberating—more than you can imagine.

Be kind to yourself. Say uplifting, non-stereotypical words to yourself. Trust your gut; you'll know when, how, and why to come out. Believe you are beautiful, inside and out.

Practice the Golden Rule. Do unto others as you wish done unto you. This means giving the same kindness that you want to receive, so don't call someone names. This also means not outing another person; they have the right to come out when or if they choose to do so.

Decide if you want a label. Ask yourself if you want a label, such as lesbian, gay, bisexual, transgender, queer, asexual, gender non-conforming, and non-binary—or no label at all. It's your decision and only you know how best to proceed.

However, fear, anxiety, and worries about people's reactions can make it difficult to think clearly. So get quiet and still and go within to discern what *you* want. Find peace inside yourself, and the answers will come.

Carol never in her life said she was gay. She said she was profoundly in love with Joanie and Joanie was profoundly in love with her, but Carol never used a label.

Select your labels and pronouns. What labels and pronouns best resonate with you? Select them, try them on for size, and change them if they don't fit, or if you feel called to identify with different words. You are free to decide for yourself, and evolve accordingly.

Find your queer tribe. Cultivate a community of queer people and allies—people who affirm you and who mirror your own beliefs and values. You can find your queer tribe in person at Pride events, LGBTQ+ bars and restaurants, community centers, meet-ups, support groups, your workplace, and through personal introductions by people you know.

You can also build an online community by following people on social media, sending them direct messages to connect, commenting on their posts, and attending virtual events that they may host.

Allow your tribe, Pride community, friends, family, work associates, neighbors, faith community, and business partners to embrace you.

Find your queer faith community. Find a place of worship that fits who you are and brings you happiness. Remember that your faith and relationship with God, Spirit, and your Higher Self is number one. Love is everything!

Together we are stronger, safer and happier. If former nuns Joanie and Carol could live and love outside the rules of their beloved Catholicism while still deeply loving and honoring God, then you can also find your place.

Be thankful! Express gratitude to yourself for charging forward fearlessly, and thank those who love you, care for you, and want the best for you.

Celebrate! Once you come out, celebrate that you have achieved the most incredible and joyful thing you've ever done. It'll just blow your socks off. It may just blow your wig off! It's beyond exhilarating when you find that real freedom.

Think of the positives, imagine the thrills, and live that way. Believe that you can do it. Remember: love always wins!

Chapter 3

You Got This, Sweetheart!

Courageously Living Your Truth

Speaking Our Truth—About a King-Sized Bed!
By Joanie

Carol and I loved dancing and singing. We danced, boogied, and sang the lyrics at the top of our lungs. We even changed the words to our own powerful lyrics and messages. We sang of making the world a better place, being true to ourselves, and of course, as Elizabeth named this chapter, "Courageously Living Your Truth!"

Two of Michael Jackson's hits, "Man in the Mirror" and "Black or White," ask the listener to remember a time when they saw their reflection and changed something about themselves as a result. Then he says that it makes no difference if you're Black or white.

Carol and I altered the words, singing: "It don't matter if you are LGBTQ+ or straight! Oh baby, yaa, yaa, yaa!"

We lived this inspiring, courageous way of life for 40 years. Most days, our actions spoke louder than our words.

We chose kindness over hate, discussion over mandates, peace over violence, love and acceptance over prejudice. We kept our joy and we rattled people's perceptions as far back as the 1980s during the height of the HIV/AIDS era when gay rights did not exist.

We were among many who carved a way to bring justice and equality for all, creating the simple things that today's LGBTQ+ people take for granted. How did we do it? How might *you* do it?

We relied on strength from three main sources:

• Our Higher Power: Jesus;

• Our allies—others who stood up with us and for us; and

• Our positive attitude and outlook on life.

We believed in being true to oneself. We accepted all people, Black or white, straight or gay, and on and on and on.

Here's an example of how we lived *Joyously Free* as gutsy lesbian trailblazers. On one of our first vacation nights, while still secret and under the vows of sisterhood, we stood up for ourselves and the world's gay community in the lobby of a motel on the Pacific Coast of Oregon.

When we checked in, the desk clerk at the locally-owned motel insisted that we have a room with two queen beds.

"No, we want one king bed," I said firmly.

The young female front desk clerk insisted again for us to accept the oceanfront room with two queen beds.

Again I repeated more loudly and firmly: "No!"

Then, naturally and lovingly, Carol placed her warm, silky hand on my forearm. She gazed at me with her gorgeous green eyes, then looked at the clerk.

In a calm, joyous, and firm voice, Carol repeated, "No. We want one king bed."

I felt so proud of Carol for her simple, intimate public display of affection with me. I could feel our heart beats were rhythmic and strong. Together we were laser-focused on a pleasant

Chapter 3 – You Got This, Sweetheart!

resolution in our favor. Internally, we were silently praying while outwardly standing up for our love.

We watched the clerk lower her eyes to see Carol's hand on my arm, and as if a light bulb switched on in her head and heart, she said, "Ohhhhh!"

Surprise twinkled in her eyes. "OK, I understand now!" she exclaimed. "Here is your room card key with one king bed. Enjoy your stay!"

I'm not sure whose smile reached from ear to ear first—hers or ours! Either way, the point was made and the results were splendid. The two-star motel was clean but creepy, and it was all we could afford for a night out. Luckily, it left us with a few extra quarters for the bed massage machine that vibrated and sounded like a freight train. Our robust, wild, and crazy laughter shook the room and the building, too. The tossing and turning was more fun than a ride at Disneyland!

Carol and I laughed at this memory for months, realizing that we were, once again, courageous warriors with a cause, dressed as lesbians wearing an armor of love and pairs of Mickey and Mini Mouse multi-colored headband ears.

Stares & Whispers

When Carol and I held hands while praying the "Our Father" out loud in a Catholic Church, people crinkled their noses with disapproval and shot disgusted glares. Their expressions said: "I don't believe you're doing this in church!"

This silent reprimand was very uncomfortable as their eyeballs raced from looking at our faces to watching our delicate hand-hold.

With silence and smiles, we were being courageous.

At first, we were slow to figure out why we were receiving these strange looks. We were absolutely comfortable with our fingers romantically intertwined. We were just being us.

Good thing Carol and I never believed in any form of guilt, Catholic or other.

Hosting the First Gay Gathering in Our Small Town

Our life journey together landed us on the coast of Oregon in 1992. Then Carol and I made history in our rural town by hosting the first annual Easter Sunday celebration in our new home and yard.

Our manicured, half-acre yard of emerald green grass and bright red and pink rhododendrons set the stage for 50 beautiful LGBTQ+ people to join us.

This was BIG! We didn't even know everyone, as we had invited friends to bring a friend to the first official "gay" gathering in Brookings Harbor, Oregon.

We truly were OUT and PROUD!

We wore home-decorated bonnets in a parade across our newly-built wooden deck. We hunted for multi-colored, rainbow-bright Easter eggs sparkling in the sunshine.

We celebrated our uniqueness, courage, and truth. Same-sex couples hugged, held hands, danced, swayed, savored barbecue, and kissed without fear, panic, or anxiety. We were living the life we all dreamed of on this powerful, blessed day.

We became a united family, and each person left the party feeling more courageous and joyful than they had ever imagined. The fun afternoon sparked memories and appreciation for this freedom to be ourselves.

Who would've thought that two former religious sisters, Carol and Joanie, would inspire courage and truth that helped create a non-judgmental, liberating world for all.

Live your truth with courage. If we could do it, so can you!

Courageously Living My Truth

By Elizabeth

Who am I?

And what do I want?

When I first heard these two questions at a professional conference, I was in my thirties, divorced, and wading through the darkness of depression.

"Ask yourself," the keynote speaker boomed over the speakers, "'Who am I? And what do I want?'"

These seemingly simple questions hung in the silent air over hundreds of people who had gathered from across America in this chandeliered ballroom. Many of these highly accomplished people appeared perplexed and shifted uncomfortably in their seats.

At the same time, I felt completely dumbfounded.

Why? Because the speaker emphasized that the answers to *Who am I?* weren't about your name, or where you went to school, or what you had accomplished in your career, or who your spouse and kids were, or what your profession was, or what part of town you lived in, or what socioeconomic strata of society you ranked in.

Likewise, the speaker explained that the answers to *What do I want?* were not about material things. They were about the things you cannot buy or quantify with numbers or dollars, and instead were about the sometimes-elusive qualities of peace, love, self-acceptance, and understanding your identity as a human being. Because only in knowing that, the speaker explained, can we find our footing in the ever-changing and flowing river of life and build a foundation for attaining material success and wielding positive influence in the world.

Joyously Free

Whoah. That was deep.

As deep as the abyss of doubts and fears that were already crashing over me and diluting my confidence around my authentic self and understanding of what I wanted in life. As a result, the speaker's questions plunged me deeper into heavy sadness and confusion.

At the time, I was coping with a bad divorce, feeling that my career as a novelist had stalled, and struggling to make peace with my identity as a white-looking, mixed-race woman navigating a very Black-or-white world.

"Um, tell me, miss, what brings you to this particular conference?" the white male taxi driver had asked while dropping me off at this event attended mostly by Black business leaders.

A short time later, in the women's restroom, a Black woman asked, "Excuse me for asking you this, but what are you doing here?"

I don't remember my answers for either person.

I only remember that my cheeks burned with discomfort because I felt singled out, misunderstood, and even unwelcome at an event where I had been invited to attend—and conduct a standing room only workshop about how to write a book!—and felt perfectly comfortable.

Those prying questions dredged up a warning that a family friend had given me before I went to college: Be careful when dating, because you could get hurt if a man "found out" that you—the girl with long blond hair and vanilla skin—are actually Black, too. If my date felt tricked, warned my family friend who had grown up during racial segregation, you could get assaulted.

That never happened, thankfully, but it sure made me feel unsafe and afraid of people's reactions when I revealed my truth.

I now know that this is similar to the terror that some LGBTQ+ people may feel about people finding out that they are

Chapter 3 – You Got This, Sweetheart!

queer. It's scary enough to out oneself to family, friends, and colleagues, and even more terrifying to get outed by others or even the media.

Yet our identities are a fundamental component to answering, Who am I? How do I identify? And why is that important?

After many years of contemplating the speaker's questions, and seeking answers through prayer, meditation, and journaling, I finally experienced revelations that fill me with peace and power.

Who am I? A mixed-race woman whose divine life assignment is to use the written and spoken word to cultivate human harmony for herself, the people she loves, and the world.

What do I want? Peace, health, safety, fulfillment, and the ability to use my talents to be a positive influence on people everywhere.

These revelations inspire me to be an ally for LGBTQ+ people, and are the reason that I agreed to co-author this book with Joanie. I know first-hand how profoundly difficult it can be to figure out one's identity, find the courage to put it into words to yourself and others, decide how to present it to the world, and to finally walk confidently through life in that truth.

As a writer, publisher, and spiritual being, I was so inspired by the speaker's questions—and how they changed my life for the better—that my sister Catherine and I created a series of workbooks called *PowerJournal*® that provide 28 days of questions that explore who you are, what you want, what's blocking you, and what action steps you need to take to create your best self and happiest life.

The *PowerJournal*® method combines my lifelong love of journaling with meditation techniques that I learned as a certified Intuitive Practitioner through Medium Lori Lipten's Sacred Balance Academy in Bloomfield Hills, Michigan.

Joyously Free

I discovered that the answers to *Who am I?* are rooted in our spiritual selves and even past lives, which can influence who we are today. I learned this through meditation and by reading *Many Lives, Many Masters: The True Story of a Prominent Psychiatrist, His Young Patient, and the Past-Life Therapy That Changed Both Their Lives* by Dr. Brian Weiss, who has been a guest on *The Oprah Winfrey Show*. (You can watch an excerpt of his interview on YouTube.)

My own exploration of past lives through meditation and Past Life Regression has shown that my soul has lived many lifetimes in male bodies. You can read about this in my memoir, *God's Answer Is Know: Lessons From a Spiritual Life*. So, it's feasible that when we meet a person in this lifetime, and feel that mysterious, soul-deep connection that unites us as friends, lovers, or colleagues, we very well may have known them as a different gender in a past life.

Likewise, from my perspective, this explains how a young child with male body parts can announce that they are a girl, and vice versa. They are expressing their spiritual identity that was born in a body that was assigned a different gender than what they feel is their truth. Lady Gaga brilliantly celebrates this in her song, "Born This Way."

So, what if we could evaluate people based on how their energy resonates with ours, as opposed to their physical characteristics or material possessions? I wrote about this concept in *Twilight*, a romantic novel that I co-authored in 2000 with *Star Wars* actor Billy Dee Williams, which explores provocative themes around race.

When we set the course for our own souls to navigate the world on a quest to attract our soul tribe, we attract amazing people into our lives. This was instilled in me by my parents, who taught me and Catherine to love and accept everyone with

Chapter 3 – You Got This, Sweetheart!

an open mind and heart. Race, ethnicity, religion, gender, gay-or-straight, socioeconomic status, country of origin—did not matter. Love and kindness mattered. Period.

In my early twenties, I lived with a gay male couple in Southern California while working at the newspaper for five months. I had just graduated from the University of Michigan with a bachelor's degree in English Literature and years of experience as a reporter and editor at the campus newspaper, *The Michigan Daily*.

There I covered the Women's Issues beat, writing stories about efforts to stop sexual assaults on campus and other topics about women's safety and empowerment. At the same time, I took many Women's Studies classes that awakened my understanding of society's imbalance of power as expressed in the feminist slogan, "the personal is political." This phrase means that the dynamics we experience in personal relationships are often a microcosm of a social, political, and economic structure that disempowers women.

These revelations stayed with me as I began an extended internship at *The San Diego Tribune*, and received the thrilling news that I was accepted into the country's top graduate school for journalism at Columbia University in New York City.

Meanwhile, living with these two men was amazing. First, they were super fun, as were their friends. Second, they taught me about gay culture. They also took me to outings in Hillcrest, San Diego's gay neighborhood where Joanie grew up. (She was living with Carol by then.)

Third, I often boarded an Amtrak train for the two-hour, sunset-over-the-Pacific-Ocean ride north to Los Angeles for weekends with a dear family friend. They took me to the joyous extravaganza of LA's gay pride parade. The crowd's electrifying energy was exhilarating as we watched from a restaurant terrace. We also danced the nights away at gay nightclubs. It was an absolute blast, creating some of my best memories, because I felt so happy and free.

So who am I, now?

I am proudly biracial, multiracial, multicultural. A sweet white chocolate fondue in the American melting pot. I am not one single ingredient, and I don't have to choose a label. I have a strong Black consciousness clothed in white skin and yellow curls. I am an anomaly. An enigma. A catalyst for human harmony as a bridge over our world's many divides.

What do I want, now? I want to use my power as a writer, speaker, publisher, and LGBTQ+ ally to help make the world a better place.

And as co-founder of Two Sisters Writing & Publishing®, we specialize in giving voice to diverse people on the pages of memoirs showcasing their against the odds success stories. Joanie's memoir, *Nun Better*, epitomizes this.

Now this book, *Joyously Free*, takes it to another level by providing stories and tips to affirm YOU as a unique individual who has the right to decide for yourself who you are, what you want, and how you identify, live, and love.

Chapter 3 – You Got This, Sweetheart!

Transgender: From Gray to Vibrant & Full of Life

By Tay Ryan

I think that often in life, we reach hardest for our best during the worst of times.

And I believe life is mostly a matter of how you think of it. So please read this with a joyous heart, as that's how I've tried to live it.

I was a child who preferred to be left to my own devices. It's not that I wasn't affectionate or necessarily lacked attention, but even from my youngest memories, I retained this feeling that there were parts of me that I had to hide.

Looking back, I can now realize that my world was like a dictionary that was missing key words needed to describe my very existence.

Femininity was incredibly rare in my world. Anything about sex was a huge taboo and my education on all things LGBTQ came from the punchlines of bad-tasting jokes that always left me with an undefinable feeling of distrust for those who had told them.

My mother, who was sexually abused early in her childhood, developed tumultuous barriers around anything feminine or sexual.

I have my suspicions that she was an autistic child in a time where that just made her seem like an easy target to those who would abuse her. This also cast her as a weird kid, prone to unpredictable eruptions of destructively defensive rage to those that she looked to for defense and care that never came.

She married young to a well-to-do Montana farmer with a level of charisma I've seldom seen outside of books or movies. I got to spend a few summers and maybe one school year with him. He was brilliant, tough as nails, and quick-witted, and he built his whole world with his hands.

In his presence, I was an alien. I was soft, introverted, empathetic, and, in his words, "prissy." The part I still, to this day, only partially understand is the anger. There's this moment with some men where you can see them experience anger because they witnessed a male express a feminine trait. It's almost animalistic, visceral, exceedingly physical—it scares the hell out of me.

It's an experience I lived through with others until I learned to mask myself behind a shield of dominance and indifference that I would carry for many years.

The homelessness that my mother and I experienced after my parents' divorce was effectively the end of my childhood. My mother was ill-equipped to handle the world alone and scrambled admirably to cope without income or any history of stability. She had been passed between family members and boarding schools most of her life, and in the moving, I think she found a hint of control and possibility.

So those were the skills she fell to: we moved. We moved so many times, that I was once in 13 schools in a nine-month school year. My education was impossible. Many teachers would just ignore me, knowing that I'd be moving along soon anyway and was already horribly behind.

At first, my mother kind of hid me from the men she dated. She always kept me occupied in another room. I had this way of aggravating them; it was like an unexplainable gift to make them act out. I didn't understand it, but I knew it was there and that she was trying to keep me safe with projects I could focus on while she did what she had to do to keep us fed and warm.

School wasn't much better. I was traumatized and heavily introverted. Add that to being effeminate and small and it was almost a given that I had a tendency to be singled out.

Chapter 3 – You Got This, Sweetheart!

I remember one town; I'd been beaten up in my last school a couple weeks before we left. It wasn't my first altercation and it wasn't really that bad. But it hadn't ended as quickly as what I'd experienced before, and school authorities wouldn't let me leave.

That gave the bullies time to mock, crack jokes, and call me names. The theme became obvious. Sprinkled between the other juvenile insults, I was called a girl, gay, and a pussy, with them threatening to kick me in mine. They made their point clear. It's not that they saw me as a girl; it was more subhuman than that. I felt powerless, and exceedingly frustrated. I think for a time, I kinda ran out of being scared.

I can't imagine anyone wanting to feel that kind of helplessness and alienation, though I don't know if that excuses me for what I did in the next town.

First day, new school. I think I heard the idea in a joke or a song. I asked who the bully was, walked straight up to him on our first recess, and though he was taller than me, I swear I was looking down at him as I squared off. I saw fear in his eyes the instant he looked at me, and I remember the jolt it sent through my body, as seeing that look scared me, too. But I swung and the fight was quick.

I don't really remember it much. I do remember, though, how I was treated by the other kids at school afterwards. I was no hero. I think a little part of me expected to be, though. I don't think they liked me much. I was pretty much avoided, but I didn't get picked on.

I lied later to my mom, claiming it was self-defense. I guess in a way, that was true.

I ran with those lessons and refined them, town after town. I learned that aggression and intensity had to be tempered, but that they worked wonders to offset how people saw me. I

Joyously Free

learned that I could manipulate people in general and that led me to my first books on psychology, a subject that would fascinate me for the rest of my life.

I began to self-educate, and treat the moving as an opportunity to run social experiments in an environment where the consequences constantly reset. I had my first positive experiences with the adult males who came through my life. I made friends, gained some wavering confidence, and kissed a girl.

I think a few words could have made a huge difference when puberty hit. If I could have passed a little note to myself, it would probably go, "Hey me. You're probably going to hide it for a while yet, and that's OK. Look up transgender, Mesopotamia, and invest in bitcoin the moment it comes out. Just don't brag about it. It gets really annoying."

But alas . . . past me had to go without. Puberty was a majestic example of how perfectly we humans can learn to lie to ourselves.

By then, I'd associated showing signs of femininity as a personal threat. Submissives were off the table, unacceptable, in any form. So, as a way to afford some confidence, I started to learn to ignore all the signs that later could have awakened me to the truth of what I was going through.

I was grateful that my stomach was small and looked generally feminine and that overall, I never developed much body hair. But I refused to think about it.

I hated my hairy legs, though, and the angular muscles, from the moment they developed. I fervently hid my body in big, baggy clothes. But really, I'm normal.

When I became sexually active, I couldn't stand anyone touching my body to the point that I read every book and article I could find to learn ways to shift the focus onto my partner and keep it away from me. But I'm still normal, right?

Chapter 3 – You Got This, Sweetheart!

Well . . . OK, maybe not normal. I'd been sexually aware from my earliest memories. That was just another thing I'd learned was best to hide, another thing that kids my age didn't seem to share, and adults got mad about. I thought it made me a pervert, but looking back, I wonder how much of it was noticing a discrepancy and hyper-focusing on gender and sexuality as result.

I grew up scouring the early BBSs (online Bulletin Board Systems that were used to exchange public messages or files) back before the Internet. I read every book I could find. By the time I came of age, I was fairly versed in alt sex culture and psychology. Or so I thought.

I never could feel normal and finally abandoned the effort. By all accounts, I became rather eccentric and disenfranchised. I can't say I'm proud of this time in my life. And I can't say that I'm not. I did my best for what I knew at the time.

Looking back, I do question my own morality and sanity, especially regarding: the moving; the poverty; all those social experiments; all that time feeling alien for a reason that just can't be defined; and all that hiding of every gesture that might give up the lie.

I became arrogant, intense, manipulative. I was known to trick people into telling me the things that they were hiding.

I tricked my mom into telling me who my real father was. I tricked a girlfriend into telling me who she cheated on me with. On hunches, it was like I could see a lie and chip at it, as long as I didn't think about it too hard.

But mostly, I used my tricks to dominate. It became my crutch and my shield. I had complete control if I were at the top. In kink culture, dominants are far more rare than submissives. Far rarer still if they're empathetic and clever. I'd found a way to be safe, a reason that I was never to be touched. And a way to be valuable

Joyously Free

to my partners without them expecting intercourse.

I lived vicariously through those I'd play with. I learned style and makeup by meticulously dictating others' attire. My suppressed feminine side gave me an intuition into what others wanted and I spent years focusing on little else.

Eventually, I branched out into the online world. I spent 10 years behind a female avatar, much of it as a professional Dominatrix. I was ruthless, clever, tender, sweet, and popular. And it ended in the blink of an eye.

You'd think by this point, I had to know I was transgender. I'd spent years in a queer adjacent community. I'd met transgender people in the communities that overlap. And I'd spent years online under the persona of a woman. But such is the power of fear, ignorance, and lies.

Something broke at that point and I became depressed. I pushed everyone away and became asexual and despondent.

My partner absorbed the brunt of my confusion and anger, and though we fought, they stayed by my side when I deserved far less.

My savior came years later in the form of my eldest child. At five years old, they came out with a very matter of fact, "I want to be a girl."

I responded in pure fear. I told them it never worked out and basically to push it down. I told them to hide.

Later while discussing it with my partner, they told me bluntly that I didn't know what I was talking about and that I should look it up.

So I did and what I found didn't match the image of an ugly man in a dress that I'd so clung to from hurtful jokes and stories gleaned from the media. I not only found beautiful pictures and stories, but noticed a prevailing theme in the timeliness of images that some would post online. I saw people I could describe as gray turn to vibrant and full of life.

Chapter 3 – You Got This, Sweetheart!

I promptly apologized to my child. Told them I loved them and that they could be anyone they wanted.

But still personally, I lied to myself and continued to hide.

It wasn't until a couple years later that a concerned friend pulled me aside and asked, "If there wasn't any form of public backlash, would you transition?"

It was like a switch had been flipped. The light came flooding in and finally I could see myself.

Transition has been hard, but kind. I've lost friends and family, endured surgeries, fear, and scorn. But for what's probably the first time, I'm present, instead of living vicariously in my own life.

Tay Ryan is an LGBTQ+ Advocate.

Joyously Free

I Don't Have to Choose: On Being Bisexual and Loved Just As I Am

By Frida

I see so much beauty in humanity, in our personalities, and in our souls. Yet sometimes life does not express that beauty back to us.

For example, a woman who is close to me said, "I'm praying for you to finally choose to be with a man."

I was hurt and angry.

Because I am a bisexual female.

This is who I am, and I did not and will not make a choice to accommodate her or anyone else when it comes to being with my partner.

You see, I am attracted to personality and what I see as physical attraction in attributes, such as humor and empathy. For my partner specifically, I simply saw my love as a person who focused on peace. I was attracted to his humor and the way he looked at me. His eyes spoke more words than any dictionary or encyclopedia. My love is quiet and reserved, but continually shows me that his affection is loud and clear.

It's hard, however, to feel attraction to both women and men.

When I'm in a relationship with a male partner, I miss the smoothness of a woman's body, her breasts, the way a woman's chest feels against mine, and the experience of a woman's touch.

But that's just my life as a bisexual person. You see, my soul is cut in two. I feel much internal divergence as a being. This is especially true when trying to explain to certain family and friends that it was not a phase when I dated women. Instead, I had to inform them that I am, indeed, in LOVE with my boyfriend, who is a biological male by definition.

Chapter 3 – You Got This, Sweetheart!

I still scream!

I scream sometimes to let me be myself, to not strip away the sexual part of my orientational identification. That would be like taking away part of what my heart beats for.

I'm still just as queer when I appear heterosexual to people who see me with my boyfriend—but this is not a role I assume. I, however, found the love of my life—a person who loves and accepts me for all of who I am.

A man who loves me for me!

My tip for people who identify as bisexual is to find a partner who loves you for your entirety . . . one who sees the real you!

Written by an introverted extrovert named Frida, who loves looking at life from many angles.

Joyously Free

Tips for Courageously Living Your Truth

Get to know a Higher Power. Seek comfort and guidance from a force greater than yourself. If you're not sure how to do that, get still and silent in a place where you won't be disturbed. Then call out in your mind to God, Spirit, Universe, and/or your Higher Self, and ask for a feeling or a message confirming that this loving energy is within and around you.

Your Higher Self is the energetic part of you that is connected to the infinity of the Universe; it knows your truth and always guides you to do what is best for you.

Elizabeth and Joanie stay in constant contact with Spirit, which provides immeasurable comfort during tough times, as well as protection in every way.

Joanie considers Jesus her best friend, and He gives her strength. She loves that His life was selfless, and that He stood up for everybody.

Elizabeth prays and meditates in a way that is "spiritual, not religious" and finds tremendous comfort and courage from her divine Source of love and peace.

Know that you are forever loved and cared for. Abundant love will guide you. Strength, comfort, and love come from the divine. JOY and love are found deep within. Even pain, disease, turmoil, and death cannot hinder, stop, or remove love.

Glean courage from others. Surround yourself with inclusive, open-minded people who support, love, and believe in you. Open your eyes and heart and follow their examples.

You can follow LGBTQ+ people on social media who express how they found the inner power that helps them, and how it can give you courage and confidence.

Hang with allies. They will inspire you to be more brave.

Envision the most incredible "dreams come true" positive outcomes for your life by being open and free. Openness to truth and courage go together. You are in for the most amazing life journey when you come out or stand up for being and sharing who you truly are.

Imagine the exponential growth of your business and profound family respect when you come out. Imagine the ginormous, delightful implications of being courageous and the ripple effect it has on others. You will be FREE and your inner circle will enlarge. You will discover who your precious, trustworthy allies and dear friends really are.

Carry on with gusto. Congratulations on your journey to live your courageous life.

Chapter 4

Kid Power!

Loving & Supporting Our LGBTQ+ Kids as Parents, Guardians & Caring Adults

What If My Child is Gay?

By Elizabeth

A baby is life's most precious gift.

And the miracle of birth is mind-blowing. Women literally have the ability to create human beings in our bodies.

This miracle involves teamwork, as one microscopic sperm from a male body sets new life in motion. With that, a person comes into the world, and one by one, we populate the planet with amazing new human beings who bring unique identities, talents, and contributions.

So, when I became pregnant, I wondered: "What if my child is gay?"

I believe most people have an inkling somewhere deep inside to explore same-sex love and/or lust. So, with every baby, there's a chance that they will grow up to experience that and even come out to live and love as LGBTQ+.

What if that became my story as a parent?

The answer comes from my first instinct as a mother with a newborn baby as I was overwhelmed with the mission to lavish

Joyously Free

this infant with indescribable, immeasurable love while protecting their health and safety.

All I wanted was for my baby to be healthy, happy, and safe. Sadly, those words don't always apply to people who are LGBTQ+.

So, I prayed that whatever identity my child expressed, they would be happy, healthy, and safe. And I vowed to nourish and protect my child's uniqueness—on their terms—every step of the way. And I did.

However, along the way, I've heard parents explode in homophobic rants, enraged at the possibility of their teenaged or young adult child being LGBTQ+.

"I'll cut them off!" This parent told me, threatening to unplug financial support for their college-aged kid to finish school.

"I'll jump off a f***ing bridge!" this parent shouted, basically saying that they could not live with the reality of their grown kid being gay.

Just as I'm unable to understand hate toward racial, religious, and ethnic groups, or misogyny, or historic brutality against masses of people, I can't understand why some people are so triggered with rage about LGBTQ+ people—especially when it's their own child.

I came to this earth to spread peace and love for everyone. As a matter of fact, when I was one day old, my father asked God to make me a "Princess of Peace" when he baptized me in the hospital room. He was ordained to perform this holy ritual, because he was a former Catholic priest who loved God and Jesus, the "Prince of Peace." My mother watched this ceremony from her hospital bed.

My parents were trailblazing renegades whose love endured a racial and religious scandal in 1966 after my father left the Roman Catholic Church to marry my mother, who was 25 years younger and Black.

Chapter 4 – Kid Power!

The bishop damned them to hell and my father's family disowned him. Then, I—as a one-year-old—crawled onto my grandmother's lap, thus inspiring a healing process that has led to beautiful harmony in our family. You can read the story in *God's Answer Is Know: Lessons From a Spiritual Life*.

All the while, my parents raised me and my sister, Catherine, in a loving home where we were free to be ourselves and follow our own paths regarding religion, spirituality, lifestyle, self-identity, and careers.

Our family was a racial, ethnic, and religious rainbow, as were our friends, neighbors, schoolmates, and acquaintances.

As a result, I grew up to be a "Princess of Peace" in daily interactions with people, as well as a writer, speaker, podcaster, and TV show host whose life mission is to cultivate human harmony for everyone. I choose to be a light shining on the ominous shadows of hate and intolerance.

So, back to the ranting homophobic parent. As I listened, I exuded peace and love, keeping the grown child's best interest in mind. My intention was to guide this parent into acceptance and love. So I spoke calmly:

- "Are you really saying that you'd rather be dead than accept that your child, your own flesh and blood, could love in a way that's different from your way of loving?"

- "You can't control your child's identity. They have their own life to live, on their terms, just as you're doing with your life."

- "It's all about love. This person was created from your DNA. How can you feel anything but pure love toward them?"

- "Do you really want to go the rest of your life with no relationship with your kid? And possibly your grandchildren?

Where will that leave you, besides alone and bitter?"

My questions slowly softened this person's stance. Their anger began to melt away. And, after having a candid talk with their grown child, this parent opened their mind and heart with willingness to accept and love their child *as is*.

Humans are Spiritual Beings Dwelling in Flesh & Bones
When my child was about three years old, they told me: "I'm so glad I picked you and Dad as my parents."

Intrigued, I asked, "Why did you pick us?"

"I looked down from heaven and thought you were nice people," my child said.

I was speechless and overjoyed!

My child has always been an "old soul" who speaks wisdom well beyond their years. So, I received this revelation as pure truth, because I am a deeply spiritual person who has cultivated a close connection to God for as long as I can remember.

This magic moment with my child happened many years before my metaphysical learnings through Lori Lipten at Sacred Balance Academy. And it was well before I read *Many Lives, Many Masters* by Dr. Brian Weiss. It was also years in advance of me learning to meditate and connect with Spirit to see that our souls live many human lives during which we learn lessons that advance the evolution of our souls.

When my child shared this, I had not yet learned that our souls choose our lives here in "Earth School" to enhance our soul's understanding of certain issues. This statement often rouses questions: "Why would anyone choose a life of suffering? And why would anyone choose to be a victim of some of the most horrific things in world history?"

Here's an example. A soul might come to earth to suffer and

Chapter 4 – Kid Power!

die from a horrific disease, in preparation for a next lifetime as a researcher who discovers a cure for that disease. Or a soul might live as a woman during oppressive times, only to be reborn in a future life as an activist who pioneers advancement of women's rights.

How does this relate to having an LGBTQ+ child who expresses at a very young age that they want to live as a gender that is different than the sex that they were assigned at birth?

When you read *Many Lives, Many Masters*, and learn that our souls' experiences in past lives can influence our behaviors in this lifetime, then it's logical to ask:

Is it possible that a soul can bring a male identity from a past life into this life when that soul returns in a female body?

And could the opposite happen? Could a soul that has a strong imprint from a past life as a woman, be born in a male body in this lifetime?

The answer is yes, when you learn the story of Jazz Jennings, an LGBTQ+ activist. She was born in a male body, but as soon as she was able to talk at age two, she told her parents that she was a girl. Now at age 23 and a student at Harvard University, Jazz says that having bottom surgery (which creates female genitalia) has ended her gender dysmorphia because her body now fully reflects her soul—how she feels inside.[2]

Gender dysmorphia is a medical term describing when a trans person feels discomfort or distress in their body because they do not identify with the gender assigned at birth.

Jazz was the first trans child to shine the world's spotlight on this topic when Barbara Walters interviewed her on *20/20* in 2007. Then in 2011, The Oprah Winfrey Network premiered a documentary about her life and family called, *I Am Jazz: A Family in Transition*. An award-winning reality TV series on TLC followed in 2015 and aired for eight seasons.

Joyously Free

Jazz, whose parents have supported her transition since she was a toddler, uses social media to educate people about LGTBQ+ topics. She also wrote a memoir, *Being Jazz: My Life as a (Transgender) Teen* and a children's book, *I Am Jazz*, which is banned in her home state of Florida.

Time magazine named Jazz one of "The 25 Most Influential Teens of 2014."

Jazz's story confirms that we are born this way, with our identities coming from our soul, the infinite energy that pulses through us and connects us to Creator/Universe/God.

Parenting is Unconditional Love; Empathy is the Healing Elixir

A parent who refuses to love an LGBTQ+ child is showing "conditional love." They're essentially saying, "I'll only love and support you if you're straight and fit into my vision for your heterosexual childhood, teen years, young adulthood, career, marriage, and parenthood."

Parenting should inherently show "unconditional love," which means loving a child just as they are, no matter what. Sadly, many parents withdraw their love and support when a child reveals they are LGBTQ+.

What is the solution that can help parents, grandparents, relatives, and adults who love and want to support LGBTQ+ children, adolescents, teens, young adults, and grown-ups?

It's **empathy**—the ability to see and feel from another person's perspective and experience.

Empathy is a miracle-making emotion, because it inspires understanding and sensitivity as we practice the idiom to "walk a mile in someone else's shoes." Only when we use our imaginations to step into their symbolic shoes and walk a distance through their daily reality, and see the world through their lens of perspective, can we really see what life is like for them.

This requires a willingness to open our minds and hearts beyond the barriers of anger, disappointment, and even rage, to see the child's perspective. One way to start this process is to remember when you were a child, and how desperately you craved your parents' approval and love, and how terrifying and devastating it would be to lose it.

Please keep in mind that your child, adolescent, teen, or young adult is probably terrified to come out to you as their parents. Also remember that fears can be amplified in young minds because the human brain doesn't fully develop until age 25, according to the National Institutes of Health. Whether a child's fears are rational or irrational, it doesn't matter; they are still scared.

So, in a calm, private environment, you can ask the child/adolescent/teen/young adult to describe experiences that exemplify how they feel about themselves. Also inquire about how they feel in certain situations, such as at family gatherings, at school, with friends, at work, in public, in their faith community, and in sports and extracurricular activities. Be patient and gentle as they respond, and listen with a facial expression that shows your eagerness to learn how to support them.

As they share details, try to imagine the experience from their perspective, not your own. Can you relate on any level with your own childhood experiences of feeling scared, different, rejected, or teased?

Use this conversation as an opportunity to ask how you can help and to emphasize that you are always there for your child to talk and assist them in achieving the best outcomes.

Pronouns and Labels Matter

An important part of anyone's LGBTQ+ journey is to announce how they want to be identified with pronouns and

Joyously Free

labels that reflect who they are. Some people, however, shun labels, and that's their choice.

As the parent of an LGBTQ+ youth, it's beneficial to allow the child/teen/adolescent/young adult to tell you their word choices to describe their identity. First, create a safe space where they can be honest and open with you. Then, ask them how they prefer to be described.

Please see the descriptions of LGBTQ+ terms and pronouns on page 46. You can also learn more about terms, identities, and news making topics on the website for GLAAD.org, which is "the world's largest Lesbian, Gay, Bisexual, Transgender and Queer (LGBTQ) media advocacy organization."[3]

GLAAD's glossary of terms explains the best words to use, which to avoid, and what to say instead. You can find this glossary at GLAAD.org/reference/terms.

The website is a treasure trove of information and resources. Formerly the Gay & Lesbian Alliance Against Defamation, GLAAD "rewrites the script for LGBTQ acceptance," according to its website. This non-profit organization founded in 1985 "works to ensure fair, accurate, and inclusive representation and creates national and local programs that advance LGBTQ acceptance."

Words are powerful! They shape the way we think, speak, behave, live, and love. The language that you share with your LGBTQ+ youth has the power to fortify their journey with comfort and confidence because it demonstrates your love and support.

Chapter 4 - Kid Power!

Celebrating Parents Who Are LGBTQ+ & Sharing Unconditional Love

By Joanie

Here's a chapter that's bigger than life itself: LGBTQ+ Parents.

Oh Lord, help me write this because my heart is so overflowing with thoughts, reflections, and experiences. I'm thinking of friends, seeing their faces, and feeling their joy and sadness. This chapter has three themes:

1. Loving unconditionally;
2. Parenting; and
3. Valuing family.

Celebrating Parents Who Are LGBTQ+

In so many cultures and scenarios in our world today, LGBTQ+ parents are condemned and not perceived as worthy caregivers. Critics spew zillions of alarmist "what ifs," making these untruths hop around like wild bunnies, such as:

"What if they force their kids to be queer like them?"

"What if we allow our child to sleep over at their LGBTQ+ house? What will they see?"

So many negative attitudes creep in, yet it is up to each of us, along with LGBTQ+ parents and allies, to throw nasty "what if" fears into the trash bucket.

We need to support our LGBTQ+ parents, erase stigmas, knock down barriers, and dissolve rumors. We need to be honest and positive as we watch a *Joyously Free* family spring forth, sparking a movement where these families are accepted and loved.

How do we do this? By using clear, honest communication, cultivating relationships, and most importantly, taking action and expressing: "We love you, no matter what!"

Joyously Free

Be a cheerleader for LGBTQ+ parents and help us all spread unconditional love.

My Family Taught Me Unconditional Love/Parenting, So I Share That

My parents demonstrated what a happy, healthy family should look and feel like, and it's my mission to spread love so that the world accepts and celebrates LGBTQ+ parents and their children.

I grew up with two straight parents, three siblings, and me, the LGBTQ+ one, for a total family unit of six. Our family exuded love in fun, responsibility, and respect, all formed around a Catholic faith that included the extension of close friends from my neighborhood, church, and grade school.

My parents were born in the 1920s, and having lived through the Great Depression, they personally knew about giving thanks, helping others, sharing gratitude with a smile, and relying on TEAMwork—Together Everyone Achieves More.

My mother, Lenore Moran, was born in San Francisco in 1924, California, and raised a devoted Catholic. She married my father, Ralph Eugene Lindenmeyer, who was four years older. Mom was spiritual, religious, and very intuitive. She could sense and see what was truly in our hearts and minds. She was open-minded, full of Irish laughter, and a fabulous listener. Her short and sweet opinions always hit the nail on the head. I thought her words came directly from God.

Our family was happy, cohesive, and bonded. We shared unconditional love and we were encouraged to be the very best in our actions and words. We grew up hearing that each of us had unique gifts, talents, and treasures given to us by God. It was Mom and Dad who showed us by example how to use and share those unique gifts of talent, time, and joy.

Chapter 4 – Kid Power!

Watching my parents interact as a loving couple, leaving daily notes on the kitchen table and kissing each other hello and goodbye every time they drove off, are just two of many ingrained behaviors that I continued to do with Carol and still do with friends today. I am glad and thankful to have positive habits.

From my parents and family, I gleaned golden nuggets such as talking and listening face-to-face, not yelling from distant rooms. I also learned to dish out compliments about each other's looks, how great the dinner was, and how nice and sweet a family member was to me.

My parents took time to plan our family outings for play and togetherness. Often there were spontaneous invites from Dad, such as, "Let's go to the beach for a quick dip," or "Who's up for a game of basketball horse?"

Even today, I schedule fun and play times for myself and with others. Like my dad, I love being spontaneous.

San Diego provided us with free outdoor adventures for family team-building with loving laughter at our favorite places: Presidio Park, Mission Beach, Balboa Park, or our backyard. From 20 years of watching and hearing my parents, I was able to apply these simple parenting skills into my own life, into a 30-year, successful and fun teaching career, when I was hanging around parents and their kids, and during 40 years of adventures with my sweetie, Carol.

Sharing Mother Love

Carol and I were honored to be aunts, friends, and mentors, and were seen by many children and adults as their temporary or lifelong primary female caregivers. In many situations, including church events, Carol and I would stand up on Mother's Day to be recognized as "mothers." Motherhood encompasses so much more than the act of giving birth.

Who do you know who deserves this accolade? It felt good to stand and I remember praying for "real" mothers, hoping they were OK sharing the stage.

As I looked around, I knew of other loving people, including divorced, trans, and bi women who were not biological mothers, yet cared for so many in maternal ways; I wished they would have stood up. But I understood that their circumstances and their identities would have opened a larger can of worms and maybe this was not the day to be exposed where church acquaintances could lash out with stares and glares of disapproval, or worse.

Oh, I continually pray for healing and the song, "Over the Rainbow," plays in my heart.

Joanie's Special Tribute to Parents Who are LGBTQ+

Meet My Dear Friends, Jana and Shacon, LGBTQ+ Parents

Jana and Shacon, thank you for permission to use your names and for being an amazing loving lesbian parenting couple.

Carol and I have been so touched by the magnitude of your individual love and the love you shower on your kids. Love keeps a family healthy and happy.

What a wonderful memory I cherish of the night that Carol and I saw you and your children as we strolled through the Christmas lights on the walking paths at the Nature's Coastal Holiday display at Azalea Park in Brookings, Oregon.

We were overjoyed to spot the clan of Jana and Shacon, lesbian lovers and parents, smiling brighter than all the acres of lights. Your family was decked out in bright red beanies, hooded sweatshirts, and warm, fluffy coats, with the older kids tightly grasping the hands of the younger ones, your newly adopted children.

Carol and I beamed with delight as we heard:

"Look at this, Mom and Mom!!"

Your children's young voices were so happy, happy as "Silent Night" played on the stereo system.

We greeted each other with big hugs, two lesbian couple friends, and your children continued to bounce their way down the magical, multi-colored, narrow-paved path of LED sparkling surprises. What a delight you all were that glorious, clear night.

We had a quick joyful chat, with Carol and I holding hands and both of you also holding hands. Then your kids shouted, "Merry Christmas," to us as you raced to catch the youngest, the two-year-old, from being swallowed by the big blue and white whale made of wires and lights on the other side of the path. The whale was a fairy dream scene with glittering lights sprouting a moving, mesmerizing whale blow.

Oh, such fun seeing all eight of you, a holy family, shining under the gargantuan white star hung atop a 90-foot-tall pine tree. In that moment and many others, I became convinced that the angels have blessed you with being a role model for other LGBTQ+ parents.

This was especially true when you and your youngest child showed up to share big hugs with me at Carol's celebration of life. It was Christmas all over!

It is absolutely pure JOY to share life with you! THANK YOU, JANA, SHACON, and FAMILY!

"I Have Two Daddies!"
Out of the Mouths of Babes: It's D.I.—Divine Intelligence.

Many times, I've been honored with being the first to hear a parent make one of the following announcements:

"I'm gay."

"I'm bi."

"I am coming out to you, Joanie!"

The parent's relief and joy delighted my heart! In most cases, my "gaydar" was well aware before they spoke their truth and I was the chosen one to witness such beauty in discovering their true self.

Most kids/youth know about their parents' love life, as well as the family secrets, coping mechanisms, and how their LGBTQ+ parents' lives affect them. But it can be risky and harsh when a child tells people that they have two same-sex parents. This can lead to extreme caution and secrecy that causes uneasiness for school children.

On the bright side, children with LGBTQ+ parents can create awesome friendships with their peers and their teachers when involved in fun extracurricular activities.

Meanwhile, I've heard questions and comments from the "mouths of babes" that have touched my heart:

"Dad, will I grow up and have a husband like you have?"

"Moms, will both of you come to my parent-teacher night?"

"I like having two daddies!"

"On our family tree, I have a lot of different last names compared to my friend Raul. How come?"

"I read about famous queer people. Mary Jones, We'wha, Two Spirits and bisexual Sister Rosetta Tharpe. Maybe my mom will be a famous mom in a queer book. That would be so cool!"

I have witnessed so many wonderful moments shared by LGBTQ+ parents and their child(ren). I love to hear the child's laughter when they see their queer parent(s) and take off flying to leap into their arms.

It's so heartwarming to see an LGBTQ+ mom give mushy kisses on a kid's face after eating s'mores of melted chocolate and marshmallow. It delights me to see the gentle nose-to-nose rubs or when a child reaches out for a hand to hold, or the parent sways back and forth while watching the child run across the soccer field and play tag in the sun rays.

How wonderful to watch the kids at a picnic or party, wearing tie-dye shirts and hats, their faces painted with rainbows, and sequins sparkling around their eyes, happily celebrating being a child of an LGBTQ+ parent. Just as they do while dancing and roller skating amidst pink strobe lights at the local roller rink with blaring music by Lady Gaga or Taylor Swift on family Pride night.

Oh, the joy of seeing the surprise cheek kisses and a sweet whisper into the ear: "I love you, Mommy!"

Oh, the fun head pats, precious hair brushing, ribbon twirls and hair braids, or falling asleep in LGBTQ+ daddy's arms and chest—safe and comfortable for hours, even when both daddies' eyes feel like closing.

Hearing the wailing and seeing the tears stream after a child gets scraped knees at the jungle gym and crushed hearts when the family pet dies and only LGBTQ+ Grandma, Mamma, or Dadda can rock them in their arms to try to make it all better.

The overflowing joys and love are so beautiful and beyond words. It's not fake, it's not AI, it's not planned, but it is DI: DIVINE INTELLIGENCE. It's the blessing of living *Joyously Free*.

LGBTQ+ Parents Are Teachers

So, here's to my friends who are LGBTQ+ parents! I admire each of you for your strength, fortitude, and expression of love with your children. You show others by your daily examples, where you smile and find a way to get through hate, judgment, and ridicule.

I admire your grace when you're dealing with another damn phone call from school telling you to please come as soon as possible because your child has once again been bullied. How frustrated

Joyously Free

you are, wondering, "Will the school ever really do something about it?"

Your child has most likely been bullied, not for who they are, but bullied because they have defended you, their loving, kind parents, and their brothers and sisters!

In your endearing actions to protect your children, you, LGBTQ+ parent(s), are for the umpteenth time teaching the school administrators, the school board members, staff, and teachers that bullying must stop. Hate and homophobia are not the answers. "Please accept, honor, and treat me, and my family with respect."

Each of you, LGBTQ+ parent(s), constantly surf monstrous ocean swells that break hard and fierce. It is each LGBTQ+ parent, who in your own way, shows ALL adults and parents the importance of patience, acceptance, honesty, and trust. It really is all about love.

I know it's tiring work to educate and reeducate others. Sometimes you need to throw in the towel and find other ways, including homeschooling your child(ren), because school becomes an unhealthy and unsafe situation.

I get it, but I don't like it. K-12 schools need to keep all students safe mentally, emotionally, and physically. They need to take a harder stance on bullying, just like they do with drugs, and truly incorporate restorative justice.

I thank the following friends for allowing me to learn from you and to be part of your extended LGBTQ+ family. You mean the world to me!

You know who you are: j, t, d/m, j/n/d, t/s, t/t, k/d, l, w/d, b/p, m, s/c, t/j, k, j/s, w, e, c, p/e, j/s, m/s, and b.

LGBTQ+ Parenting is a Vocation, a Call from God

Parenting as an LGBTQ+ person is a vocation, a calling from

Chapter 4 – Kid Power!

a higher source. It's all about love! A selfless love where actions speak louder than words. It's a lifetime commitment!

It's the same way Jesus lived: all inclusive. And I believe Jesus learned that from His parents . . . all three of them!

Let's celebrate LGBTQ+ parents.

I'm exuberantly sharing high tens, chest bumps, and praise to my plethora of friends who are parents of tiny sleeping babies, rambling toddlers, school-aged kids, teens, and fired-up adults.

Parenting is a lifelong blessing, commitment, and responsibility.

It makes no difference if a parent is biological, surrogate, adopted, friend or family, part-time, full-time, single, straight, bi, tri, gay, trans, lesbian, or multi-everything.

Hats off to all parents! I am so grateful to have a variety of great friends who proudly strut their parenthood. No labels, no boxes, just a mission to protect and provide! Here's to my plethora of LGBTQ+ parent friends who have babies, toddlers, children, youth, and adults whom they nurture.

Some LGBTQ+ parents were in heterosexual marriages and became biological parents. Others have adopted, fostered, or jumped into helping friends and family in the calling to become parents.

Queer parents create family dynamics that are unique and full of love, but sometimes conflict can arise with relatives who are steeped in mainstream traditions. They may ask: *How do we handle this? What do we say or not say? Are we accepting or not? Why are some LGBTQ+ parents disconnected from their larger families? How do some LGBTQ+ parents integrate into their larger families and friends circles in healthy ways? What makes the difference?*

With whom and how do we celebrate special days with LGBTQ+ parents? Is there tension or ease? Can we love without limits?

If one LGBTQ+ parent is single, is it okay for them to bring a "plus one," a partner, a date, a lover, a person with a different skin color/ethnicity/language or culture, to a family/friend celebration without causing a clash of values?

Will the LGBTQ+ parent feel free to introduce a significant other and share this person's importance to their family?

Are there other LGBTQ+ people who need to be included and welcomed—not shunned—into a circle of friends and family?

As an LGBTQ+ parent, are personal LGBTQ+ relationships accepted within my family, with my children, with my parents?

Every situation raises unique concerns, questions, and unknowns. The best solution is to talk about it, and to listen with compassion.

We can do this! LGBTQ+ parents are made of pure rainbow glitter. They are the bright stars. They face challenges that many of us cannot imagine. So as we share love and support for our LGBTQ+ kids, let's also shower queer moms, dads, and parents with understanding, kindness, and allyship. They have the most important job in the world—parenting—and we can all help them succeed in raising the healthiest, happiest kids possible.

Chapter 4 – Kid Power!

A Father's Story: Loving & Supporting My Gay Son

By Scott Eason

I met my son Joshua when he was eight years old. That's not a typo. His mother needed some help with her Cub Scouts. Being an Eagle Scout myself, I started helping her and got way more out of the adventure than I thought I had contributed.

When I met my son in 1987, I knew he was gay. He was only eight, but there were "tells." He was a good, honest kid and had a good, kind heart. As my relationships progressed with him and his mother, I was drawn into their little family. I married his mom, adopted him, and grew our family when his brother was born.

Like most kids, Joshua was picked on in school. His easy-going personality was ridiculed as being a "sissy." He was chubby, and was picked on as being "fat." As a redhead, well, you know.

I, too, was picked on a lot when I was a kid for having asthma, being skinny, being white, having divorced parents.

Joshua played several city league sports: football, baseball, soccer, wrestling, and volleyball. He really didn't find his passion in sports.

We also went on several trips together on my motorcycle.

As he grew up, I tried to teach him that he would be judged in life on his behavior. It was very hard to get him to understand this in the midst of all the other things that came with being a kid growing up. I would tell him about times in my life where I had good things given to me—opportunities, jobs, whatever—because of what I did: working hard, being honest, and treating people well.

I want to express how much I love my son by telling this little story. I had a friend who was struggling with a decision.

Joyously Free

His niece was getting married, and he wasn't sure he would go to the wedding. As we talked about it, I could tell he really loved his niece, but struggled with attending the wedding because she was gay.

He just couldn't see himself going, because it would show that he supported her lifestyle. He believed that his Christian faith would not allow him to love and support her because she was gay.

So I shared with my friend how much I loved my son. And because my friend and I practice the same faith, I emphasized how our faith teaches us that God the Father, Jesus the Son, and the Holy Spirit love each and every one of us unconditionally. We are called by our faith and by God to do the same. My friend attended the wedding.

My son has seen *his* faith tested by the prejudices of the church and the people in the church. Despite this, he has kept his relationship with God.

My son has grown into a good man. He treats people well, has found true love, has become successful in his employment, has loyal friends, and maintains his faith.

I am very proud of my son.

By the way, Josh attained the rank of Eagle Scout. I am still proud of him for sticking it out and achieving this.

Scott Eason loves being retired and traveling with his wife, Joyce, in their RV to visit friends and family.

A Mother's Story: Wanting Love, Happiness, and Safety for My Gay Son

By Joyce Eason

Our oldest son, Joshua, graduated from high school in 1997 and went on to college at Southern Oregon University in Ashland, Oregon, to study English and French.

In the year of 2000, Josh had the chance to study abroad in France for 10 months. Josh was still living at home with us at the time of his departure. As I was cleaning his room and getting his car cleaned and ready to be stored for winter during his time abroad, I came across a *Playgirl* magazine.

My heart sank, and I was confused. I had suspicions that he was gay, but didn't know for sure. I always try to give everyone the benefit of the doubt, so I put this unfathomable thought in a special compartment in my brain, and tried not to go there very often. Unfortunately, I thought about it every day and every night.

From the time I found the magazine, there wasn't a night that I didn't get down on my knees before bed and silently and emotionally pray to our good and gracious God:

"Dear Lord, please don't let Joshua be gay, but your will be done."

It wasn't the gay part of being attracted to a man that bothered me. All I ever wanted for Josh was to be happy, but what really upset me about him being gay was to think that Josh could be ridiculed and abused and end up like the young man in Wyoming who was beaten and hung on a fence post to die because he was gay.

That was my nightmare. So each night while Josh was in France, I prayed. And prayed. And prayed more earnestly and fervently than the night before.

Joyously Free

Ten months of his studies went by, and finally Josh was home.

I have a beauty shop in our home, which I have had since Josh was a year old. Of course, our boys were with me in the shop during the years before they went to school. After they started school, the first thing they did when they came home on school days was plop in one of my chairs in the shop and visit. I got to hear about all the happenings in class, on the playground, and at lunchtime. I loved that aspect of having my own shop. I always knew where my boys were and loved every minute of their lives.

So, after Josh got home from France, one night we were sitting in my shop talking about his trip, his friends from France, and his travel. Somewhere in the conversation he said:

"You know I'm gay, Mom."

I said, "Yes, I know. What do you want me to do about it? You're my son, and I will always love you."

That's when I told him that I didn't have a problem with him being gay and being attracted to men, but the thought of him being ridiculed, abused, or hurt by many was a feeling as a mother I never wanted to have. We hugged, and he said he would be just fine. Joshua also asked if I could not tell his dad, as they were in a good place and he didn't want to mess it up. I said of course, but wasn't sure how I would keep that secret from my husband.

As time went on, my heart was in a good place with Josh. He and I had always had a special relationship and now was no different. He moved to Massachusetts the next year to pursue his life. Not sure if he knew what that would look like, but he was up for the adventure. I missed him terribly, and especially missed him sitting with me and talking about life. I have always thought that when your kids get to the point when they are on their own, then you've done your job as a mother.

Some time later, a year or two perhaps, my husband, Scott, and I were talking about the kids and life, and he asked me if I thought Josh had a girlfriend.

Oh boy, what do I say? Do I give up the secret?

This is what came out of my mouth: "I don't think this is his persuasion."

Scott said, "I didn't think so."

From that time on, everything was out on the table. Life went on as usual and we kept no more secrets.

Since that time, Josh has fallen in love with a nice young man, Nathan. When they married, Scott and I attended, along with our son Bret and his wife, Taylor, and one of Josh's best friends, Jennifer. The wedding was lovely, happy and very joyous. Josh and Nathan have been happily married for seven years, and through a surrogate and good friend, they brought a child into the world in October of 2023. They have big hopes and dreams for another child very soon.

I feel that God has blessed each player in this Love Story. I always conclude my prayers with, "God's will be done." God is so good. I feel God's will has definitely been done.

Scott and I talk often about how blessed we are to have such wonderful children. God has given Josh and Nate a life of love and happiness to each other and those around them. God has blessed Bret and his wife, Taylor, with wisdom and understanding to be a part of Josh's life. Bret and Taylor asked Josh to officiate at their wedding in 2020.

As a mother, seeing my two boys in this situation was one of the most gratifying, joyous, and love-filled moments of my life! Our siblings and friends are all very understanding and loving towards Joshua and his lifestyle, but mostly they see our son as a loving and kind human being who is very knowledgeable, full of wisdom, very patient, and very loving to all.

That's my boy!

Thank you, God!

Joyously Free

On Being the Mother of a Gay-Drag-Trans Adult: Stumbles, Regrets & Love

By Markaye Simpson

Born in Fairbanks, Alaska, on August 6th, 1992, Alex was our self-proclaimed "loud and proud" transgender daughter. She was like the Aurora Borealis—full of color, forever changing, dancing, a show in the sky for the world to see.

Her journey in transitioning was cut way too short. On September 22, 2022, Alex passed due to complications from juvenile diabetes.

Gratefully, God was guiding and sending signs, though we missed many, to help us give the love and support Alex needed to know we loved her, period. Maybe sharing some snapshots of pivotal moments with Alex, including major missteps, will ease the worry of getting it all right in the moment.

Stay the course with love, education, giving space and using your God signs!

★

The room was seriously still, drenched with sunlight on a late June afternoon in 2010. Alex and I sat across from each other. I knew what was going to be said before the words came out:

"Mom, I want to tell you something."

A long silence.

"I'm gay."

I felt this conversation was long overdue, yet I still had not prepared. Alex had gone from being a starter on a competitive soccer team to not wanting to play. She had started wearing clothes that had a feminine touch and using feminine mannerisms. Subtle changes.

Chapter 4 – Kid Power!

My response: "I don't care what you are! We love you no matter what. But you still need to give me those ten grandkids you promised!"

Not the best response and not the worst. I asked if her father or I could do anything. Alex just wanted to get out of the conversation as quickly as possible and said, "I have a friend to meet," and that "all is good."

Flip and wit were normal at our house, and I wanted Alex to know that all was still normal. My response should have included questions like:

- How can we as parents be a support?

- Do you want to talk about it?

- Do you feel safe?

- Do you have friends or a community you can talk to?

At the same time, I wanted to let her know that we would always be there, and we would love her the same, regardless of her sexuality.

Instead of making Alex feel less burdensome and unconditionally loved, my blunders created a wall of dread when we started any conversation regarding her transitioning journey.

That September, Alex moved to Oregon to start college, where she would go on to find her authentic self, building a community in the process. Her dad, brother, and I followed her in January of 2011 so we could be closer to her and support her struggles with diabetes. Unbeknownst to us, God was guiding.

Alex joined a dance troupe in 2015 that solidified her love of music, comedy, and performing in front of an adoring audience. This introduced her to the world of drag, and her next transition began.

Joyously Free

When Alex mentioned she was doing drag, I asked if she was still identifying as male and if we should still call her Trey, her middle name that we had used since she was a baby. She laughed and said she still identified as he/him and that when people hear her middle name, they think it is odd. Unfortunately, these questions would put Alex on the defensive and prevent her from being open with us regarding her transition, rightfully so. Anyone coming out will need to do so in their own time.

Alex founded a drag troupe in 2018. This kick-started Alex's calling to loudly advocate for a community where all could feel safe and welcomed. The shows were as much for entertainment as a space where no judgements were made. In 2019, the troupe put on a western play, and it was such a hit they were invited to perform in Portland! She shared her success with enthusiasm. This opened doors for her professionally and for us personally to start asking questions.

What we learned is:

- Drag is an art, a form of self-expression that pushes one to think past preconceptions;

- Not all drag queens or kings are gay;

- While in drag, it is only appropriate to use the drag name;

- A queen or king who mentors another is called a mother; and

- Performers also headline bingo, brunches, and other events that want interactive entertainment.

Alex encouraged drag queens, kings, and other queer performers to use their creativity and talents unabashedly. We asked:

- How did you come up with the concept?

Chapter 4 – Kid Power!

- How long does it take to produce the show?
- How long does it take to personally prepare for the show?
- What do you love most about performing?

Phone calls and texts became more frequent with her sharing successes, failures, her foray into comedy, articles and interviews, her advocacy and a love for her fellow performers and fans. Our responses always included that we were proud of her and loved her.

During a too-short, 25-minute phone conversation on December 29, 2020, Alex came out as trans-gender. The 200 miles separating us felt like a million. This time I did ask her questions and none of them made her feel secure in that moment. I inquired about things that should have come later as topics naturally arose, such as:

- How long have you known?
- Why haven't you told us?
- Are you on hormone therapy?
- How long have you been on hormone therapy? How did you come to this decision?
- What about our history?
- What do we call you now?
- Do you have a therapist to help through the transition?
- Do you feel safe?

And . . . I sobbed. I cringe thinking about it now. I did tell her we loved her no matter what, and that she was still Alex. That is all I should have said.

Joyously Free

I learned:

- she would keep her name Alex, but lose the name Trey (when a transgender person sheds a given name, that name is considered a "deadname");
- her history and photos should be shelved for now;
- that she wanted me to use the pronouns she/her; and
- that she had a "chosen family" and they were her community to help through transitioning.

I had known this was coming. But I did not realize the fear I would have for her future, the sadness of how she had 28 years of never being her true self, and how her dad and I would not be able to protect her.

Tip: If you have a transitioning adult child, you may want to talk with someone from your local LGBTQAI+ online community. Also know that your role as the parent of an adult transitioning person is very different than a parent's role for a young child who is trans. Do not let the burden of worries fall on your transitioning child, no matter their age.

Two days after this conversation, Alex messaged, "You always wanted a daughter!" True! A God moment!

We would get together for lunches and dinners, but Alex was always restrained. She knew she was loved, but we were not doing enough to gain her trust and prove that her health and happiness were all we wanted, regardless of gender.

We stumbled on Alex versus Trey and her pronouns. We blamed it on 28 years of programming, plus not seeing Alex much, due to her needing space. Excuses.

For Christmas of 2021, she stayed with us in the small city of Yachats, Oregon, on the Pacific Coast, along with her brother and sister-in-law, Donna, who had no issues using the proper

Chapter 4 – Kid Power!

pronouns and calling her Alex.

Alex looked forward to our family Christmas gatherings. We wanted this one to be perfect for Alex. We prepared her favorite foods, purchased the best gifts, and practiced using the proper pronouns while forgetting her "dead" name.

Through twinkling lights, smells of roasting beef, Christmas music and best intentions, we failed. So, we tried harder. Since we did not talk to Alex often, my husband Garrett and I role-played with each other. We practiced using our daughter's preferred pronouns while pretending to be talking to our daughter without using her deadname. It was working!

Through the winter of 2022, Alex started opening up. She showed appreciation, even humor, for how we were trying. She spent more time with us. We noticed that she constantly wore a crystal necklace that we had given her at Christmas.

At 29, she had the first and only love of her life. She had a heartbreak. She shared it with us. She talked about her "kids" in her troupe and her love for them radiated. Her comedy shows had picked up. After a show that sold more than 450 tickets, she called, ecstatic! After a show undersold, she called, devastated.

On June 19th, 2021, Alex's older brother married his girlfriend of 10 years. It took some convincing, but Alex came to the wedding. It was so fun discussing whether she should wear dots or beautiful florals to the ceremony. She thoroughly enjoyed attending the wedding and visiting with extended family who loved and cared for her.

This was the last time we would all be together as a family. She was now fully engaging us as any grown child would in her life. Loving her, her loving herself, and educating ourselves—all with divine intervention—had come full circle.

The following is a text exchange from three days before her 30th birthday:

Joyously Free

Me: "I think we need to set the premise that I never mean anything poorly—even if I "poorly" express what I am trying to say. *Laughing Love emojis."*

Alex's reply: "I think it is safe to say that I assume you have good intent every time. Did you do everything perfect for a kid like me? No. But I also fully acknowledge that you did the most with the tools and resources you had and every single thing you did to raise me was done out of love and care. I hope you know that's my viewpoint. And hey, I'm pretty amazing, so you didn't do too bad!"

Open communication continued to bring love and forgiveness.

On September 22, 2022, Alex left this world. Everything around us felt colorless. During the week when Alex's life was celebrated several times, we met her troupe. Their love for Alex/their Drag Mom was palpable. We, in turn, fell in love with them. Their comments were balms to our souls as they told us:

"Alex knew you loved her."

"She loved you both."

"She was dreading that wedding and had a blast."

Yes, we were and remain full of "could have, should have, would haves," but she did not doubt our love.

Several weeks later, I mentioned to Garrett how I wished I had kept the crystal necklace that we had given to Alex for Christmas, because it kept her close to me.

The Friday before Mother's Day 2023, I was washed in grief when flowers in brilliant blues arrived from her drag kids with a lovely note. On Saturday, a package arrived, and I recognized the name of one of her drag children. In a beautiful box was the crystal necklace and a poignant letter explaining how it had been easing a friend's grief. The letter went on to describe what the crystal was used for, how Alex always wore it, and how they felt it needed to be home, with me. I cried, knowing Alex was with me, in her colorful, dramatic way she would want to be. Her troupe had no idea it had been a gift from us, why we had given it to her, or that it was the only thing of hers I desperately wanted to have with me.

Alex used her platform in her community to spread love. She was a vocal advocate for the LGBTQIA+ community, the unhoused, and anyone she felt was underserved.

As Alex and as her drag persona, she volunteered tirelessly on boards and community panels. She devoted herself to guest speaking, leading protests, organizing community events, and participating in a documentary now used in some college curriculums.

She tirelessly gave her time and love to leave a legacy in her community. Amidst it all, she was a daughter who loved her family dearly and needed to know they loved her.

We are grateful to God for guiding us, to ensure Alex knew she was loved, and our love would never waver. Above all, we are grateful to God for continuing to let us know that Alex loved us, and her spirit and color will always be with us through them.

Markaye Simpson is a proud mom of a trans daughter, drag queen artist, and community activist who is now in heaven. Married since 1985, Markaye adventures with her husband and volunteers in her community.

Joyously Free

Thank You for Being My Gay Son

by Janai "Grandma Boom" Mestrovich, M.S.

"Thank you for being my gay son," I exclaimed. "I love that you are gay!"

He smiled from his 42-year-old heart. Even though he already knew I loved him, it was very meaningful that I expressed those words.

And actually, I really don't care either way. Straight, gay, or any possible identity, he is a phenomenal human being. He is the kindest person you can imagine. With great integrity, he is brilliant and funny!

He accepts me with my idiosyncrasies and my outrageous creativity, and he revels in the fun and deep conversations that we share. I feel very fortunate to have him as a son.

"STOP LOOKING AT MY BUTT" is a sticker on my water dispenser showing a little bear with the cutest butt, standing with its back to the viewer. I laugh every time I fill my water glass.

Darion places funny stickers like this in many places when he visits. I find surprises in every room that always generate smiles and laughter. Of course, I leave silly little items for him to discover when I visit him . . . or hide in his suitcase when he is leaving.

Several years ago, I was tired of feeling sad after Darion would leave after a visit. We would have such a great time and it got discouraging to end the visit with sadness.

"We're going to transform sad to glad this morning," I announced while driving him to the airport for his flight back to the state where he lives.

"Mom, it's eight a.m." He was not game at first. After he checked his luggage, I asked him to give his cell phone to a

Chapter 4 – Kid Power!

stranger to take a picture and to trust me. (You should have seen the look on his face!)

He knew my hard-headed gumption was not to be messed with, so he reluctantly followed instructions. Then I got down on the airport floor, grabbed his ankles, and told him to act like I was trying to keep him from leaving.

He could NOT refuse as he witnessed me lying down on the dirty airport floor! He played along and it proved to be the perfect answer to transform sad to glad. He got more than 200 Facebook likes, which broke a record for his page. This has become tradition for the past couple of years. He even buys costumes to enhance our blasts of sad-to-glad transformations during his departures.

I truly believe that the families who PLAY together and have FUN, create a strong relationship glue for special bonding that helps to balance out life's challenges. That goes for any relationships with any identities. It's no different for anyone. We are all the same with hearts/minds/bodies/emotions/spirits. How wonderful that we can inspire each other with our individual expressions of who we are and have fun, regardless.

Creating joy is a highly prized experience to share. And it's free! Fun opens the doorway to lightness in any relationship.

An advantage that I witness with Darion's gay orientation is that he is very open with people from different life expressions. He knows what it is like to be discriminated against. AND he is supportive of my eccentric ways to express myself, being true to the spirit that I am . . . which is straight and unconventional in the way I dress, behave, think, and interact. He encourages me to never lose my zest for life.

All of these things come from goodness and love, which have NOTHING to do with how a person identifies with herself, himself, or themselves in terms of gender or sexual preference.

Love IS Love!

When Darion was 10 years old, there was a slumber party with some boys and a trek to the park the next morning. Darion shared that the boys kept making fun of him, especially his name. I asked him how he felt about that. His answer was a profoundly accurate reflection of his self-worth.

"Mom, I couldn't figure out why they wanted to spend so much time making fun of MY name," he said, "because it's just my name!"

He was unscathed emotionally! Boy, was I ever proud of his response and happy for him!

Discrimination occurs when people are either insecure with their own self identities, are afraid of things that differ from their orientation, or are ignorant of the spiritual approach to unity in diversity with mutual respect.

Individuals who live with higher values are able to walk, talk, live, and see a wider range of human potential. Those individuals have greater freedom in how they live and see themselves, so it is easier to not be judgmental. Everyone has a story, a childhood, a background. Seeing beyond the surface is a gift of the seer for those being seen from the inside-out.

In our culture, we have dismissed the fact that we ALL have male and female attributes within ourselves. Society has dictated exactly how we are to march to the tune of a collective idea of how we should "ACT." However, society has not permitted the individual in the societal beehive to be true to the spirit of who they are. Consequently, we see an extreme situation that is out of balance, due to judgmental attributes, profound ignorance and fear, and loss of true connecting beyond the surface with heart-to-heart communication, inclusion, unity in diversity, equity, and mutual respect.

By propagating higher values, we weave a new fabric for society on a global scale and we create new possibilities for peace on earth. We first must remember that we all have the same human make-up; we all breathe and have cells/organs/minds/hearts/bodies/emotions/struggles/dreams/needs/desire to belong/quest for purpose.

Tips for Parents/Grandparents/Relatives
1. Have FUN together! Nothing connects in such a joyous and free way as having fun.

2. For heaven's sake, PLAY and LAUGH a lot! It not only releases tension, but it creates an unforgettable experience that is high-caliber relationship glue.

3. Offer an open-ended invitation that you are ALWAYS available to LISTEN and talk, sit in silence, and explore topics or whatever is on your child's mind, regardless of age. Once a parent, always a parent.

4. Being gay or any other life expression is beautiful and can weave a relationship fabric from love. When human beings exhibit higher values in the way they live, it does not matter how they identify with the spirit of who they are.

5. Share. Talk about your discomforts in your growth as a human being. We all have them, and even though they may be different experiences than our children have, it still shows there are struggles, challenges, lessons, and accomplishments in the psychological human growth curve. By sharing YOUR experience, you open a doorway for your child to walk through with deep sharing. It creates a mutual respect through greater understanding and trust. This will also assist your child in realizing that others project

Joyously Free

their discomforts onto those they do not understand while they are in their own confusing adaptation of finding meaning in life.

6. Let your child know that you TRUST who he/she is or they are.

7. Get creative with artistic expression by "coloring feelings"—use crayons, pens, pencils, and paint to express your emotions on paper or on a canvas. You can also make up new games to share and leave funny or loving notes in places to surprise your child. The sky is the limit on how we can connect in fun and meaningful ways, so CONNECT with every opportunity possible.

8. Give space. You may be ready to have a discussion, but it is important to honor when your child is ready to talk about any part of the process that your child is going through. Be patient.

9. Enjoy each other with movies, books, walks, adventures, and new foods. Discuss feelings about different topics that open the relationship to a larger field of understanding. And it is always a great idea to agree to disagree.

10. Be grateful you have this child who offers so many opportunities to learn and share, which is true of any child's gender identity. All gender identities really are "normal" in the human spectrum of possibilities. Be open and proud of your child and it will encourage our culture to begin opening up with acceptance, clarity, and value of all humans.

Chapter 4 – Kid Power!

Love really is love. When human beings exhibit higher values in the way they live, it does not matter how they or anyone else identifies with the spirit of who they are. Buddha once said: "There is no way to happiness. Happiness IS the way."

English poet Samuel Taylor Coleridge also shared profound wisdom by saying: "What comes from the heart, goes to the heart."

How beautiful to imagine a world culture that connects from heart to heart . . . then no labels are needed. We can all be grateful for who we are and who our children are. After all, they give us the gift of bearing witness to the magic of their unfoldment as we participate in their nurturing and learn so much from them.

Janai "Grandma Boom" Mestrovich is Executive Director of Superkid Power, Inc., a nonprofit, tax-exempt 501(c)3. As the author of nine books, she is a pioneer in experiential life skills for children ages three-plus. She provides food/basics for the unhoused and poverty-stricken. Learn more at www.superkidpower.org and on Facebook.

Joyously Free

A High School Counselor's Support: No Room for Homophobia

By Sally Roy

During the early 2000s, I decided to have a more secure, full-time job after working at the local community college branch campus in the rural northwest corner of California. So I went back to finish my credential to become a school counselor. The following summer was hired at the only local comprehensive high school.

I inherited the office of a young school counselor who had relocated to the beaches of southern California. As I surveyed my new office, I noticed a slightly faded orange letter-size copy paper sign on the bulletin board. It said: NO ROOM FOR HOMOPHOBIA.

Hmm, I thought, *that's pretty hokey.*

However, I agreed with it, so it stayed.

Fall semester started and as I was learning the ropes, one particular student visited my office. I recognized his name in my Outlook calendar as coming from a prominent family known for being culturally involved as leaders in one of the local Native American tribes.

He arrived for his appointment, and I immediately felt at home with his warmth and smiling demeanor. He was of medium height and a bit heavy, and appeared at ease talking to me. He sat in the only other chair in my small office next to my desk and leaned forward towards me as he talked.

He asked to transfer to the homeschool program. At that time, referrals to the "homeschool" program in the district required a counselor's referral and meetings. This was in the era

Chapter 4 – Kid Power!

before charter schools created more movement without needing a stated reason for a student to transfer between schools.

He was a good student and I was curious about why he wanted to switch schools, when he had more opportunities with us and was doing well. I pressed him for a reason. I was hoping I could resolve his issue and have him stay with us.

He told me he was being harassed because he was gay. Oh.

My first thought was to convince him to bring in administration to address this and make the other students back off. I knew many things went on between students that were out of sight of the adults, and this was absolutely not acceptable. I believed our school provided the best education in the county and that he should remain at our school where he would have the benefit of our school's resources and a likely superior education.

I could see that he was not willing to have the administration step in and solve the current problem. In hindsight, I had underestimated the social ramifications of him coming out; he would have been ostracized and endlessly harassed by his peers in the school that had 900 students. I believed the other student(s) should have been reprimanded!

He was adamant. He did not want to pursue any retribution. He just wanted out of an environment where he felt unsafe. It was not my decision if he would transfer or not. It was his decision!

I could see that I was not going to change his mind. So, while respecting his decision and honoring his confidentiality, I started the process for transfer. I scheduled an after-school meeting with him, his father, his teachers, and myself to discuss if he should be allowed to transfer.

I don't remember now, so many years later, what reason was given for the transfer, but his being harassed for being gay was never mentioned in front of his dad or his teachers. He was not willing to acknowledge the true reason, that he was gay. It was

Joyously Free

too high of a price for him! Committed to honoring his privacy, I sadly signed the paperwork authorizing the transfer, and he left our school.

His experience of intolerance and my helplessness stuck with me for the next 14 years while I worked at the high school. I saw homophobic and unkind attitudes soften as time went on, but I never took down that sign. It was there when I left. I wanted that message to be there, loud and clear, as a reminder to others who came after me.

Sally Roy is a school counselor who works in rural Northern California.

Tips For Parents, Guardians & Adults Who Love & Support LGBTQ+ Youth

At Home. Home is where the heart is, and as adults who love our LGBTQ+ youth, you can empower them to face life with courage, confidence, and support to create the best possible present and future.

Create a safe space. Your child, adolescent, teen, or young adult is probably afraid of how their parents and relatives may react when they come out. Welcome them to talk with you, openly and honestly, by assuring them that you are there for them, no matter what, and that you will do everything in your power to understand them and protect them while providing space for them to evolve into the unique individual that they are.

Join PFLAG—Parents, Families and Friends of Lesbians and Gays—the United States' largest organization dedicated to supporting, educating, and advocating for LGBTQ+ people and those who love them. PFLAG National provides support for nearly 400 chapters across the United States, with more than 350,000 members and supporters. Visit PFLAG.org to find a chapter near you.

You are not alone, and many professionals along with parents who have walked this path are eager to guide you.

Explore The Trevor Project. Introduce your youth to this international organization that provides a safe social networking site catering to LGBTQ+ young people who are between the ages of 13 and 24. Visit TheTrevorProject.org to find counselors, crisis services, and abundant resources that can enhance your ability to support your young person and their siblings.

Their website offers a free, 40-page guidebook called *Coming Out: A Handbook for LGBTQ Young People* that is a downloadable pdf. Reading this booklet as a parent can provide insights into what your child may be feeling. And sharing it with your young person to explore with you or in private can equip them with a powerful tool to process their coming out experience.

Find a therapist for your youth who specializes in LGBTQ+ children, adolescents, teens, and young adults. A therapist can provide solid guidance and tools for LGBTQ+ youth to use in the throes of challenges. It's hard enough being a kid, adolescent, teenager, and young adult who's trying to figure out who they are and how to navigate in the world. It's even worse when they experience fear, potential rejection and ostracization, bullying, and even being kicked out and disowned by parents.

Support siblings. Your child's siblings can also benefit from seeing a skilled therapist who can help them understand and cope with the fact that their little brother is now identifying as a girl, or that their teenaged sister is dating girls, or that their sibling is now expressing a non-gender-conforming identity. Your other kids may need assistance adjusting to new names, pronouns, and experiences at school, including teasing and bullying. A therapist can help them process their emotions and equip them with coping skills.

Chapter 4 – Kid Power!

You can also include siblings in family conversations where everyone is free to ask questions, share feelings, and acknowledge challenges. Set parameters before people begin to speak so that everyone feels respected and safe to express their honest emotions.

Get therapy for yourself and be gentle with yourself. Change can be hard. There's grief in releasing the dreams you had for your child since before they were born, to fit a certain profile of what you think a happy life looks like. This includes your hopes for a wedding with a male groom and female bride whose heterosexual union produces grandchildren. Process your feelings in a way that does not further burden your youth, who is already grappling with so much. Focus on accepting your child's vision for what a happy life looks like for them. It's their life.

Honor identities, names, and pronouns. Ask your loved one how they would like to be identified, as well as what pronouns they prefer. Practice saying and using those pronouns and terms. Also, your child may announce that they're using a new name to replace their birth name, which they may refer to as a "deadname."

Be patient and give yourself grace to release your vision for your child's future and allow their vision to manifest. At the same time, accept and celebrate your child's vision for what a happy life looks like for them. Help your child do the exercises in the earlier chapters of this book to create a clear vision, along with self-confidence and courage, to make their best life a reality for them as an individual and for you as a family unit supporting them.

Learn LGBTQ+ terms and vocabulary at GLAAD.org/reference/terms. You can also find a list of LGBTQ+ descriptions and pronouns on page 46.

Communicate. Acknowledge and accept that your child is marching to the beat of a different drum. Many LGBTQ+ youth struggle with words to describe themselves or their friends, so be patient and gentle, and do not condemn, make harsh assumptions, or express judgment.

Tell them frequently, "I'm here for you," and, "You can talk to me about anything, anytime." Mean what you say, so even if your child, adolescent, teen, or young adult wants to have a tearful talk at 3 AM, wake up and be there for them.

Create a safe space where what they say is totally private. Turn off your phone, computer, and TV. Assure them that they can say whatever they want and get your feedback that's honest, genuine, and supportive.

Listen more than talk. Practice the art of thinking before you speak, because you cannot "un-say" something; once it's heard by a child or young person, it could leave a lifelong mark—or scar—on their mind and heart.

At the same time, be aware of your facial expressions; a scornful or disapproving look can be just as scary and scarring as harsh words.

Have family discussions. When your child, teen, or young adult evolves with their new identity, it will affect your family and life outside the home. So have a family meeting on a regular basis about how to face these changes together. Make it fun, perhaps over pizza every Tuesday evening, and allow each family member to ask questions, vent, and share. Ask open-ended questions that start with how, what, and why, such as: "How can I help you? What do you need? Why do you think that?"

Decide if the family should see a counselor together.

Also discuss how to reveal changes, when appropriate, to: your extended family and friends; your young person's teachers, sports coaches, leaders of extracurricular activities such as Girl Scouts and Boy Scouts, and managers at after-school jobs; your neighbors; your faith community; your colleagues; and anyone else who is part of your lives.

Within your family, set boundaries on what you will or will not discuss with people outside the home, and practice how each of you will respond to questions, criticism, ridicule, or bullying. Talk about how to report any such behavior to the appropriate authorities.

Emphasize safety first. Sheer terror for your child's health and safety may be your first response to them coming out as LGBTQ+. Acknowledge the fear and speak with a professional counselor about how to process your anxiety and fears of the unknown. Explore apprehensions that may be rooted in news reports about deadly violence toward LGBTQ+ people, along with bullying, discrimination, and the risk of HIV/AIDS. Speak with your youth, as you would with any child, teen, or young adult, about the importance of putting safety first—always and everywhere.

Allow space for self-expression. Your child, adolescent, teen, or young adult may want to dress differently, decorate their room in a new way, display symbols of their evolving identity, and bring new friends into your home. Discuss the parameters of your house rules that allow their age-appropriate freedom while respecting your home. At the same time, open your mind to how youth express themselves with hair colors and clothing styles, tattoos, or body piercings that you may not agree with.

Social media. First, emphasize safety first to set boundaries about what is and isn't appropriate for your child, adolescent, teen, or young adult to post on social media. Emphasize the importance of never sharing personal information, nude pictures or videos, or your home address.

Also reinforce that it can be dangerous to communicate with strangers online, because someone posing as another child or teen may actually be a predator with criminal intentions. That person may know all the right things to say to manipulate a young person who's exploring the new terrain of being queer. For that reason, emphasize that your youth should never meet up with someone they met online.

Understand hormones and surgery. If your child, adolescent, teen, or young adult wants to take hormones and/or get surgery, research the topic, consult with medical professionals, and, if you can, talk with other parents and youth who have gone through this process. Learn the reasons and risks to make informed decisions.

Be involved in their life. Cook together, share meals, sit on the sofa and talk, watch movies, go bowling or roller skating, go camping, and do any activities that are fun and provide time to bond. Make time and be present!

Shower them with love. Lack of love and nurturance for LGBTQ+ children or teens can cause devastatingly low self-esteem, mental and emotional problems, and suicide. So, help LGBTQ+ youth deal with fears and depression by showering them with love, and by providing a guiding hand to find LGBTQ+ resources and activities with other youth in their "tribe."

Chapter 4 – Kid Power!

Know the risks. Your response to your child, adolescent, teen, or young adult's evolving identity can be a matter of life and death, because 40 percent of trans kids contemplate suicide and end their lives, according to The National Institutes of Health.[4] That's four in 10. Imagine a room with 10 youth, then four disappear because they died. If you've ever been to a funeral of a child or a teenager, it is heart-wrenching. Your love and support can save lives!

It's vital to support and love all kids, especially our most vulnerable ones. You can help lay the foundation for a solid future in our world where 82 percent of transgender individuals have considered killing themselves, with the majority of them being transgender youth.[5]

Continuously emphasize to your youth that you're here for them. If they're in emotional crisis—especially if they're threatening to harm themselves—stay with them, schedule an emergency session with a therapist, and seek emergency mental health services. Emphasize that every problem has a solution, and that suicide is not one of them. Tell them they were born for a reason, and you're there to help them get through this, no matter what it takes.

You can find an abundance of suicide prevention resources at TheTrevorProject.org.

Include the extended family. Create open dialogue and opportunities for grandparents, aunts, uncles, cousins, and close family friends to help your LGBTQ+ youth grow mentally, spiritually, and physically. Get involved and organize events for your youth to have fun with your family's inner circle: go kayaking, zip-lining, video gaming, music listening, and dancing. Maybe it's time for you to just be silly and be a big kid with them.

Outside the Home

As adults who love LGBTQ+ youth, you can advocate for them outside the home, especially in places and situations that directly affect them.

Network with other parents of LGBTQ+ people who have learned lessons that they can share with you. You can meet other parents through social media sites, at in-person support groups, at Pride parades, and at other events.

Enroll your child in affirming activities. Summer camps, play groups, and other activities can enable your child, adolescent, or teen to meet and befriend other youth who are like them. Founders of these groups aim to build community and confidence among young people who are LGBTQ+. The experiences can lead to friendships that provide companionship and belonging long after the camp or activity ends.

Support gender-neutral bathrooms. Everybody needs to use the toilet. Let's make sure that we can all go into a neutral bathroom. Change signs accordingly. Examples are: bathroom, restroom, family bathroom, gender neutral, what you are, and the best sign that Joanie saw said, "Whatever!"

Advocate for viable medical and mental health services. If your pediatrician is homophobic, then find a new physician for your child, adolescent, or teen. Get referrals to local pediatricians who are LGBTQ+ affirming from other parents, perhaps those you meet through a local chapter of PFLAG.org. Similarly, you can find the best mental health services for your youth through networking and referrals.

Stop conversion therapy. Many professionals consider this a form of child abuse, and it's illegal in 27 countries, 26 states, and more than 100 municipalities across America.[6][7]

Conversion therapy involves cruel methods that try to force a person's sexual orientation or gender identity to conform to heterosexual norms. The methods have included: "brain surgery, surgical or hormonal castration, aversive treatments such as electric shocks, nausea-inducing drugs, hypnosis, counseling, spiritual interventions, visualization, psychoanalysis, and arousal reconditioning," according to Wikipedia.[8]

The consensus in the scientific community is that this does not work. Instead, it's considered torture that causes grave, long-term harm. So, what can you do?

First, if you're thinking about forcing your child/adolescent/teen/young adult to undergo this, please stop and research how it does all harm and no good.

Second, if your faith community, extended family, or others are pushing for this, inform them that this form of child abuse is illegal in many places.

Third, investigate whether your country, state, and municipality have a law or ordinance prohibiting conversion therapy. If it does not, then contact your government leadership and ask them to propose legislation to ban conversion therapy.

Sports! Allow and support LGBTQ+ kids to participate in sports and activities, such as a girl playing football and a boy taking ballet classes. They are athletes and performers who are free to enjoy their sport or activity.

Support schools and libraries to provide age-appropriate LGBTQ+ literature. Speak up against book bans. Organize a committee and even a protest to counter any efforts in your local school district and/or town to ban

LGBTQ+ books. Meanwhile, read affirming books with your children or read them yourself, then schedule time to talk about the books with your kids.

Social events. Help LGBTQ+ youth navigate peer pressures around school events such as prom and homecoming dances that traditionally focus on male-female coupling. Support your teen's choice to attend with an LGBTQ+ date. If the school prohibits same-sex prom dates, meet with school officials to advocate for getting rid of that rule. Call the local media to force pressure for change. Lead a protest. If the school district won't budge, keep trying. Meanwhile, organize a city-wide LGBTQ+ prom for your child, their date, and teens from across town! Change has to start somewhere, so let it start with you!

Be the change you wish to see. Become the resource that you're needing right now, but that you can't find in your town or on the Internet. Make a list of exactly what you're seeking and become that source. You can do this by starting a social media page where you post tips for other parents, based on your own experiences. You can start a support group in your town or online. You can organize an annual pride event—such as a parade, picnic, outing to an amusement park, camping trip, you name it—for LGBTQ+ youth and the adults who love them.

Write the book that you needed, but couldn't find. Chronicle your journey and list questions that went unanswered because the resources you needed were not available. Tell your story in your book and share your advice to other parents and guardians of LGBTQ+ youth. Every LGBTQ+ journey is unique, so you may be able to share insights that can help people and even save lives.

Likewise, for example, if you have ideas on how

teachers and schools can better help kids on their rainbow paths, then write a book about it. You can team up with a professional therapist to co-write the book so that their credentialed expertise adds credibility to the guidance you are offering along with your own personal experiences, which are golden unto themselves.

For Allies & Advocates

Become a parent or guardian for an LGBTQ+ child, adolescent, teen, or young adult whose biological parents have rejected them and evicted them from the family home. This is especially a problem for trans youth who often become homeless, which puts them at high risk for drug addiction and crimes that include being trafficked for prostitution.

Advocate by posting LGBTQ+ affirming signs and symbols, including Pride flags, online and in public and private places, such as offices, places of worship, schools, community rooms, gymnasiums, businesses, etc.

Sponsor events that showcase diversity related to LGBTQ+ history, art, fashion, music, books, films/media, and sports. Invite local out and proud LGBTQ+ youth and adults for a panel discussion, drag show, or symposium. Organize a writing workshop for LGBTQ+ youth.

Learn and discover ways to be a great ally and advocate on websites such as GLAAD.org, PFLAG.org, and TheTrevorProject.org. Please see more resources at the end of this book.

Encourage school districts to provide ongoing LGBTQ+ training for school board members, parents, staff, and teachers.

Get involved with your local Pride planning committee.

For Parents, Grandparents, Guardians, and Relatives Who Are LGBTQ+

Cultivate honesty. Young people are learning and watching your behavior. Do your own self-check regarding how you live your life truthfully. Remind your child, adolescent, teen, or young adult that you are open to talk about anything on their mind, and that they are free to ask questions that you will answer honestly.

Read and share books that show having two moms and two dads is more common than you think. Celebrate their families.

Chapter 5

Be an Ally & Advocate

Teamwork Makes the Dream Work

Allies and Advocates: Learn, Listen, and Lead!

By Elizabeth

Allies and Advocates.
 Who are they? How are they different from each other? Why are they so important? And what exactly can you do as an ally and/or advocate?

Let's start with knowing what allies and advocates do.

An ally, according to The Human Rights Campaign, is "...someone who is actively supportive of LGBTQ+ people. It encompasses straight and cisgender allies, as well as those within the LGBTQ+ community who support each other (example: a lesbian who is an ally to the bisexual community)."[9]

An advocate, according to the Oxford Language dictionary, is "a person who publicly supports or recommends a particular cause or policy."[10]

Allies and advocates are part of the team that helps LGBTQ+ people win respect, acceptance, and freedom in our world.

"Teamwork makes the dream work!"

That's one of my favorite sayings, and it profoundly applies here. Because there is no "I" in "team." It's all about "we."

Likewise, a meaningful life is all about relationships.

"What is the meaning of life?" I asked my father when I was 19.

"Love," he said. "Giving love and enjoying it when you receive it back."

Period!

So, **teamwork in the spirit of love is a great way to think of being an ally and/or advocate for LGBTQ+ people.**

Let's continue the team metaphor.

An ally attends the game to help fill the bleachers with fans, friends, and family members who cheer on their team and show the opponents that this team has the backing of a loud and loyal crowd. An ally's presence helps the players feel supported. Team members may go to the ally for advice and guidance, hugs, and words of encouragement. An ally makes the team feel valued, affirmed, and empowered.

An advocate takes action to advance the team's cause. An advocate may lead a fundraising campaign to build a new gymnasium, buy new uniforms for the players, and pay for the team's travel to out-of-town games. An advocate may speak at a school board meeting if a player or team is receiving unfair treatment, or if an antiquated rule is hindering the team's progress. An advocate may even travel to Washington, D.C. to testify at a Congressional hearing on a topic relating to a problem that the team is experiencing.

Now, more specifically for LGBTQ+ allies and advocates, here are some examples.

An ally who is straight might wear an eye-catching, colorful Pride rainbow T-shirt while running errands around town, showcasing support for LGBTQ+ people.

An ally may donate money to organizations that work to promote the health, safety, and freedoms of LGBTQ+ people.

An ally invests time to learn about issues and the best terminology that fosters acceptance and support.

Chapter 5 – Be an Ally & Advocate

At the same time, an advocate takes more direct action to create positive change. An advocate may meet with a school district's superintendent to propose that LGBTQ+ students be allowed to bring LGBTQ+ dates to the prom and other school events. This advocate would ask the superintendent to banish any rules that say only male-female couples can attend the prom and other school events. The advocate may even approach other parents to collect signatures and garner support to show the superintendent that the majority of parents support same-sex dating at school events.

An advocate may picket the Vatican in Rome with the hopes of inspiring the Pope to allow the Catholic Church to sanctify same-sex marriage.

An advocate may attend a meeting at the local library to speak out against book bans that aim to remove LGBTQ+ literature from library shelves.

While there's power in numbers, there's also power when someone in the majority speaks out and takes action on behalf of someone or a group in the minority.

As an ally or advocate who is straight, you may have extra power of persuasion to help people open their hearts and minds to accept and celebrate LGBTQ+ people as well as influence decision-makers on issues affecting the queer community.

As human beings, we inherently trust people whom we perceive to be like us. We strive to find common ground as a way of connecting, then growing together. As such, if you are a straight person speaking up and taking action to help LGBTQ+ people, then another straight person may be more open to listening to what you're saying and doing.

When someone in a privileged group advocates for people who are disempowered, the person with social/political/economic privilege has tremendous power to appeal to and influence people who share their status and power.

For example, white and Jewish people were among the many Black founders of the NAACP back in 1909. These white individuals understood that they could use their social, political, and economic privilege to advance the cause and dismantle the institutional racism that legally discriminated against Black people.

Likewise, the reality is that cisgendered men (people who were born with male body parts and identify as male) hold the majority of power in government, corporate America, and higher education. When these men advocate for equal pay and advancement for women, other men in power may be more likely to listen and take action to promote women to leadership positions and pay them equal wages. One example is that an all-male U.S. Congress passed the 19th Amendment in 1919, granting women the right to vote.

How to Become an Ally and/or Advocate

First, **understand what's inspiring you**. Do you want to help a family member? Are you outraged about recent crimes against LGBTQ+ people? Are you disturbed by laws, education trends, and book bans that are encroaching on our freedoms?

Take time to **explore how you want to help**. Get quiet and still and contemplate how you want to become an ally and/or advocate. Explore what particular topics and actions pull on your heartstrings. Ask your Higher Self/God/Spirit/the Universe for guidance on what to do and how to do it.

Seek clarity on your **why** and write it down with a description of all the emotions and experiences that may be inspiring you at the time. Then, if you face opposition or criticism that makes you question why you've chosen to become an LGBTQ+ ally and/or advocate, read what you wrote as a reminder to strengthen your resolve to courageously persevere on your mission to help

Chapter 5 – Be an Ally & Advocate

people who need and appreciate your allyship and/or advocacy.

Next, **learn the history and culture of LGBTQ+ people** from trusted sources.

The National Park Service presents a robust collection of information in its online "LGBTQ Heritage Theme Study" series called, "Telling All Americans' Stories."[11]

The American LGBTQ+ Museum in New York has a traveling exhibit called *Queen Justice,* created as a collaboration with Lambda Legal.

Do an online search for "best books to learn about LGBTQ+ history and culture." Narrow your search for specific topics that interest you and your mission to help, such as "trans children" or "Two-Spirit."

Very importantly, before you speak up, **learn the best terminology** that you can use as an ally and/or advocate. You can boost your credibility and impact by using the best terms to describe LGBTQ+ people and issues.

This will enable you to counter adversaries who deliberately use hurtful, inflammatory rhetoric to spread hate, fear, and opposition.

For example, anti-LGBTQ+ politicians, protesters, preachers, and everyday people use the term "homosexual." This word is considered so derogatory and offensive that respected media outlets such as *The New York Times, The Washington Post,* and *The Associated Press* strictly limit its use on their news pages, according to GLAAD.org.[12]

Imagine an ally or advocate being unaware of this, and even though they have the best intentions, they stand up in a meeting and announce, "I support the homosexual lifestyle."

That's a double whammy, because nobody says "the straight lifestyle," so applying it to LGBTQ+ people implies "otherness" and that a person's internal gender or sexual orientation is a choice, when it's not. Can you see how using outdated, offensive

Joyously Free

terms could potentially do more harm than good, and detract from an ally's or advocate's good will if they are criticized and ridiculed?

So, what's best to say instead? First, give people the opportunity to tell you how they prefer to be described. Simply ask them. Please go to page 46 for descriptions of Lesbian, Gay, Bisexual, Transgender, Queer, LGBTQ+ and other terms, as well as pronouns.

An enriching stop on your learning journey as an LGBTQ+ ally and/or advocate is the website for GLAAD.org, "the world's largest Lesbian, Gay, Bisexual, Transgender and Queer (LGBTQ) media advocacy organization."[13] In addition to their Glossary of Terms, they list words to avoid and what to say instead. You can find this glossary at GLAAD.org/reference/terms. Words are powerful! They shape the way we think, speak, behave, live, and love.

Formerly the Gay & Lesbian Alliance Against Defamation, GLAAD "rewrites the script for LGBTQ acceptance," according to GLAAD.org. A non-profit organization founded in 1985, it "works to ensure fair, accurate, and inclusive representation and creates national and local programs that advance LGBTQ acceptance."[14]

GLAAD's many resources include the latest news pertaining to LGBTQ+ people, that can equip you with information and understanding as an ally and advocate.

I'm an Ally as a Podcaster, TV Show Host, and Publisher

When you're an ally and advocate, you can support LGBTQ+ people in all that you do.

I do that as an award-winning journalist, author, podcaster, and publisher.

On The Goddess Power Show with Elizabeth Ann Atkins®, I interview LGBTQ+ people such as queer author Marissa

Alma Nick, author of *Rebel in Venus,* and bisexual journalist Rachel Krantz, author of *Open: An Uncensored Memoir of Love, Liberation, and Non-Monogamy—A Polyamory Memoir.*

As a newspaper, magazine, and TV journalist, I have interviewed LGBTQ+ people, including a transgender person and their mother, as well as couples who married at a big-city Pride event.

As co-founder of Two Sisters Writing & Publishing®, I publish books by LGBTQ+ people such as Joanie Lindenmeyer, including this book, *Joyously Free,* her best-selling memoir, *Nun Better,* and *Healing Religious Hurts.*

We also publish my erotic novels that feature lesbian and bisexual characters in my trilogy, *Husbands, Incorporated,* and in my upcoming series, *Eleven Women* by Sasha Maxwell, my *nom de plume.*

My "why" is crystal clear: it's my divine life assignment, as indicated by my father's baptismal request for God to make me a "Princess of Peace," to cultivate human harmony with the written and spoken word. Blessed with the gift of writing and speaking, and my parents' renegade spirit to defy convention, I use the power of the pen as a publisher to amplify diverse voices, including those of LGBTQ+ people. I also do this through daily interactions with people, by expressing kind words that help people feel seen, heard, and valued.

How can you do this as an ally and/or advocate? Think about areas where you have influence and power to make a difference, then explore how exactly you can do that.

Joyously Free

My Straight A's (Allies): Armored Friends & Family

By Joanie

Did you get straight A's in school?

I did not!

I was a B student all the way, often telling my mom, "There is plenty of room for improvement! Be patient with me, Mom!"

She would smile, affirm me, celebrate my accomplishments, praise my efforts and cheer me on while complimenting my sincerely honest character and behaviors. All of which are my greatest gifts of truth, joy, and trust in the Lord.

I like being the kind, positive, best me to others in our world where skepticism, fears, judgments, and bigotry can derail so many organizations, institutions, and people. I believe that love "all ways" wins!

That's why I believe friendships are golden, and I never take them for granted. I have deeply cherished friendships throughout my lifetime with my nun friends, sports teammates, neighbors, work colleagues, students, my blood family, and my LGBTQ+ family.

I affectionately call my friends, family, allies, and advocates "my straight A's." Over the years, they have supported me, loved me unconditionally for who I am, and challenged me to be more and do more. They accepted my quirky weirdness, and my super-high mood ecstasies of loving life to the fullest.

We enjoyed each other's uniqueness, never competing for attention. Complimenting and bringing out the best in them raised the bar for all of us. My cheering Straight A's packed the bleachers at my San Diego State University volleyball games. In my Catholic Church communion lines, my Straight A's and I

Chapter 5 – Be an Ally & Advocate

shared the same sacramental host and chalice. In my teaching career, the Straight A's changed their classroom decor and culture to be more rainbow-like, all-inclusive and accepting. My colleagues even removed their husband-wife portraits from their desks after realizing that I didn't feel safe displaying the love of my life, a woman, on my desk.

Safety first, was how Carol and I lived and behaved for years. We didn't go against the grain publicly because of our fear of tires being slashed, graffiti destroying our reputation, and knowledge that could lead to a loss of our jobs. Laws of equality would come later, to protect me and Carol and all people in employment and in health care. Note: Pay attention to the legislative acts that promote or deny civil rights.

During my youth, when my single friends began to be couples as boyfriend and girlfriend and in straight marriages, I was still involved in friendships as a trio. When Carol and I were a couple, we were accepted by our Straight A's: Aggie and Bud, Sheila and Rob, Carolyn, Charlene, Tim, Doris, Fred and Veronica, Bill and Cindy, Dick and Mary, Hal and Chris, and Duke and Heidi. She and I were just another couple for dinner outings, picnics, shows, concerts, ball games, travel, road trips, and countless conversations where we could speak our truth and be celebrated!

Carol and I chose to be smart and savvy, not pushing the envelope in the 1990s and 2000s. We were not publicly affectionate. We saved our intimacy for our home, bedroom, and travel. But our true friends knew that Carol and I liked our intimate moments as we would sit in the back of their cars, caressing, and holding each other's hands and fingers.

At an event, we would sit as close as possible, shoulder to shoulder, our legs and arms touching and feeling warm and snug. Giggles would erupt and our huge, joyful smiles garnered respect and showed we were a happy, fun-loving couple. Some of our Straight A's didn't have a clue we were a couple and that triggered fun winks between me and Carol that were even more special. Giggles, snorts, and pure silence were signs of our hormones that bounced like jumping beans! We believed that someday they would ask or we would tell. We trusted our intuition to know when to say something, and when to know that it didn't matter, because they loved us as we were.

I can't even imagine life without my "Straight A's."

Once, my "Straight A" dear friend, Tim, stood up at a large school conference and spoke about how courageous I was to come out to my fellow teachers, staff, and administrators. The crowd of teachers roared with applause and gave me huge hugs. I cried tears of freedom. I shOUTed for joy and felt absolutely free—no more secrets, no more hiding the true me and Carol.

In a dark, small place in my apprehensive brain, I still wondered if there would be any repercussions or consequences to taking the unapologetic stand of being a lesbian—monogamous and ever so happy. However, every day I interacted with many school employees and colleagues who belonged to extreme anti-gay, homophobic churches and held staunch negative, demeaning, and conservative views about LGBTQ+ people. About me!

In my heart, I knew my Straight A's would protect and defend me. I imagine there were times, behind the scenes, unbeknownst to me, that my allies did speak up for me.

My allies epitomize what Dionne Warwick sings in "That's What Friends Are For."

Oh, what a joyous feeling! It gave me goose pimples that more and more people smiled at me and greeted me in the high school hallways, on the city streets and in the businesses I frequented.

I was no longer invisible. I was "out." I was as Carol had always been, covered in a holy aura with our guardian angels watching, defending, and protecting us.

I like being me, a lesbian, if you need to put a name or label on me. It does not define me and surely it does not limit the multitudes of friends who bring me joy, love, and adventures.

Carol never used—nor did she want—a sexual identity label. She did not believe in putting people in boxes. In fact, in all of her 79 years, 40 of which we were intimately together, her life, her world of love, and her joy were completely boxless. She was a free spirit with total love for humankind. She had a way of seeing and living in both a spiritual and earthly way. We were kindred souls.

As I did with Carol, I absolutely love laughing, playing, praying, and sharing silly, scary, wild, precious, and adventurous life moments with my variety of friends. I thrive when we are together in person and on Zoom, or when communicating through texts, phone calls, emails, and posts on Facebook and TikTok.

I thank—from the top of my heart—all of my "Straight A" friends for being in my life. You are my shield, my hope, and my peace as my head hits the pillow each night. In case I haven't told you lately, I love you!

My dear friends of all sizes, shapes, genders, colors, ethnicities, and faiths, I hope I have been as good a friend to you as you have been to me! To have a friend is to be a friend!

Your "bestie blessed" friend, Joanie.

Joyously Free

A Loving Ally & Joanie's #1 Fan: Her Big Sister

By Gail Baker

I'm Gail Baker, Joanie's older sister. We've always been close, despite our age difference of 12 years. While our physical distance has varied, our hearts have always touched and our communication has never lapsed. We're good friends and blessed to be family, too.

My first recollection that Joanie might be gay was in 1968. This is the year I got married. In planning the spring wedding's color scheme, I chose a sunshine yellow and brilliant lime green that was all the rage at the time.

Of course, being the bridezilla that I was, I asked the family to participate by using those colors in their attire for the wedding. I chose adorable floral lime and yellow dresses for my little sisters and the prerequisite fishnet tights to finish the ensemble. I was so excited and knew how cute they'd both look.

Well, Joanie wasn't loving it! "Yuck!" was her response. Getting her in a dress, let alone a frilly one, was a long shot, but after much bribing and urging by our mother, Joanie reluctantly agreed. She did look super cute, and I was grateful that we had a cohesive and colorful family photo to enjoy. Thank you for taking one for the team, Joanie.

Joanie's resistance to wearing a dress was my first inkling that she was on her own path in life. Many years would pass before she came out officially. When she broke the news in 1981, I was living in Chico, California—married with two kids, aged 6 and 13. She told us in a phone conversation about Carol and the life they were planning together. She sounded excited and we in turn were happy for her. We weren't surprised at the

Chapter 5 – Be an Ally & Advocate

announcement, and neither were the kids, who commented, "We already knew that, Mom. We just want her to keep coming over to play with us."

We ALL knew and accepted Joanie for all the love and joy she contributed to our family. For us, it was no big deal that she was gay. I've since learned what a struggle and big deal it was for her. I think I can speak for the family by saying, "We love you, Joanie, for who you are! Just keep coming over to play!" This joyful woman is a gift to us and we just want her to be happy.

And she is.

I am so grateful to have witnessed the power of love from my front-row seat for watching Joanie's life's story unfold. We have always been kindred spirits, so viewing her progress as a proficient writer doesn't surprise me. She has a boundless energy and a joy that is contagious.

I had the pleasure of witnessing Joanie and Carol's deep love for each other in June 2017 when I drove the exhausting 900 miles from San Diego, California, to Brookings, Oregon.

I made the trek solo to help out as Joanie needed foot surgery and it could only be done at a larger medical facility, rather than the one in the tiny town of Brookings. Joanie needed an escort to drive over the mountains with her and get her home safely. The operations on both feet were scheduled in Medford, Oregon, about two-and-a-half hours east and over the beautiful scenic Smith River and the fir-covered Coastal Range Mountains.

Carol had had a stroke a few years prior and was confined to a wheelchair. She needed constant care and Joanie had arranged with a neighbor and friends to stay with Carol while we were gone.

As planned, Joanie and I left early for her surgery on a beautiful summer day and thoroughly enjoyed our time together on the road. Looking forward to her medical success, Joanie was happy and relaxed. We yakked and sang and laughed as silly sisters do.

The surgery went smoothly and by late afternoon, Joanie was all bandaged up on both feet and released. We called Carol with the good news, and she told us that friends were coming over to play cards. Joanie was grateful that Carol was happy and that she seemed to be handling her absence well.

Joanie and I headed back to the coast around 3 PM, and as we got closer to Brookings, the daze of her medication was wearing off. Joanie's hunger pangs ensued. That called for a pit stop at one of her favorite Mexican restaurants in Smith River just north of Crescent City, California. We ordered the most fabulous, fragrant dishes and took them "to go" and share with the folks back at the house.

We were so happy to look forward to yummy food while celebrating a medical "mission accomplished" with the others. Joanie's pain killers were still doing their job, and being the trooper she is, never complained.

We made it to their home around 6 p.m. and saw the kitchen table was busy with the quiet chatter of intense card players. We yelled hello and all of a sudden the normally sweet and thoughtful Carol, just "lost it." She lit into me in a loud, scolding voice:

"Where have you been, Gail, and why did you make Joanie stay out all day?!"

She was furious with me, and if she could have jumped out of her wheelchair, I'm sure she would have loved to have slugged me.

Whaatt? I thought as tears streamed down my face.

Unaccustomed to reprimands, I was dumbfounded. The guests rushed to hug me, as they, too, were alarmed at Carol's outburst and felt bad that I was the recipient of her anger.

Joanie immediately went to Carol, hugged her, and reassured her that all was fine and that it wasn't my fault that we were gone all day. She diffused the situation with love and comforted her. I could almost see Carol's heart softening. Her tense face relaxed, and a relieved smile and quiet prayer replaced her fear.

From my perspective, I was astounded by the power of love to alter a really intense experience. Kudos to Joanie and to a love so strong and accepting. Witnessing love through adversity made me admire my sister even more. Of course, Joanie reached out to me as well and acknowledged the hurt that had transpired. Even after a long day packed with medical concerns, Joanie showed resilience and selflessly cared about others while forgetting her own pain that was encroaching.

The accusations still stung as I was helping Joanie bring in food and supplies from the car. I had never faced Carol's wrath before and I didn't understand it. My feelings were hurt at the time, but as Joanie explained later, that since Carol's stroke, her behavior had changed and huge, emotional swings and outbursts were common.

Whew! How hard to live this way . . . never knowing when the scales might tip. Joanie later explained that Carol was jealous of our relationship and worried that I'd take her away. The thoughts of losing her anchor to life must have been so profound that they stirred up the resulting anger and resentment. As I understand it, some stroke victims don't have what we call a "filter," so they say and do things that we would not consider doing.

Love isn't always easy. These two women had the whole package, though. They enjoyed many years of laughter, adventure, and joy. Their strong love for each other, God, family, and friends kept them close through the hard times. I'm grateful to have witnessed the whole picture and have a deeper connection to my sister as a result.

Love you bunches, Gail

Gail Baker is one of Joanie's sisters, as well as her dear friend and #1 fan.

An Ally & Advocate Empowers a Teen's Transition

By Diane Weir with Bob Weir

I was raised in a strict Catholic home, and my future was pretty much dictated by a domineering parent. School was miserable, because I was forced into classes I had no interest or skills in.

So, as an adult, I felt it would fulfill me to become a career development specialist. My job allowed me to help high school students identify their interests and skills, and then further help them research possible career options.

In 2012, the high school was implementing a new career interest inventory system at about the time when one particular student was beginning a transition process (with the help of very supportive parents). I was formatting student records to be uploaded into their Career Interest accounts and called the student into the office, because I knew a new name was in their future. I offered the student the option of having me upload their current name or their new chosen name.

With a little finagling of the student record formatting, I succeeded at uploading the student's new name. This way, each time the student logged into their Career Interest account, they would be greeted by their chosen name and not one that they preferred not to be reminded of, especially while they focused on their future plans.

It was a simple thing, really, but having a choice empowered the student even more AND it helped me realize that we all, in ways large and small, can offer support and advocate for those who may not know what options are open to them. Or that they even have options.

Diane Weir is a lifelong believer that we should all be able to live the life that brings us happiness. She is happily married to Bob Weir.

Chapter 5 – Be an Ally & Advocate

Allies Committed to Changing Lives for the Better

By William Burse

While growing up, I was taught to be very conservative. Throughout my childhood and teen years, certain churches said that homosexuality was wrong, along with all kinds of derogatory stuff.

Me, going to prison, that whole battle, was also about homosexuality being a bad thing! That's all I want to say about that.

Coming back, out of prison, into my new way of life, I have learned that all people are people and I want to help them all!

No matter who they are.

Simply put, I am an LGBTQ+ Ally now!

I want to help people all of the time.

I think that the LGBTQ+ population is just like any other population, and I don't even see it or notice it. Who cares what people's sexual labels are!

I was mostly influenced to be an ally because of my Aunt Carol and Aunt Joanie, who are LGBTQ+. We didn't talk about it. It wasn't a bad thing that we didn't talk about it. It just didn't matter to us.

While I was growing up, Aunt Carol and Aunt Joanie were my favorite people. They inspired me to love everyone and to stay positive and to have a wonderful outlook on life.

I love them for who they are as people. I have a lot of great childhood and adult memories of them. They were always there for me, my sister, and my mom and dad; we all grew together as family.

I witnessed and saw just a tip of the iceberg of how Joanie cared for and loved Aunt Carol.

Joyously Free

Before Aunt Carol died, I spent a week with them at their same house where we would vacation every summer. I knew Aunt Carol was just weeks away from death; my parents had already died. These two women were my precious family. I came to hug Aunt Carol goodbye, and I collapsed into her as she lay in the hospital bed in their bedroom. There is a picture, taken by Aunt Joanie, that shows my head buried into her neck and she is smiling. When I was a baby, I had probably buried my head into her neck the same way.

It was only recently, during the last few years, that we've talked about LGBTQ+ issues. We are forever family.

I thought other friends of mine were and are LGBTQ+. I don't know for sure, but it didn't and does not matter. They are my friends.

Today, I own and operate addiction treatment centers that include detox and transitional housing. I've been helping straight and LGBTQ+ people in Northwest Arkansas for several years. We, True Self Recovery, currently serve many adults: male, female, parents, single, career-oriented, retired, straight, LGBTQ+, and veterans.

One of my goals is to open a center in Palm Springs, California, to serve the LGBTQ+ community. I feel that LGBTQ+ people are the most underserved population in that area in regard to addictions. This is an untapped niche, so we want to be the one to step in and help. We want to help LGBTQ+ people be sober and live as their true selves.

I am, we are, your allies!

Will Burse will soon marry Brittany Poe. They are the proud parents of a baby girl. Will, who's in his forties and loves to travel, is founder of True Self Recovery, the #1 top rated addiction and mental health treatment provider in Northwest Arkansas. You can contact him at trueselfrecovery.com.

Chapter 5 – Be an Ally & Advocate

My Adolescent Confession & Apology

By Kyle Clausen

This story is from Facebook messenger from Kyle Clausen to Joanie Lindenmeyer and reprinted with permission from Kyle.

Kyle: I was heading into Crescent Elk Middle School in Crescent City, California. I was in 7th grade, maybe 8th grade, but somehow, I had heard that you were lesbian or gay.

I was whispering to my good friend at that time that you were a lesbian. I was young and dumb.

My mom asked what I was whispering about, and she made me tell her. I think after my friend was out of the car, she shamed me, rightfully so, and said something to the effect of, "You don't get to do that. That's her life; it's not funny."

Something like that. You were probably the first queer person I had heard of and I was very glad it was early on . . . and then I met you.

Sorry for the shitty comment when I was 12 or so. Lol. But also, thank you for being an example to be who we are, no matter what.

Congrats on your book! There was an older guy carrying it on the plane. From what I could hear, eavesdropping, he was from Brookings or Gold Beach.

Joanie: Oh wow, Kyle, thanks for sharing.

Your mom is a true ally!! Strong and compassionate. Hope I get to meet her. You are welcome. And yes, we are examples, role models of faith, hope and love. Keep being You!

Joyously Free

Allyship: A Call to Action

By Pamela Ross McClain, Ph.D.

In an eclectic world, where humanity is encoded with diversity
Expecting gender conformity should not be our reality.

Inclusion can bring peace to a world that's unjust
When we learn to love everyone like the God we trust.

Being an LGBTQ+ ally is a sacred art
Allies advocate for equity with an open heart.

Allies offer support with deeds, both big and small,
Allies fight the good fight for the long haul.

Standing firm as an ally is a call to action
Allies dispel perennial lies by disrupting their traction.

Allies join forces with the marginalized and assuage their fears
By respecting their truths and drying their tears.

Allies learn lessons from struggles the powerless face.
Knowing subjugation and hate should have no place.

Allies seek justice with intentions that are pure
Unified in solidarity, knowing love is the cure.

Allyship will silence injustice's deafening roar
Across the globe and forever more.

Tips:
- Allies unite;
- Educate yourself;
- Expand your view.
- Be worthy of the faith entrusted in you.

Dr. Pam Ross McClain is a career educator and community builder who wants to advance a new research tradition, vulgar scholarship, which will resonate truth and speak to the sensibilities of everyday people. In other words, Dr. Pam wants to empower others to find their truths and shame them devils. She can be reached at prossmcclain@umich.edu.

Tips for Being an Ally and/or Advocate

Financially support businesses and organizations that are LGBTQ+ owned, founded, and friendly and that are empowering the queer community.

Boycott companies, restaurants, and organizations that have anti-LGBTQ+ policies. Flex your power with your dollars to send a clear message that their intolerance will not be tolerated and spread the word amongst people you know to join your boycott. Read about recent controversies that major companies have faced around LGBTQ+ commercials.

Be a mentor for an LGBTQ+ person. Provide words of encouragement. Take them out to eat and talk about whatever's on their mind by creating a safe, confidential space. Help them get a good job and/or advance their career by: guiding them to get clarity on what they want to do, helping them create a great resumé, writing a recommendation letter, putting in a good word for them to people you know who are hiring, helping them prepare for interviews, driving them to interviews, celebrating with them after they get hired, and providing advice as they work and ascend in their career. You could also connect them with people you know in the LGBTQ+ person's chosen field of work who could mentor them.

Stay informed on current events. Find trusted online sources to learn how and where your help as an ally is most needed. Know what's happening in the news regarding legislation, protests, trends, crimes against LGBTQ+ people, public opinion on relevant topics (such as hormones and surgeries for trans youth). Visit GLAAD.org for up-to-date news affecting the queer community.

Knowledge is power. It provides you with a good understanding of how to help, how to voice an informed opinion, and what to say when challenged by critics.

Volunteer at LGBTQ+ events in your town. Learn about them through local chapters of national organizations such as GLAAD.org that you can find online, visit community centers and ask how you can volunteer, check out bulletin boards for flyers about events that need volunteers, contact the organizers of your city's Pride parades and festivals, and ask LGBTQ+ people you know how and where you can get involved.

Give hugs! Join the 14,000 volunteers for FreeMomHugs.org, a nonprofit organization founded by Sara Cunningham, who struggled for years to accept that her son was gay, because his truth conflicted with her Christian beliefs. When she accepted and loved her son as he is, and began attending queer events, she saw the depth of pain that many LGBTQ+ people were experiencing.

So in 2015, she went to the Oklahoma City Pride Festival wearing a homemade button that announced: "Free Mom Hugs." That simple act of kindness grew into an organization that has chapters in 50 states with volunteer moms giving hugs to those who deeply appreciate them.[15]

Start or contribute to a college scholarship fund for LGBTQ+ students. PFLAG.org provides scholarships and lists them by state. You can see the list on their website and contribute accordingly. You could also start your own scholarship at your alma mater or at a school where the need is greatest.

Consider the importance of a scholarship covering room and board for four years, in the context of many LGBTQ+ youth becoming homeless after they come out and their parents force them out of the family home. Having guaranteed housing on a college or university campus ensures that the student can stay in school and earn their degree, which leads to secure employment and financial independence. With that, they can create lives that are *Joyously Free*.

Speak up everywhere! Write letters to legislators, submit guest editorials to local and national newspapers and magazines, blog, write books, attend protests and parades, and express yourself wherever you see the opportunity.

Speak up against anti-LGBTQ+ businesses, organizations, and leaders.

Get involved nationally and locally, in your faith community, at your local library, in your place of employment, at school board meetings—wherever you can use your voice to dispel hate and promote inclusivity and justice while promoting that "love is love."

Chapter 6
How to Heal

Don't Listen to Naysayers

Stop Throwing Tomatoes!!!
They Only Bounce Off My Joan of Arc Armor

By Joanie

Why are some people so hateful with words and actions about me and my LGBTQ+ friends? Why is there a deafening silence in the room when the topic about gay people arises?

Sometimes the statements and stares are so rude, crude, violent, silent, and thick, they could crush a mountain. These powerful emotions stem from ugly accusations that are point blank directed at me, LGBTQ+ people, my friends, my surrogate family, my fellow church mates, team members, school colleagues, students, neighbors, and those who are not even "out"—not even to themselves!

In my youth, I was an excellent poker face bluffer at card games, but I was even a better mask wearer as I attempted to protect my personhood. This is a theme for many of us LGBTQ+ people as we try to cope with rejection and hate.

So I prayed and prayed, "When will discrimination stop? How can homophobia end? Will I always have to explain myself, defend myself, and cope with hate and rejection?"

Joyously Free

Three specific examples come to my mind, two of which are detailed in *Nun Better: An AMAZING Love Story*:
- tomatoes flew at me on pages 111 and 112; and
- locker room graffiti expressed hate on pages 164 and 166.

The third hurtful story involves a dear friend, and I'll share later. Maybe you have a similar story about a rift with a family member, a friend, or a colleague.

What I remember most from the first two harrowing experiences was feeling victimized, repulsed, and hated for being my absolute true self, a gay woman in the 1980s and a lesbian teacher in the 2000s.

In both traumatic situations, I was still closeted, only "out" to a few close friends. In Washington state, Cathy, Amy, Susan, Joan, Alice, and most of my health department staff colleagues knew I was gay and had my back. I was definitely "out" to dear friends Suzie, Brad, Karen, Mark, Joan, Beth, and Scott.

In California, working within a rural public school district, my comrades and allies were Tim, Sherry, Joyce, Kirk, Bob, Leah, Colette, Colleen, Sally, Megan, and Marc; they were a small and mighty, trustworthy and confidential handful of teachers and colleagues.

During my 25 years of employment and service for the Del Norte High School community, I gained dramatically more friends who were trusting, accepting, and celebrating my truth. This mutual understanding opened doors for them to share about their families, friends, past and current relationships, failures, and coping skills during challenges. We all discovered that everyone copes with rejection—internal, external, or both. That life can be difficult, hope can seem far away, and that each day is a brand-new day . . . never been lived before. It's each and everyone's responsibility and choice to make every day worthwhile or not.

Chapter 6 – How to Heal

My deep pains were not visible to the public eye. I thought I was good at masking, faking, and hiding my sexual orientation in the 1980s.

One night, while doing my job as a community health education specialist, coping took on a new meaning. Though I stood tall at 5'8", and proud to represent LGBTQ+ and straight people who were infected with HIV/AIDS, the tomatoes left enormous stains on my psyche and soul. Did they know that I was gay? I'll never know.

The pungent red splotches on my clothing disappeared in the washing machine, but PTSD tainted the reels in my mind for months, possibly years.

I can still vividly see a man, age 30 or so, with scraggly, dirty blonde hair. Wearing blue jeans and a gray hooded sweatshirt, he bolted up from a metal chair. He was part of a large crowd of elementary, middle, and high school students and parents who had convened that cold night to understand the law stating that certain grade levels of students could opt out or receive prevention education about this new disease.

As the man stood, hate glowed in his eyes. His eyebrows scrunched and deep creases formed in his forehead. He cocked his arm to heave something red and round at me. Within seconds, a deluge of tomatoes flew at me.

About 20 of the 75 parents formed a ferocious gang, an uncontrollable hostile united team, an organized club of dissenters standing up, taking their positions and voicing their fears, frustrations, and hate at ME. More tomatoes flew, splatting on and around me. I ducked, squatted, leaned, and avoided most of the flying blobs.

"Go to hell, fags!" they shouted.

"AIDS is a gay disease!" someone yelled.

"We need to ship you to your own island," another screamed.

Joyously Free

This was my first experience of being targeted by a mob hate crime. And I was not even an "out" lesbian.

I was only providing scientific information mandated by Washington State's community health department. Yet, I was the target of deep-rooted homophobia. Somehow, I remained poised and peaceful.

When Jesus was being persecuted, he said something like, "They do not understand me." That raced through my mind on that wild and frenzied night less than a year after I had left the convent.

The next most traumatic experience happened one morning when I entered the girls locker room at the high school where I taught Physical Education and Health classes. High on the walls in black spray paint, the following was written multiple times:

"Lindenmeyer is f____ gay."

I immediately locked the doors so the girls would not see this and so that I would not be outed. I could not let the girls lose their trust in me, as my sexual orientation had nothing to do with them, and my role as a teacher was sacred and trustworthy.

I phoned the athletic director and my male physical education colleagues, my voice quivering as I explained what happened. They all arrived, full of compassion while giving me big hugs. Pain and shock burst out of me in tears. Maintenance staff immediately painted over the graffiti.

They say, "Sticks and stones will break my bones, but words will never hurt me." So not true! I was angry and hurt. Words can make or break someone.

It was a mystery how anyone got into the locked locker room to do this. And this points to that nebulous, faceless force of hate that we know is lurking in the world. These haters hide behind graffiti, write editorials, post hurtful information on the Internet, spread gossip and lies, spew inflammatory political rhetoric, picket, print anti-LGBTQ+ messages in church bulletins, and propose anti-LGBTQ+ legislation.

I still feel the painful sting, as it is personal, like when someone insults your momma. You would speak up and defend her. But you can't if you don't know who said it.

I wish haters could see us as loving human beings rather than targets for hate rooted in fear and intolerance. I pray for a world that is inclusive and calm as we talk, listen, and meet face to face. I want people to ask questions of me and give me the freedom and respect to not answer. I will grant the same to you.

How to Cope

I cope by hanging out with my LGBTQ+ family. We relate to each other and don't have to talk about the struggles. We can just be ourselves, no questions asked. We all know that we have felt the hateful stings and our joyous, free moments. We bond as a team wearing our rainbow-colored jersey uniform.

Listening to music also soothes hurtful memories, and the song "Don't Worry Be Happy" by Bobby McFerrin helps me focus on joy and hope rather than dwelling on the naysayers.

Coping with specific incidents requires responses that are best for that situation. During the tomato bombardment, for example, I walked away. Thankfully, I was not alone. My school allies and bodyguards quickly escorted me out of the room.

Your best strategies for coping in situations like this are to walk away, rely on friends and allies to help you, and pray for peace and love.

That night, I began praying: for the haters to come to their senses; for people infected with the human immunodeficiency virus; for people on their deathbed with AIDS complications; for people to make good decisions regarding their sexual health; for churches and more inclusive leadership and policies; for

Joyously Free

religions and countries to make their laws, rules, teachings, and regulations be loving and inclusive of all people; for people to use condoms (I even sent condoms to my teen nephews as Christmas presents); for drug users to have access to sterile needles; for people to be healed from sex and drug addictions; for gay people to live safely, act smart, and not push the envelope by flaunting their identity during this dangerous era.

As I drove home in the pouring rain, even I succumbed to fear about HIV, wondering, *As a lesbian woman, could I catch HIV? It wasn't worth donating my life to a cause tonight. Well, Joanie, what was that negative last thought?* Yikes, that disgusting thought lasted about 10 minutes on my 45-minute drive home. Now I was even more upset by my own thoughts. Oh boy . . .

I concluded that this mission to help create a more loving world was not about flaunting or pushing the envelope, or wondering, *Is it worth my life to help others? Oh my God!*

My new thoughts came like lightning bolts, the same divine intervention that dropped St. Paul off his horse. I told myself, "Joanie, be Joan of Arc, a warrior on a mission to dispel hate and bring compassion. Be willing to take more risks! If I can dive on the floor to save a volleyball, I surely can dive through life for a bigger reason."

My inner voice spoke in a mellow tone: "Joanie, you can handle this. Be not afraid." As I released angry tears, I sang the Catholic song, "Be Not Afraid" by John Michael Talbot, which played over and over in my head. I felt renewed, charged up, angry, and protected from all harm and mental anguish. All I had to do was hang on to Jesus. *That, I could do!*

I arrived home to the loving arms of my sweetie, Carol. She greeted me at the door with the porch light on. The tears gushed out of me as I collapsed in her arms. I was a little kid with a big *owie* and I needed a Band-Aid of love. I told her everything.

Chapter 6 – How to Heal

Together, we coped. We both released our pains, wiped our tears, and intimately rubbed each other's soft hands and forearms while cuddled on the sofa, our legs intertwined, with the living room lights dimmed.

Here I was cocooned in a healing cradle of everlasting love, as happiness engulfed me from head to toe. She understood me, she intently listened to me, she barely spoke, and she was 100 percent there for me. She nodded and let me ramble. We cried together, sharing the frustrations, anger, and hopes in the form of "what if's."

"You did good tonight, Joanie!" she said.

That night, as we snuggled in our warm, sloshy waterbed, we made a decision. Looking deeper into each other's eyes, the way to our souls, we, Joanie and Carol, committed partners, women totally in love, would always stand up against homophobic bullies and for "Love in Any Language" as sung by Sandi Patty and the two of us.

We vowed to spread hope and encourage people to be their best selves, then let God do the rest. We were called by God on a mission to spread happiness as His designated couple. Our love and joy would shine and last forever. We believed!

It's very easy to retreat and create a cemented heart! To not trust in others anymore, to not risk making new friends, to not upset a safe daily routine, to not leave a protected fortress, and to not let love take hold of a heart. Carol and I knew—and I still know people today—who live inside a brick heart. At the same time, some people cope by turning selfish, retreating, and burying their heads in the sand to stop the pain, and becoming a recluse. They may think they are happy, but it also may be a façade.

Not our style!

Over the years in our relationship, Carol and I continuously pledged our love. We thanked God more. Our hearts had doorknobs that could be turned to open those doors at all times and from either direction. We did not want our lives to be blockaded walls and we did not want to walk on eggshells. This took patience and smarts, honesty, and trust in our growing relationship.

We were still young as a couple, yet we trusted in higher spirits that were way bigger than us, and that all would be fabulous in our lives and with those we met. We exuded love far and wide! Yes, for 40 years, that was us.

We wrote letters, talked, shared, forgave others, asked to be forgiven, and said, "I'm sorry." We strived to always be better, not bitter.

We invited people to tell their personal stories and be relatable. Carol was a pro at asking, "How did you meet?" Then it was game on, ears opened and smiles beaming as we would listen, engage, and love them. It was fun!

We inspired people to find peace, listen to love songs, and say kind words:

You are sweet. You're adorable. I appreciate your time. Thank you for calling. It's great to hear your voice. I'm excited to see you. Let's get together. Want to go for a walk? How can I help? I have some apples to share with you. You are so kind. I prayed and thought of you today. You make me feel happy. I love you.

These are all coping mechanisms to live *Joyously Free!*

Coping When You Experience a Conflict in a Friendship

A longtime friend recently told me that she did not support LGBTQ+ people—trans people, to be specific. And she expressed reluctance to support me, my stance on LGBTQ+ issues, and my next two books: this one and *Healing Religious Hurts: Stories & Tips to Find Love and Peace,* coming out in October 2024 from Two Sisters Writing & Publishing®.

Chapter 6 – How to Heal

This friend is someone with whom I had reconnected after Carol's passing when I was creating new friendships and rekindling older ones.

This was important, because I no longer had Carol's strong shoulders to lean on, her hand to hold and be caressed by, her warm body to cuddle and sleep with, or my partner who shared my joys and disappointments. However, I have Angel Carol and I always have my Jesus! Life has changed, not ended.

Thankfully, I am blessed with a few people with whom I can honestly and safely divulge my fears, doubts, excitements, aspirations, and hopes. I am so grateful. They have not replaced Carol, but they are my salt of the earth, my life coaches and spirit guides, who are sturdy boulders supporting and loving me unconditionally.

I had thought that one particular friend was all of the above. Until she expressed her belief that trans people are unnatural and not created in God's image. That we as a society should not support trans youth, not encourage medical interventions, and definitely not allow trans people to compete in sports that pit "male" versus "female" athletes.

Shocked, a tornado of questions swirled in my mind.

What was the real issue? Did it stem from my gaydom? Was it difficult for a person to have a friend who is an outspoken lesbian? Was my friend being pulled by her family or friends, while feeling stuck in the middle?

Something felt off, the air seemed thicker, and we would delve into these questions in time. I valued my friend too much to let this slide. I wondered what information they might need to feel comforted. And I wondered how we could be close friends, yet have such different perspectives?

My friend does not personally know anyone who is trans and I have several trans friends, adults and youth.

Joyously Free

My friend seems to be very judgmental of trans people and I am not judgmental, and am so glad to have friends that are trans.

My friend is straight and I'm a lesbian.

My friend has a few lesbian friends. I have many lesbian friends.

My friend's circle of friends is 99 percent straight; my circle of friends is 50/50 straight and LGBTQ+.

My friend is happily married to her husband and I am single (lesbian marriage, widowed after 40 years).

My friend looks at things from an academic point of view and I look at things from an emotional, relational point of view.

My friend is very dedicated to specific religious and faith traditions and I believe there are many ways to be spiritual and that one religion is not the only way.

We are both honest, caring, and happy people. We like the outdoors, travel, sports, music, and food, and we both honor our family and friends.

My friend has always supported me and my projects and I have always supported her endeavors.

I concluded that for the first time in our friendship, we would have to agree to disagree.

I am standing up for my philosophical and spiritual beliefs that God makes everyone unique and in God's image. I am *Joyously Free* in my sexual identity, my sexual orientation, and my true self.

I also believe in miracles, because I have experienced them and witnessed them, and I have faith that my friend can open her mind and heart to accept and love all people. The power behind these miracles is my belief that God is all loving, all forgiving, and always alive in me and every life form.

My proof is that I've been miraculously cured, with no medical explanation. I've died and lived. My deceased mother and I

Chapter 6 – How to Heal

had a conversation in the kitchen in front of my siblings. We've held hands with imprints of hers in mine. Carol experienced numerous miracles—her hearing returned and her cancer disappeared. Angels, saints, and Carol's spirit from heaven have shown me light and voices, too!

Dead people have spoken to me, appeared to me, and been present with me. Angel Carol has walked in my home; after she died, I heard every step of her walk from the kitchen into the bedroom.

I've seen a statue come alive and Jesus' eyes met mine. I feel Jesus' presence. I heard Jesus' voice in my heart, in my mind, and in the air, as real as can be.

These miracles and acts of divinity happen out of the blue, with no explanation. It's faith, it's bizarre, and I love it!

How often do they appear? A lot! Have you ever been thinking of someone and then they call, show up, or text you at that exact moment? Have you ever lost something, prayed, or meditated, and then, voilà, you knew where it was . . . like magic!

Cultivating peace within ourselves helps make great things happen. Like a powerful volcano, or an ocean roar or the wind in the trees or the honk of a horn, or a smile, or in the still of quiet, God is there, everywhere all the time. You are blessed!

So, with this miracle-mindset, I chose not to distance myself from my friend. Whether the heaviness of the rift would come to a head or not, I would cherish my core belief that life is love and love is God. I would continue to support my trans friends—and love my dear friend as well.

I'm sharing this story because you may encounter similar difficulties on your LGBTQ+ journey. Is it best to not talk about certain issues with particular people, hoping that peace will prevail and that they may have a change of heart? And how can we find common ground where we learn that queer people and straight people are more alike than not; we all want to live and love in peace and harmony, just as we are.

The rift with my friend weighed heavily on my heart and inspired questions. Maybe trans athletes could have their own trans competitions. Maybe it does not matter if my friend does not support my book. Maybe my friend and I would spend less time together, talk less, and let time heal all, while we find more reasons and ways to say, "I love you, my dear friend." Maybe this was a chance for using one's voice, for being a better listener, and for improving myself. Maybe God would take care of it. As the saying goes, "Let go, let God."

I believe that this rift can be cured. Miracles do happen. There is a bigger reason for it and it's time for me to trust in the Lord with all my heart and say, "Thank you, God, for making me, me!! Thank you for making me *Joyously Free!*"

"Thank you, God, for making my dear friend! Help my friend to become *Joyously Free.*"

Chapter 6 – How to Heal

Find Power in Your Pain

By Elizabeth

Every human being experiences some form of rejection, trauma, fear, shame, isolation, guilt, disease and/or death of a loved one. It's part of life.

When these painful experiences are related to being LGBTQ+, it can be difficult to heal, because the wounds cut so deeply into our psyches that they can scar our souls.

Good news! I'm going to teach you a healing method to identify, release, and remedy this pain, and even heal you on a spiritual level. What does that mean? Well, it can feel miraculous, so please, keep reading.

Here's the gift in it all:

The most difficult issues of our lives can become our most empowering gifts. Take it from me, because I turned **pain into power** to heal myself, then made a career of showing others how to do the same.

The issues that you may be struggling with right now, could very well inspire your life's purpose, passion, and mission. And when you commit to transforming your pain into power, and do the hard work to heal, you could create a career of it as well. Imagine supporting yourself financially with your passionate calling to change the world, all inspired by the pain that you may have experienced as an LGBTQ+ person.

You can do this when you're *Joyously Free*. But getting there requires releasing the emotional baggage that threatens to block or bog down your ability to fly into your healthiest, happiest life.

So let's talk about how to transform your pain into power, which can lead to your passionate life purpose.

Here's my story as an example, with **pain** rooted in:

177

- racial identity;
- battles with food, fat, body image, and self-worth; and
- a horrible divorce that triggered 16 years of awfulness.

How do these issues relate to my gender/sexual identity? In every way, because they are also core identity issues that influenced how I lived and loved—or not!—at the time. Navigating the treacherous terrain of love and romance while standing on quicksand relating to my own identity and lack of self-worth made the experience fraught with fear and anxiety, which made me want to avoid dating altogether—until I resolved and healed these other issues.

Thankfully, my **power** was born during hellish struggles with these issues and became my life mission as a changemaker on planet earth. How?

First, inspired by my racial identity, I became an award-winning journalist, best-selling author, and popular speaker on the topic of mixed-race identity, interracial families, and race in general.

My articles for *The Detroit News* as the race relations reporter were nominated for the top journalism award, the Pulitzer Prize, back in the mid-1990s.

A portion of my master's thesis at Columbia University's Graduate School of Journalism was published in *The New York Times*, which led to interviews on The CBS Evening News with Dan Rather, Good Morning America Sunday, Black Entertainment Television, and NPR.

Likewise, inspired by my battles with food and fat, I committed to a super healthy lifestyle of exercising and eating a plant-based diet, got into the best shape of my life, became certified as a fitness trainer with ISSA, and now motivate others to begin and sustain a wellness regimen. My motto is, "Make the rest of your life, the best of your life."

Chapter 6 – How to Heal

Before that, when I viciously criticized my bloated body and felt miserably trapped in a sugar addiction and the unstable moods and wavering weights that it caused, I didn't love myself enough to be able to truly love another, so I spent a lot of time alone on my sofa, crying and soothing my sadness with more ice cream that only made me feel worse.

Then, thankfully, inspired by my horrible divorce, Spirit awakened my Goddess mission that enabled me to peacefully and graciously endure 16 years of verbal abuse and turmoil from my ex-husband. Then he had a near death experience during which he credits me for saving his life and now views me as an angel.

This experience birthed my Goddess platform with new books, retreats, meditations, and *The Biss Tribe: Activating Your Goddess Power*, a six-part series of books that teach how to manifest your best self and best life.

In addition, knowing that I did not fit society's oppressive mold for a traditional and stifling structure for how women should live and love, I felt constantly pushed by forces, seen and unseen, to squeeze my free spirit into their stifling boxes where even the most luxurious packages made me miserable.

Fearing a repeat of my horrific divorce trauma, and the depression and isolation that it caused, I became extremely squeamish and reluctant to try love and relationships again with others. I was always asking, "How, when, and with whom will I ever feel fulfilled in terms of romance, love, and pleasure?"

If you're still wondering, what does this have to do with healing LGBTQ+ rejection, trauma, fear, shame, isolation, guilt, disease and/or death of a loved one . . .

The answer again is, everything.

Because the healing and empowerment methods I'm about to share with you have worked magic and miracles to free me to live and love as I truly desire, and they will for you as well. Here are my tried-and-true tips for becoming *Joyously Free* by healing whatever is hurting you and holding you back.

Healing Tip #1
Immerse in the Safe Space of Therapy.

A great therapist can be an amazing guide on your LGBTQ+ journey, because they can guide you to face fear and questions around your identity, explore if and how you come out, help you heal from trauma, and define what living *Joyously Free* looks like to you.

If you want to pursue potentially life-changing counseling, please find someone you really vibe with, because therapy only works when you can be *graphically honest* about your feelings, experiences, and dreams.

The best way to find the perfect fit for you is through word-of-mouth referrals and/or online reviews that you trust, to connect with a counselor, social worker, psychologist, or psychiatrist who specializes in your specific LGBTQ+ identity.

Also, since we don't experience our gender identities and sexual orientations in a vacuum, it's imperative to explore and unravel other issues in your life—especially hurtful ones rooted in childhood and family dynamics.

Working with therapists over the years has been profoundly beneficial for me. These trained experts help us connect the dots and provide perspectives and guidance that we're unable to see for ourselves. In addition, these empathetic counselors are skilled in helping us identify and address anxiety, depression, shame, anger, regret, guilt, grief, and the long list of emotions that can explode from life traumas that include LGBTQ+ hurts, fears, and anxieties.

Yes, therapy can be expensive. But it is the best investment in yourself. You can't buy happiness, peace, or confidence in a

Chapter 6 – How to Heal

store, but when you invest in therapy, the payback is all of the above and more.

If you're on a budget, find a clinic in your area that provides free or low-cost services, and/or can help register you for state-funded programs that cover mental health services.

I have witnessed the remarkable success of people whose life-threatening struggles could have ended it all for them, yet the power of therapy and accompanying treatments have made them champions for their causes while showing others that help is available and that it works wonders.

Remember, there is **no shame** in getting the mental health guidance that you may need, for any reason. Your dream life awaits on the other side of trusting a professional to help resolve whatever issues you may have.

In the resources section of this book, you can find organizations that specialize in helping LGBTQ+ people, parents, and allies, and that may be able to refer you to therapists.

You can also contact local or national LGBTQ+ advocacy groups and ask for recommendations for the best therapists in your area. Better yet, thanks to private telemedicine that became commonplace during the COVID-19 pandemic, many therapists now use secure online video portals, so you can meet with them privately from any location.

Healing Tip #2
PowerJournal for Healing with Archangel Raphael

Look at the words "meditation" and "medication."

Notice how only one letter is different.

Medi-**c**-ation.

Medi-**t**-ation.

For me, these words are one and the same, and they can be for you, too. It's an honor to introduce you to the idea, or emphasize it if you already know, that meditation can heal you emotionally, physically, and even spiritually.

If something has been blocking you from coming out and being *Joyously Free*, then we can clear your path with the help of my "PowerJournal for Healing with Archangel Raphael" technique, as described in my memoir, *God's Answer Is Know: Lessons From a Spiritual Life*.

This healing experience can help unblock anything that's obstructing, delaying, or derailing your LGBTQ+ journey. Coming out is a courageous expression, so in a moment, I'll share how failing to speak up literally made me ill, and how this healing technique gave me the courage to overcome fear and express myself.

Likewise, meditation can help you find inner peace, tap into your creative genius, sleep better, lower your blood pressure, boost your mood, connect with Spirit, amplify your intuition, and even help you have longer, stronger orgasms.

You are about to experience my "PowerJournal for Healing with Archangel Raphael" technique that I conceived during my year-long spiritual retreat in 2013, when I healed and released many emotional, physical, and ancestral wounds by combining journaling and meditation, while calling upon non-denominational, all-loving Archangel Raphael.

Please note that angels are not human and therefore do not have genders. Even the most powerful angels—known as archangels, who sometimes have traditionally gender-specific names, such as Archangel Michael—are neither male nor female.

Very importantly, these angels who include Archangel Raphael are all about spiritual power that is bigger than the doctrine of a single religion. They are always with you and available for you to call upon their power to protect, heal, and manifest.

You also have at least one guardian angel who has been with you since birth; you can get silent and still and ask them in your

Chapter 6 – How to Heal

mind to reveal their name and signs of their presence in your life.

This might sound woo-woo or airy-fairy. Especially if you only believe and trust what you can see, hear, touch, taste, or smell with your five physical senses. That's OK. We've been programmed to live in 3-D since our souls left the higher, invisible dimensions and came into the physical world at birth. We've been taught to ignore our intuition and not believe that humans have supernatural powers, or that angels and spiritual beings are real.

Why? Because for centuries, the "powers that be" haven't wanted the masses of humanity to know that we have access to a sixth sense—the supernatural power of the Universe—to heal, receive psychic knowing and downloads, find power, and conceive innovative ways to do bold, brave things in the world.

They want us to be followers like sheep behind the "leaders" who know and use this knowledge to their advantage for power, wealth, and control. Some of these same leaders may have condemned LGTBQ+ freedoms as yet another way to manipulate people and stifle our individual birthright to decide how we live and love.

If it sounds too far-out and bizarre to trust invisible forces to help change your life, please feel free to skip to the next section.

But if you're curious about how to harness this power and live your best life with it, then please, read on.

The Universe is charged with infinite energy and information that we can tap into and use. This energy is invisible. It's "the force" that Obi-Wan Kenobi made mainstream in *Star Wars* movies.

Let's explore this in terms of something you do every day. You trust your cell phone to wirelessly connect you with people, information, videos, music, and so much more, from sources around the world.

These sounds and images are beaming through the air—invisibly!—all around you on energetic frequencies that match

Joyously Free

with your phone and other devices. These frequencies are being transmitted from towers that carry voices and images to your specific phone number.

All thanks to the unseen magic of electrical energy currents known as wi-fi. Wi-fi that you trust and know is there—electrifying the air!—as something we take for granted in this digital age.

You also know that all you need to tap into this magical information source is a wi-fi network and password to receive those frequencies that enable you to talk with anyone and receive any information from anywhere, 24/7!

Likewise, similar frequencies from the Universe are also pulsing through the air—and through you. Our souls, which live in our physical bodies, are individual starbursts of this Universe/God energy that is the pulse giving life to our human bodies.

In fact, the spark that's keeping your heart beating and your brainwaves moving is an electric current that can be measured by monitors. If you doubt what's keeping your heart beating, remember that a person suffering cardiac arrest is brought back to life with **an electric jolt** from a defibrillator.

This electricity is the starburst of God energy inside you and it is your soul. Your soul is your true identity. Not your name, your appearance, your family's history, your education, or your job.

This soul-power current of energy in your body is connected to the energetic frequencies of the Universe all around us. We are transmission towers that can send and receive information. Have you ever thought of a friend, and they immediately texted or called you? That's not a coincidence. That's confirmation of the energetic connection that we have with each other, and the more we hone it, the stronger it becomes.

You can access this cosmic, divine source of energy and information when you connect to its frequency, just like

Chapter 6 – How to Heal

when you turn a radio dial to receive the clearest reception of a channel.

So how do you tune in? With meditation. It's the best way to activate this power and use it for your benefit, starting with healing and/or unblocking you from anything that has hindered your path to being *Joyously Free*.

Two other ways that you can tap into this empowering energy are:

1. Cultivating a high-vibe mindset and lifestyle* that elevate your "vibrational frequency" to make it easier to connect with this Universal power.

2. Dwelling on the high-vibe feelings of peace, joy, and love for yourself and others. Every emotion carries a vibrational frequency, and when you dwell in the highest ones, you can tune in to the cosmic channels where you may literally hear angels sing. Of course, it's only human to experience the low-vibe emotions such as anger, shame, guilt, and fear. That's why this book is showing you tips on how to lift yourself up into a joyous mindset and lifestyle.

*You can learn more about how to cultivate a high-vibe lifestyle in the *Ascend: 8 Steps to an Infinite You* section in my book, *God's Answer Is Know*.

Before we do the meditation, here's an example of how this has worked for me. Let's call this story: "How failing to speak up literally made me sick."

This experience happened after a business meeting with a male client who gaslighted me about money that was promised but would not be paid to me. As a single mother, I really needed that money, and I was doing excellent work to earn it with impeccable professionalism.

Joyously Free

But as a people-pleaser who was afraid to create conflict in an on-going business relationship with this prominent person while meeting in a prestigious restaurant, I bottled my rage inside. I silently fumed behind a professional facial expression.

As I drove home, all that bottled up fury exploded inside me as a horrific migraine headache. The excruciating pain hammering behind my eye triggered the urge to vomit. With a migraine, light hurts your eyes. Smells make you nauseous. And sounds are terribly amplified and irritating.

"Archangel Raphael," I prayed while driving, "please take this pain away."

I immediately "heard" Archangel Raphael saying: "It's your client. Go home. Have chamomile tea, meditate on the couch, and go to bed."

A short time later, in my living room, as my tea brewed, I sat with my legs crossed on the sofa, and typed my intention into a journal entry on my laptop:

"Archangel Raphael, please heal this headache and make my head feel normal."

I closed my eyes and breathed deeply. The room was silent; my body was still except for deep inhales and exhales. Amazingly, the pain began to subside. Then I envisioned myself floating up a golden beam, and passing through the lavender veil that separates the physical realm from the spiritual dimensions, to meet Archangel Raphael in a heavenly dimension.

There I saw a giant angel with outspread wings, standing over me as I laid suspended in the air, as if I were in a supernatural operating room. Archangel Raphael hovered their healing hands over my abdomen. These hands became magnetized, pulling out bright blue splinters from my liver as if they were metal nails. These glass-like shards looked like tiny blue light sabers lodged in all directions in the maroon expanse of the

Chapter 6 – How to Heal

organ that detoxifies our bodies.

Archangel Raphael said, "Elizabeth, you have to express yourself. Failure to express yourself is toxic. Otherwise, the words, the communications you fail to speak, the thoughts and feelings you keep bottled up inside, become splinters lodged in your liver and they're toxic. They make you sick. They hurt you."

Archangel Raphael is a spiritual alchemist, who transmutes hurting into healing with the mystical, violet flame of St. Germain. When we call upon Archangel Raphael, this divine being brings their transformative fire in a large, shallow, brass dish that resembles the Olympic flame.

So Archangel Raphael cast these blue shards into the lavender flames. As the fire transformed the negative energy, it crackled upward in a spray of golden sparks. Then this sparkly geyser arced back down to my body, sprinkling into me as healing energy. And the migraine pain stopped.

"It is done," Archangel Raphael announced.

"Thank you for healing me," I said.

I descended back through the lavender veil and slid down the golden beam into the physical realm. I became aware of my body sitting on the sofa. Then I journaled about the experience:

"Thank you, God and Archangel Raphael, for this miraculous healing!"

Messages from the divine are deeply symbolic, and provide the answers to why we're hurting, and how to avoid future pain.

This situation involved blue shards in my liver because our livers detoxify our bodies. And the turquoise color of the shards that he removed represent the energy center in our bodies that rules communication and our "divine right to speak and hear our highest truth." Our throat chakra is one of the seven main energy centers in our bodies that rule every aspect of life.

Joyously Free

As directed, I drank the calming tea and went to bed. I woke up the next morning refreshed, pain-free, and determined to speak my mind when necessary.

Why had I been so terrified to express what I really felt? First, thanks to explorations of past life experiences in meditation, I knew that my soul had experienced deadly consequences for speaking up and doing what I was divinely guided to do as a spiritual healer, as a storyteller, and as a woman.

And in this life, I've craved approval. For good grades, for being nice, for doing a good job, for being sweet and agreeable. This Good Girl Syndrome is a disservice that society imposes on girls and women and can affect all genders and identities. It brainwashes too many of us, so that we don't speak up, we don't argue, we don't disagree, and we don't say something that might offend someone. As a result, we tip-toe through life playing nice—and playing small.

And being scared to come out.

"Be louder. Roar!" my spirit guides instructed during many meditations guided by giant lions symbolizing courage. I prayed for the courage and confidence to let Elizabeth roar. (I know this sounds psychedelic, and no, I wasn't smoking anything or drinking Ashwagandha. Meditation really will take you there, into fantastical dimensions that provide insight into your everyday life.)

This story emphasizes the need for LGBTQ+ people to speak up and speak out. Keeping our truths bottled up inside does not feel *Joyously Free*.

Instead, the message here is that failing to speak up and express our truths can make us sick while suffering in pain! We have to heal and release the fear of expressing ourselves by being more concerned about our own well-being than other people's feelings. That's not selfish. It's strong.

Chapter 6 – How to Heal

Disclaimer: Please consider potential consequences regarding your physical safety and reliance on financial support that may be jeopardized by speaking your truth. Safety first!

How to PowerJournal for Healing with Archangel Raphael

You can try this healing meditation technique to follow my guided meditation by using this QR code:

Meditation

Or you can follow these instructions:

Get comfortable in a space where you will not be disturbed. Open your journal or laptop, and write:

PowerJournal for Healing with Archangel Raphael.

Date, time, location

Intention: "Archangel Raphael, please help me identify, release and heal anything that's blocking me from living and loving Joyously Free."

You can also write something more specific, such as, "Archangel Raphael, please help remove the fear of telling my parents that I'm gay, and help me find the right words to courageously express myself."

Sit comfortably with your spine straight. Close your eyes and take deep breaths to relax. Become aware of any tension in your body and imagine your muscles softening like warm butter.

Ponder your intention as you envision a golden beam or the side of a rainbow that you can ascend into a higher dimension where you're free to converse with God, angels, ancestors, divine beings, your Higher Self, and/or the wisdom of the Universe. Imagine yourself floating up this beam or colorful slide, into a heavenly dimension where you're safe and surrounded by pure love and peace.

Then call out to Archangel Raphael, by repeating what you wrote: *"Archangel Raphael, please help remove the fear of telling my parents that I'm gay, and help me find the right words to courageously express myself."*

You may hear words, feel an impression, or see visions. You may experience a healing, as I described earlier, in which Archangel Raphael removes symbols of what's causing the fear to come out to your parents. He may give you guidance, and you can ask questions. When the conversation concludes, thank Archangel Raphael for helping you.

Then descend along the golden beam or rainbow, back to your physical body. Observe any more messages or visions that you receive.

Now write as many details as you can remember in your journal, especially instructions for you to follow to heal, speak up, and live your truth.

Healing Tip #3
Define a New Identity for Yourself with Systems for Success

Please read or listen to *Atomic Habits* by James Clear. Here are the two biggest take-aways from this bestselling book.

You need systems to succeed. You can set grandiose goals for yourself, but they will never be reached if you lack *systems* to achieve them. For example, if you want to write a book, but have no system for committing time to write, learn how to structure your chapters, or keep you accountable to your writing and publishing schedule, the book will never be completed.

What systems do you need to heal from whatever is holding you back from living *Joyously Free?*

The Google dictionary from Oxford Languages defines

systems as: "a set of principles or procedures according to which something is done; an organized framework or method."[16]

You can create whatever systems work for you. They can include daily habits that affirm who you are, such as:

- Doing a three-minute morning meditation where you sit in silence and stillness and envision yourself coming out and going through the day with courage and confidence, then acting out those visions throughout the day;
- Pampering your body with a daily self-care routine;
- Reciting a morning monologue in private that you wrote yourself as a self-styled pledge or declaration of who you are now and how you live; or phoning or texting someone—call them your *Joyously Free* Mentor—every morning for a burst of affirmation and encouragement to face the day as the new you.

Your system can be any action you can take every day that helps you stay in the present and appreciate it as a gift, and that keeps you looking forward to a bright future, rather than reliving the past that you're leaving behind.

Recreate your identity for lasting change. The author James Clear says in *Atomic Habits* that the best way to re-invent yourself is to change your identity. He uses smoking as an example.

Instead of saying: "I'm trying to quit smoking," tell yourself, "I am a person who does not smoke."

In terms of living *Joyously Free*, think about replacing this self-talk: "I'm trying to speak up for myself and express my truth," by saying, "I am a person who speaks up for myself and who expresses my truth with confidence and courage."

See how it's much more solid to replace the wishy-washy concept of "trying"—which implies potential failure—with saying, "I'm a person who . . . "

Healing Tip #4
Create an Alter-Ego of Your Boldest Self

You can create an alter-ego or avatar—which is like a secondary personality that you create—who is brave and bold enough to be as wild and free as you really want to be. Start by conceiving this version of yourself by creating a clear picture in your mind. Then decide how you can bring your alter-ego to life.

I do this as a writer, using the pen name or *nom de plume* of Sasha Maxwell when I publish my erotic fiction novels, *Husbands, Incorporated, Eleven Men*, and, coming next, *Eleven Women*.

Sasha is the sassy, braver version of me who has zero fear or concern about bluntly speaking her mind during her wild adventures.

Sometimes if I feel timid or afraid to speak my mind, I ask, *What would Sasha do?* That helps me boss up and say or do what's necessary. When you create an alter ego that's bolder and braver than yourself, you can take on its identity at times when you need an extra dose of courage. It works!

Healing Tip #5
Rescript Your Thinking & Reprogram Your Mind

Have you read *Think and Grow Rich* by Napoleon Hill?

This is one of the most powerful success books ever written, and it contains golden nuggets that can help you on your journey to being *Joyously Free*. (Please read the updated edition that is more inclusive than the original 1920s version. There's a similar book, *Think and Grow Rich: A Black Choice and Daily Motivations for African American Success*, by Dennis Kimbro, PhD.)

Napoleon Hill's chapter on "Autosuggestion" inspired a method that I've used to lose 100 pounds and get more fit and healthy than ever, write dozens of books, maintain a peaceful mindset and lifestyle, attract amazing relationships and

Chapter 6 – How to Heal

experiences, be a guest on TV shows that include *Oprah* and *Montel*, and manifest many goals and gifts.

To use this technique, write down what you want, then recite what you wrote every morning and night. This reprograms your brain to motivate you to take action to acquire what you want and how you want to think, feel, live, and love.

I took this a step further, by writing a detailed script—like a mini movie scene—then recording it with my own voice in a microcassette recorder (before cell phones) and now into the audio app on my phone. I'm always writing a new script, which I record and listen to when I first wake up in the morning and while I'm falling asleep.

This works! It activates something inside you and in the Universe to deliver what you want on a silver platter while transforming the way you think and feel. It can even help you create outcomes for situations that you feared would turn out badly, but instead resolve in ways that are bigger and better than you ever imagined.

So, think about what you want. How you want to feel, think, speak, and behave as Next Level You. Write it out in great detail. Describe your lovestyle, your relationships, where you live, what you're doing for work and/or advocacy, how you're having fun—where and with whom. Detail how you're living out and proud and loving it. Then record what you wrote with an excited tone of voice and enthusiasm as if it's already real. Envision yourself being and doing all the things you're describing and feel the thrill of it as if it's already happened.

When you listen to your own voice describing what you want as if you already have it, in a spirit of gratitude, your mind believes it and activates something inside you and in the Universe that helps it become reality.

Believe and make it happen!

Joyously Free

A Gay Man's Transformation Through Trauma

By Anthony Martinez Beven

I'm Anthony Martinez Beven, a certified nutritional detox specialist, naturopathic practitioner, and clinical hypnotherapist, and I've made it my life's work to share my story of hope and healing, as well as stories of how I've led others through the healing journey to bring about awareness and change in how not only patients, but medical doctors and society view chronic illness.

"Show me how to save my life, and I'll live my life for you," those are the words I uttered to God and the universe in a dire moment of desperation after receiving news of the status of my immune system after an unimaginable medical diagnosis that shattered my world but allowed for entry into a new one. Transformation through trauma has been part of my life since I was baby.

At 10 months old, an adverse reaction to the Pertussis vaccine left my body inflamed. Being so small, I had no veins. A small incision was made in the back of my head to get an IV in me to hydrate my body and bring the inflammation down.

At 34, my life took an unexpected turn when I was diagnosed with HIV and anal cancer within a short span, leaving my immune system severely compromised with only 27 T-cells. T-cells are a type of white blood cell crucial for the functioning of the immune system, and a count as low as 27 signaled a serious health crisis.

At 40, I battled through a second undiagnosed bout with anal cancer that was more intense than the first time, and during this time, I battled two bouts of shingles and COVID. It was through this experience that I realized I wanted to move from the coaching platform to more advocacy.

Chapter 6 – How to Heal

In 2024, I authored my first book, *The Self-Healing Blueprint: Learn How to Become Your Own Health Expert*. This book shares details of how I embarked on a transformative journey of self-healing and personal empowerment. In this comprehensive guide, I also share my knowledge, experiences, and practical strategies to help readers take control of their health and well-being.

These health events not only challenged me physically, but also sparked a profound transformation in my career path. Previously a journalist covering health and medical topics, I transitioned to marketing executive roles. However, my journey didn't stop there. Driven by my personal health challenges, I ventured into professional health coaching and advocacy when I identified a gap in medical diagnosis.

In late 2017, I opened a detox spa, aiming to provide holistic support to individuals facing cancer and chronic illnesses. Through my coaching and advocacy work, I've assisted thousands of people in overcoming various health issues, shedding light on the importance of cellular-level functionality, DNA, and genetics in accurate diagnosis and treatment. The spa closed in December 2022 after the COVID shutdown.

Through social media, my voice and my story have reached hundreds of thousands of people seeking guidance and answers in their own journeys. I have rebranded myself with the tagline "Become Your Own Health Expert." This allows me to offer my expertise in the forms of books, online communities, and educational tools, at an affordable price point.

My efforts have garnered national attention, with features on TV, radio, news sites, and podcasts, amplifying critical conversations surrounding health and wellness.

In 2023, fueled by a desire to combat misdiagnosis—the third leading cause of death in America—I founded The Chronic

Joyously Free

Illness Foundation to "change the diagnosis on misdiagnosis." This nonprofit organization focuses on providing educational resources and training for medical professionals treating cancer patients and those with chronic illnesses. You can learn more at TheChronicIllnessFoundation.org.

My book, *The Self-Healing Blueprint: Learn How to Become Your Own Health Expert*, is available on major online retailers like Amazon, Kindle, and Barnes and Noble. Through this book, I aim to empower individuals to take control of their health journey and advocate for their well-being.

Anthony Martinez Bevin is an author and entrepreneur. Learn more about him at DetoxDaySpa.com. Follow him on Facebook, Instagram, Twitter/X and TikTok at DetoxDaySpa and DetoxDayCoaching.

Chapter 6 – How to Heal

Trans Triumph:
The Hurricane Is Finally Over & I Love Being a Man

By Will Jaster

"Alright, LJ. Looking things over, we can write you a prescription now, and that would be finalized in about four weeks. So, in a month, you can begin taking the lowest dose of testosterone for HRT."

The first time I heard this, my heart was doing cartwheels and backflips in my ribcage, and upon landing after a momentous leap, it slid right down onto my stomach. My heart was laughing in joy the entire way down. The only words that could escape my mouth were, "Are you serious?"

I can't tell you what the day was like when I first received the news that I was permitted to begin hormone replacement therapy, or HRT for short. All I remember was that it was at the end of June of 2023. It could have been snowing in the middle of summer for all I cared. The whole world revolved around that one moment in my mind.

Years prior to this, I had only just come out as a trans person. And even then, I could only call myself a person, not a man. I had yet to feel comfortable saying it out loud fully, because I didn't want the weight of my existence to crush me yet. I much preferred being a silhouette of something vaguely queer, rather than to speak the words outright. There were some who accepted me, though many more who shunned me. This was one of the perks of growing up in a small town.

The town is fairly rural. It's rather interesting to be a part of this community. If I could define this town in a few words, I'd call it a "terminator line" town. In space, the terminator line separates day and night; when you see celestial bodies, and half the planet is dark with nighttime, and the other half is in the light of day, the terminator line is between them. It's also called the "grey line" and the "twilight zone."

Similarly, my hometown is a place where two stark halves meet and blend into one another. Though instead of the light side of a planet meeting its shadowed side, I'm witnessing the modern practices of the younger generations blend with the older. I enjoy watching the younger generations here grow and add more character to this place I call home.

However, plenty of older people in this town prefer to keep it frozen in time, for better or worse. I've witnessed them spread hateful messages in the Letters to the Editor column of our local newspaper, and call for book bans at our library with occasional threats of violence. It is still surreal to me to look back on one meeting I had attended in which a veteran from World War II presented a picture of Nazi book burnings as a warning of where these bans could go, only for the majority of the protestors to trample over his pleas.

Even more surreal was the fact that only months before that meeting, I still lived with my father, who sided with the people who didn't care to think about how much violence they were willing to commit just to get a couple queer and sex ed books removed from the public library shelves.

I found that with people who still saw me as a girl, the cuts from their words hurt me, but were easy to deal with. While witnessing a heavy amount of hatred being thrown at people I identified with, I wondered if I had suffered enough to count as one of them. I asked myself question after question, worried that I was taking up time and resources that could be used by someone who deserved them more than me.

"Am I really trans? Am I enough of a man to be one? Am I faking this?"

Chapter 6 – How to Heal

I decided that to prove that I deserved my identity, I needed to view myself under the same lens of hatred that the transphobes of my town viewed me with.

I had already felt dysphoric about my body. This hadn't been a problem when I was younger, because I was only familiar with the experience of girlhood. However, with the start of puberty, I found that womanhood was much more unbearable. When I was younger, the world cared less about my body, as had I. I was a blank canvas, and I had the power to paint myself however I pleased. But once I started to become a woman, the world ripped the brushes out of my hands and painted me in the "correct" style that I should have been using this whole time.

This created dysmorphia that felt like my skin was becoming too tight for me to wear. I was suffocating in my own body, a place that should have been my safe haven. When I looked at my naked reflection, it felt like my face was disconnected from the rest of me. I was fine looking at my body, then my face, as if they were separate. But I just couldn't look at the whole picture by applying my face to the rest of me. It felt like a censor bar was covering my visage.

The dysphoria was bad enough, but I forced myself to lean into it. I had to be miserable if I were actually a trans man, right? So, what made me uncomfortable was that I hated my feminine body, particularly my chest and hips. I despised my voice, and the fact that my face always seemed a little too soft to be a man's. Eventually, that hatred affected more than my identity. It seeped into every aspect of my life.

All this emotional turmoil followed me to that fateful meeting with an endocrinologist in June. After jumping through hoops with therapists, finding a recommendation for a clinic with a physician, and agonizing for months while waiting for a screening call, I eventually found myself at an appointment to talk with an endocrinologist.

Joyously Free

The fact that they gave me an answer so quickly was astonishing. I thought I'd have to wait at least another year. In fact, at first, I was in denial that it was real. This had to be some joke, right?

During that call, I was grounded back in reality by my mother. She hesitantly placed a hand on my back, worried I'd flinch at the contact. With a smile, she said, "You've been waiting long enough, dove."

My mother has been one of my biggest sources of support since the beginning of my transition. She was there for all of it, every single messy stage of coming out and finding myself. At first it was hard for her, but she was willing to learn. Afterward, she became one of my fiercest advocates as I made my journey to find myself.

I think that's all any transgender person could ask for from friends and family: someone who takes time to learn before judging, and someone who is there to support you during the challenges of identifying as trans.

The next month of waiting flew by. I went to the local pharmacy, and in a few minutes, I was given my freedom—one that came in four bottles of testosterone cypionate, and four matching needles to administer the 0.13 mL dose. The dose itself would be taken subcutaneously, meaning under the skin and into a layer of body fat, and I would be injecting it myself.

However, I needed to be supervised by someone experienced in giving shots to make sure I was administering the testosterone safely. Additionally, since I was new to the world of self-injection, I was hesitant to start HRT immediately. So, I decided to wait a week to mentally prepare for what I considered—and still consider, honestly and playfully—to be stabbing myself. No, this was not self-harm; it was self-love and self-care, because I was finally free to transition. During that time, I had a chance to think about my future, and my mother had a chance to think about the past.

It started at nighttime. What hour, I couldn't say, but the sky outside was pitch black, and the crickets had begun their evening overture hours ago. I had left my room to make sure the doors were locked, and as I returned to my room, I found my mother in hers, crying.

She was sitting on the floor, buried in memories. She was encircled by boxes, books, and picture frames. Staring back at me from those pictures was myself. No, that detail wasn't correct. That wasn't me in those pictures. That was *her*.

That little girl with light blonde hair and blue eyes so big she could have been mistaken for a cartoon character come to life. She always had such a big smile, one that could light up a room. She was a pretty little thing. Everyone thought she'd grow up to break a lot of boys' hearts. She'd also grow up to do something big, like become a nurse, or a mother, or . . . I don't know, some sort of "woman" job. But yes, she'd do that, and she'd be perfect at it. After all, she always was a perfect little girl. That's what all the adults seem to remember about her, anyway.

The little girl I remember was temperamental, filled with hatred for the way everyone saw her, but trapped with no way to speak it out loud. Every now and then, I'd have a chance to spend time alone with her while looking in the mirror. She never seemed to smile much when she was my reflection. I never really smiled back at her, either. It always felt like she didn't belong there.

When I saw her in those pictures, a thick slime coated my insides. I wanted to cough that slime up, and purge it from my body as quickly as it arrived. To my dismay, it only bloated my body more, once my mother took note of my presence.

We met eyes, and I could see how glazed-over hers were behind her glasses. Her wrinkles etched heartbreak onto her face, and her tears were fresh. She wasn't fully there. She never is when she's in pain. I was familiar with her being in this sort of state.

Any time my mother is dealing with stress or pain that she refuses to talk about, there's always a strong chance that she will be sleepwalking the following night. Sometimes, her bouts of sleepwalking can last for days on end, even through the sunny parts of the day if the pain she's feeling is intense enough. It always felt like I was met with another person, someone filling in for my mom while she was away on a business trip to her subconscious. She was a far less deadly and much more sorrow-filled version of the Other Mother from the dark fantasy horror children's novella, *Coraline*, by British author Neil Gaiman.

While I wished to run away as soon as she noticed me, I was pulled right in like a fish on a lure. My lure was the weight and obligation of family. It always was.

We sat together on her floor, and she told me the story of that little girl as though I hadn't been there to witness it myself. All the while, I balled up my fists so tight, my hands began to ache. My legs were twitching as though they were trying to come to life and drag me away if I wouldn't do the job myself.

Despite the way I flinched, my mother clung onto me, and told me a truth I didn't want to hear.

"When you call it a deadname," she said in shaky breaths, tears returning, "it makes me feel bad for loving this little girl. Because you think she's dead."

(A deadname is a transgender person's birth name that they replace with a new name that's more aligned with their gender transition. Therefore, their previous name is "dead.")

I left my mother's bedroom after that. I responded with as much grace as I could, explaining that I wasn't going to be upset

Chapter 6 – How to Heal

at her for having those feelings. My transition was a big moment in her life as well, and I wanted to respect that. With that distance, it was easier to lie and tell her what would comfort her.

It's not as if I don't understand that transition affects more than the transitioner's life. It's a change that everybody close to them has to get accustomed to. However, I would be lying if I said that I didn't despise the way in which some people will say that transition is also a struggle for the loved ones. Unless a loved one is also transgender, there's going to be a stark difference in the struggle that both parties face. The person transitioning is changing their whole life, and even in the safer places to do so, they are still putting themselves at risk of harassment or murder by making that change.

All a loved one changes is their language around that person. And I won't deny it's hard to change your language; every now and then, I slip up on saying the right names and pronouns, too. But it infuriates me when people treat changing their language like a grieving process. You didn't lose anyone; the person you love is still there and needs that love now more than ever. If anything, the only thing you're losing is an image of the person that you believed to be accurate.

At the end of the day, transgender people are still the same human beings as they were before transition. It's just easier for them to outwardly express who that human being is now. We aren't stealing loved ones' memories by transitioning. We aren't mindless zombies, or pod people from the 1956 sci-fi movie, *Invasion of the Body Snatchers*. We are still human.

After that run-in with my mother, I returned to my room, and promptly locked my door.

It rained for days. I sat in my room, attempting to escape into work or mindless distractions. Anything to drown out my mother's mournful cries. The walls of our little house are fairly thin. So, it felt as though she was right there in my room as she cried over losing her little girl.

All the while, those waves of questions returned. I began to look at those vials of testosterone differently. They weren't freedom anymore. All they looked like now was a method of euthanasia for that little girl. I'd become her killer, in that sense, and I couldn't handle bearing that title. I loved my mother too much to know that she'd only see me as the killer of her little girl. At the same time, I also hated myself too much to keep living like this.

I was angry at that little girl for how she caused this strain between me and my mother. It all seemed like her fault. If she had never existed, I wouldn't be trapped in this situation.

Eventually, it became too much. I had to let these feelings out somehow, and I did it the only way I could. I began to write.

I decided to write to the little girl who had been haunting me. It wasn't like she would receive those letters, but I had to tell her what was going on. I had to confront her about the pain she was causing everyone. I was tired of watching her smile at me, mocking my misery with her picture-frame glee.

"Everything about you existing makes it to where I feel like my right to exist is challenged every day," I wrote. "Why couldn't I have just been born Will and save both of us the trouble? You could have continued being dead without the burden of being grieved, and I could just live. I may not hate your name, but I hate the concept of you. You make me feel like a shadow. Your shadow. All anyone sees in the presence of me is the absence of you. At the same time, I am so desperate to be you. Not because I want to be you, but because I want to spare myself and everyone else the pain of being me. You should have never existed in this body. You are nothing but a parasite."

One sharp-tongued letter was written with ink and tears.

Chapter 6 – How to Heal

One moment of release from all that built-up pain. In the bitter silence of my room, I finally took my chance to breathe.

Of course, there was no little girl in that room with me. She was once me, after all. But in that silence, I could hear my heartbeat. And in that heartbeat, it was like I could hear her speak to me. It was a quiet little message, but it was still there:

"I'm sorry . . . for you and me. I'm just sorry."

At that moment, the cracks of a breakthrough began to form. It took days after to notice, when the emotional hurricane calmed and everything settled.

Eventually, my mother came to her senses again. She apologized, explaining that she just needed to process this change. She held it in too much for my sake, and the way it had finally come out had been disastrous.

What my mother said in her apology made me think about the hatred I felt towards the little girl I used to be. After talking with my mother, I looked back on that letter. All I could think of was how cruel my words had been. Especially to a child.

Whether I like it or not, I was once that little girl. I knew what kind of pain she had been through. She already thought she shouldn't exist. Why on earth would I tell her she was right? She hadn't done anything. She was a child, one who needed care that nobody knew how to meet. She was afraid of being a burden, and here I was telling her she was nothing but a parasite.

She didn't need that kind of hatred. She'd been shown enough of that to last a lifetime already.

For years of my life, I had rooted my entire being within hatred. I had to be a transmasculine person because I hated being a girl. At the same time, my mother seemed to hate losing her daughter, and I didn't want my mother burdened by that hatred. I never realized that I would have a more fulfilling life if I allowed myself some love.

Joyously Free

The truth is, I love being a man. I love the ability to grow a beard and have a deep voice. I love finding a feminine way of presentation within a masculine identity. And my mother loves her child, no matter what that child grows to become. But she also loves the past and can't let go of it easily. She could love both without one bringing a feeling of hatred towards the other.

It was my love for my mother that gave me the patience to return to that conversation, to make sure that I truly understood her. It was my love for myself that kept me pushing through the hesitation to take that big leap. It was my love for that little girl to finally allow her a chance to rest in peace.

The day I got my injection training was a glorious one, just like the first time I was told I'd be allowed to start taking testosterone. I sat there, staring at my exposed belly, more than ready to take that first dose.

Testosterone cypionate, 0.13 mL dose. It may seem like euthanasia for a little girl, but I saw it as a way to let go of her. Here and now, she'd finally have the chance to fly away, just like she always wanted.

My mother sat next to me as I prepared the needle. Just like she did when she told me I had waited long enough. I had, hadn't I?

The dose was administered, and in that instant, I could feel that little girl's presence all over again. We said our goodbyes to each other, and thanked each other for those times together, both the good and the bad. And in that moment, we were finally free.

Tips:

For LGBTQ+ people: Do not root your identity in what you hate about yourself. If you only focus on the traits that you think "undermine" your identity, you won't see all of the wonderful things about yourself that affirm who you are.

For Allies: be patient and open-minded. You don't have to be correct about LGBTQ+ topics all the time; all you need is to be willing to listen and learn.

Will Jaster is a 17-year-old high school student graduating in 2024. He is also a trans masc individual who aspires to write his own novels one day. After graduation, Will plans to continue his education through community college, and eventually become a mortician.

Joyously Free

A Bisexual Woman Navigating Life with Gaydar and Road Stand Signs

By Jenny Leffler

I was 10 years old when I became aware that I was attracted to girls as well as boys. It was 1980, and I was in the fourth grade in a small Upstate New York farming town called Hubbardsville. The population of the town was only a few hundred people, and the majority were Caucasian, Christian farmers.

The town was not exactly a place where you could expect open minds and progressive hearts. I remember hanging out with my friends, listening to music as they talked about which boys were cute and who they wanted to marry. I went along with the dialogue, agreeing that the boys were cute and adding my own opinions in the mix, all the while wondering in the privacy of my own mind, "What about the cute girls?"

Living in a small Christian town, I knew nothing about the LGBTQ community. I didn't even have words to describe my attraction to girls, and I spent several years wondering what was wrong with me. I was a private, introverted child and never in a million years would I have told anyone how I was feeling.

I was an observant child, and I looked at the other people in my community. I didn't see anyone else "with" a girl, so I assumed that I was supposed to only like, and be with, boys. This is how my simple mind worked because, realistically, children have simple minds and cannot understand complex feelings or express them with words.

So, I ignored my attraction to other girls and hoped it would go away as I got older, as if it were something I would grow out of, like old socks. I chose instead to focus on riding my horse, playing softball, and averting my eyes in the locker room so I

Chapter 6 – How to Heal

wouldn't look at the developing bodies of my female classmates. I got my first boyfriend in seventh grade. For a while, thoughts of girls were shoved to the back of my mind, because I was giddy about having a boyfriend, and I could finally feel like I fit in with my friends who all had boyfriends.

My family was originally from Utah and we moved back there in 1986. My stepdad worked as an engineer for a Utah company, and we moved to Mexico for five years before moving back to the United States, living in Hubbardsville, New York, for five years. We went from living in that small Christian town, to living in a big Christian state, whose citizens were predominantly of the Latter-Day Saints (LDS) faith. I was 15 years old. My hormones were running rampant, as they do for any teenager, and I was trying to find my identity.

I started watching more television and movies and listening to music of the era. I began to understand my attraction to females and finally had a word for it: bisexual. But having a word for it didn't mean that I was brave enough to wave that word around like a sword. I was living in Utah, after all, a place where the LDS faith was king, a faith that absolutely condemned anything but heterosexuality as a sin—something they still do today.

In high school, my "gaydar" started working, and I confidently began to get to know other students who were LGBTQ, though I still kept silent about being bisexual. I longed to tell someone, to be a part of the LGBTQ community, but fear kept me silent. Fear of societal judgment, fear of judgment from family who were members of the LDS faith (I am not a member and never have been), and fear of being "different." People were being thrown out of their homes by their loved ones, beaten, and murdered because of their sexuality, and as a 15-year-old, that scared the hell out of me.

Joyously Free

High school graduation came and went and I was off to college and too busy really to think about anything but trying to navigate the world as an adult. I entered my early twenties, still trying to figure out my path in this world, with traditional, patriarchal views battling with feminist, independent views in my mind and in my heart.

I wanted to explore the fun-loving, feminist side of me; I wanted to let loose and tell the world I didn't care what they thought of me, that I will love who I want to love, woman or man. But that fear had a strong hold over me, and I let it hold me back. I missed out on having wonderful intimate relationships with lovely, intelligent women because of fear.

I didn't want anyone to hate me. I was an introverted person and the thought of opening up to others and attracting attention to myself brought on near panic. So, I once again hid that part of myself like it was a shameful secret, and I spent my twenties not really feeling like my genuine self. And, really, I *wasn't* my genuine self. I was pretending to be like all the "normal heterosexual" people and I was ashamed of myself, filled with guilt.

Because I chose to hide who I really was, I became depressed and began using food to cope with my emotions. I spent several years alone and lonely, only leaving my home to go to work. I was too embarrassed about my expanding waistline and too ashamed of myself to be out in public.

It was at work that I met my future husband, Keith. I was working the graveyard shift, as was he, and we struck up a friendship. He told me years later that he knew when he first saw me that he was going to marry me. I couldn't understand why. Obese and depressed at the time, I didn't believe anyone could ever love me, because I didn't even love myself.

Keith said he saw the light in me, really and truly "saw" me, and he knew he was put on this Earth to love me. And he did.

Chapter 6 – How to Heal

He loved me unconditionally and because of his love and support, I learned to love myself, be secure within myself, and gain a self-confidence I never thought possible.

Keith was the first person I "came out" to, and the relief and joy I felt when he hugged me and told me he loved me was indescribable. This was the first time in my life that I felt seen and heard, that I felt important. In that moment, the fear of being my genuine, bisexual self, left the room. I embraced my sexuality and spent time on introspection and what finally being my genuine self would mean and what it would look like to the world.

I don't go around announcing to everyone that I am bisexual, nor do I keep it a secret. If it comes up in a conversation, I'll mention it. I don't walk down the street questioning who is heterosexual, who is gay, who is lesbian, who is bisexual, etc. That's not how I go about my life. What consenting adults do in their bedroom is none of my business. Who they love, is who they love. I don't question it, and I don't judge it. I am not a person who yells loudly with a bullhorn about LGBTQ rights. I make quiet, behind the scenes efforts to affect change and advocate for my LGBTQ community.

Love and sexuality are fluid. They don't fit into a neat little box with black and white instructions. I feel that traditional views of love and sexuality suppress the genuine happiness and sense of self inside people who may be exploring their identity.

Each person's journey is unique, and the ways I coped with my fear, and with hate and rejection, may not make sense. Each individual has to choose their path, and as you walk the path, I hope you will see the "roadside stands" of support from your LGBTQ community. We are here for you and you are not alone.

As the actor and producer Elliot Page—the first openly trans man to appear on the cover of *Time* magazine in 2021—said, "We deserve to experience love fully, equally, without shame and without compromise."

Jennie Leffler's Tips to Cope with Hate and Rejection:

1. Limit your social media. I didn't have to worry about social media when I was a kid, because it didn't exist. Remember that social media is not reality, and people are only putting their best face forward to give the illusion that their lives are perfect. It is also being used as a platform to spread hate and ignorance and this is toxic. Our brains absorb this information, and mental wounds are more difficult to recover from than physical wounds.

Please reduce your use of social media and avoid reading and responding to hateful comments.

2. Find a supportive person or community to guide your LGBTQ+ journey. Change is challenging and you don't need to go all in all at once. You don't have to come out and yell it from the rooftops. Find a person or a community of people who can be a support system for you and start by telling them.

So many people have already gone through, or are going through, what you are, and these amazing individuals can be your mentors and guides on your journey. You don't have to quit going to church, change your religion, or leave family and friends.

Don't ignore and avoid your feelings like I did. It makes the journey that much harder, and it can be really lonely. Be patient with your process, and you will figure out which path is yours and how you want to walk it.

3. Tend to your mental health. So many mental health resources are available, with many more in recent years, thanks to the growing popularity of telehealth. Use these resources. You can find therapists who specialize in providing counseling for LGBTQ+ individuals. And many places of employment offer free counseling. Social media can also be beneficial, because you can join private groups where members support each other.

Chapter 6 – How to Heal

4. Make self-care a priority! Be mindful of what you are saying to yourself. Make sure you are getting enough sleep, eating three meals a day with two small snacks in between, and drinking water. Treat yourself to fun activities regularly, and don't be afraid to spend time alone.

Loving yourself and enjoying your own company goes a long way to developing self-acceptance, security, independence, and identity. Oh, and get some physical activity in there somewhere! It can be as simple as taking a walk in the park, or as unique as goat yoga, or as difficult as climbing Mount Everest. Our minds and bodies are happy when they are active and stimulated.

5. Expand your LGBTQ+ social circle. Use an app like Meetup to pursue your interests with people who share them. Yes, Meetup has LGBTQ+ options, and it's free. Attend Pride events! These events are the hub of your community.

6. Never give up! If you are having thoughts of wanting to die or of killing yourself, please call the National Suicide and Crisis Lifeline by dialing **988**. You are not alone, and we need you here with us.

You've got this!

Jenny Leffler is a Licensed Clinical Social Worker who enjoys helping homeless veterans get back on their feet. She has a passion for traveling the world, reading, and spending as much time as possible with her two dogs.

Joyously Free

A Gay Man: Celebrating Love & Loss with My Forever Person

By Michael Martin

Our eyes met in 2020 on a Sunday during the San Diego gay pride event. I saw a happy, laughing and smiling guy sitting by himself across from the bar. He wore a fox tail with a fanny pack and matching Crocs. He quickly became my fox prince.

We did everything together, dancing everywhere we went, and showing the unconditional love that we had for each other. It was only a short year together, but anyone who saw us just assumed it had been a lifetime of love that we shared. Our passion was so strong, we made each other shine.

Andrew Phillip Holland was hard of hearing, but it didn't matter, because we communicated through touch more than words, and by simply being present with each other. We had both overcome so many challenges before we met, and together we were empowered and comforted to do this even more.

Andrew was from Atlanta, Georgia, and had always been shunned or disrespected, because people perceived him as too small, gay, or just too weird.

When we met, none of that mattered, because he was my human. On August 9th, 2023, while he was getting ready to pick me up from work, he was killed in our apartment in downtown San Diego. A neighbor we did not know was ordered to stand trial for murder.

I lost my person, someone whose very being dwelled within me. Yet I coped with this horrific loss by remembering the phrase that Andrew and I had taught each other:

Never lose your sparkle.

Chapter 6 – How to Heal

Your sparkle is your joy and your love for yourself that radiates from within and brightens the moment for everyone you encounter.

I have been holding on to that, and it has kept me going.

I have so much support from my close friends and Andrew's online community of friends. My faith has also provided some comfort, although it's been challenging. Growing up as a Catholic youth minister's son in San Diego, on top of being a middle child of six, I was not one to speak out. So I just went with the flow.

When I met Joanie, the author of *Nun Better*, and shared what happened to Andrew, she suggested that my story is something that needs to be heard.

Real love is out there and given to us by God and by a spiritual force. The purpose of this gift is for us to teach others to never give up. You don't have to forget or move on from this love; you can keep it alive inside you.

And with it, you can move forward by spreading your sparkle.

Meanwhile, never stop loving yourself and help will come if you just ask or speak out.

Stand strong in your truth.

Be the sun or smile that someone in your path needs.

Don't judge, because you do not know their story.

Andrew's and my love will never stop. It will morph into something bigger and brighter, something more expansive than the cosmos.

I will always love you unconditionally, Andrew Phillip Holland.

I am yours forever.

Michael Martin is a San Diego native who is part of the sunny town's vast LGBTQ+ community. You can reach him at mikeepants21@gmail.com

Tips for Healing & Ignoring Naysayers

Prepare a "first aid kit." Be ready to heal from any hurtful words or experiences, by knowing who you can call for comfort, what you can do for self-care, and what affirming words you can use to diffuse the negativity.

Hate, rejection, and persecutions can tear an LGBTQ+ person apart in seconds and the devastation can last for decades. So, now's the time to prepare your "first aid kit" of tips that you can use in a natural, loving, and joyful way. Joanie and Carol believed in being proactive and facing challenges with courage and grace.

Your "first aid kit" could include the phone number or email address for a close friend, relative, and/or trusted counselor or therapist to talk through disturbing experiences. It can also include physical action that helps you vent anger, such as hitting a punching bag at the gym, taking a run, lifting weights, screaming alone in your car, or riding your bike. Hobbies can be soothing as well. Laughter is the best medicine, so watch funny videos or movies.

Your metaphorical "first aid kit" can also include soothing tea, a soft blanket for cuddling on the sofa, and a playlist that always makes you feel better.

It's also OK to release your emotions by crying, and engaging in comforting activities such as journaling, meditating, or praying.

Imagine a Teflon shield protecting you. Have you

Chapter 6 – How to Heal

ever seen drops of water on a nonstick pot? The droplets roll and don't stick. The non-stick Teflon coating does not allow even the stickiest food to stick to the pan. This makes for easy clean-up.

Now think of this same phenomenon happening when you face naysayers or haters. Envision around yourself a Teflon bubble that their mean words and hateful stares cannot permeate. This way, you don't react or argue with haters in public. Walking away to safety may be your best option.

If you are in danger, leave the situation as quickly as possible. Keep the non-stick deflection shield erected over your thoughts and your heart, so that their hate remains away from you.

If a hate crime has occurred, call the police immediately and phone the FBI hate crime number: 1-800-CALL-FBI or 800-225-5324. Put this number in your phone.

Believe in karma. Know that you get what you give. Dish out kind words and they will probably boomerang back to you. What goes around comes around, and you reap what you sow. So, be kind. Speak nice words. Believe that what you give will come back to you.

Say "thank you" a lot. Be grateful for little things that are really big things, such as breathing, having clean water, eating fresh food, giving and receiving smiles, etc. Start a gratitude list and practice reading it. Every day, write 10 things that you're grateful for. When you flex your gratitude muscle, it will get stronger, and giving thanks will become an automatic thought process that uplifts you.

Find comfort in God and Spirit. Prayer and meditation are powerful elixirs for hurt feelings. Take time in a quiet place to connect in whatever way works for you and ask for comfort and guidance. You can do this at home, at your place of worship, in nature, and anywhere that you feel safe and free.

Your Higher Power is always there for you, so allow its infinite love to embrace and soothe you.

Your Higher Power is always there for you, so allow its infinite love to embrace and soothe you.

Thank you to our powerful, courageous writers

You added extra sparkles for making *Joyously Free* burst with inspiration!

Chapter 7

I Do, I Do!

Gay Marriage

You Are a Match Made in Heaven

By Joanie

"Are you married, Joanie?" came the question for the umpteenth time. Before I could respond, the second question always came quickly: "Do you have kids?"

Oh, how judgmental, I thought as my face probably turned bright red with discomfort, fear, and shame that no one understood the true me.

I did my best to keep a poker face, a gay one, and not blow up and show my anger and disgust. I touched my short, sporty, natural blond hair style, thinking, *They just don't see the real me—a gay, a lesbian woman who is secretly partnered and living with the love of my life who is a woman.*

While growing up and becoming an adult, I was adamant that: *I do not want to date or ever marry a man. I don't need or want to have a boyfriend to look good in front of others for their lofty, sexist opinion or my acceptance in society.*

For Christmas parties and dinner dates with my straight friends, I had no desire to show up with a male escort. Yet,

Joyously Free

I was at a loss for words as their simple questions deflated my confidence.

Personally, it felt like, *Oh golly, how am I going to wiggle my way out of this one, because I don't have the strength, yet, to tell my whole truth.* Plus, I needed to respect Carol; she was still a nun. We did not want our reputation of kindness and joy to be tainted. God was calling us to do something really, really BIG!

But when and how, dear Lord?

For me, these two powerfully disturbing questions, which were asked frequently, were churning deep within my gut. I dreaded this. It felt like an attack from forces that wanted me to conform. So my mind raced: *I bet my friends, my colleagues, my churchmates, probably don't even know that they're attacking me.*

I wanted to boldly proclaim:

"No, I don't want kids, I'm gay, and I actually have the love of my life standing at my side. She's still a sister in the Catholic religion, but we are so very happy and we absolutely love living together. We share the same bed, we kiss, and make love for pleasure and intimacy! This is the true me and the true us! God put us together."

Oh, how I wanted to scream that to their faces and from the mountain tops. But I was so weak.

Meanwhile, our life was remarkable with careers we loved, talents we shared, and friends we enjoyed.

We were "forever" in our personal commitment to each other, yet our government made it illegal to be a same-sex couple and it was even more forbidden and denied by our beloved Catholic faith.

From the time we fell in love, we believed that our union was God-ordained, because we met after we had each committed our lives to the church as vowed sisters, nuns. That took us both to the small town of Lewiston, Idaho, where our epic romance began in 1982.

Chapter 7 – I Do! I Do!

The following year, Carol and I had our first "real conversation" about our love and commitment to each other, and this conversation became a marriage proposal of sorts.

It happened as I lay wearing blue athletic shorts and a white logo T-shirt, relaxed and sprawled on her twin bed in her convent bedroom. It was covered by a multi-colored, cotton quilt made of four-inch squares of orange, blue, red, and pink patterns with knobs of purple thread as accents.

This soft cocoon of cotton, virgin and holy, sacred and profound, had been the site of our first intimate moment as Carol's warm soft, strong hands massaged and caressed my shoulder, which was sore from playing softball. Oh, the comfort and the pain relief were heavenly, as if she were touching and soothing the inside of my soul. Warm and happy, I felt dazed by her compassion and unconditional love as she tenderly guided me to collapse onto her chest and lay my head on her heart. She cuddled me close, her large squishy breasts sending tickles all over my body. *Lub-dub, lub-dub,* our hearts were beating with the same rhythm!

Two hearts beating one beat, I thought. *This is EXTRAORDINARY! This is INTIMATE! This is REAL LOVE!*

As we sat there, she rubbed me as a few tears streamed down my face. She wiped them with her gentle fingers and I cried even more. We laughed and held each other for a good while. Time disappeared and life had changed.

Then, our legs and arms wrapped tightly around one another. Our fingers intertwined in our signature love hold, her gorgeous green eyes and my hazel eyes diving deeper into our souls. We knew this was bigger than big! As our bodies, minds, emotions, and thoughts quietly ricocheted back and forth in a sweet synchronicity, we cuddled, safely and privately in this forbidden embrace. As two women, sisters in the Catholic Church, living and proclaiming our vows of celibacy, poverty, and obedience to ourselves, families, friends, our dear congregation of the Sisters of St. Joseph, and to the world, we knew change was coming. A great kind of change that would bring peace like never before.

Bold and sincere, honest and vulnerable, I said, "Carol, I need you and I want you! For me to be complete, I need you!"

Tears streamed down my face, releasing pent-up emotions and welcoming a peace that would resonate forever in my soul.

"No, you don't need me, Joanie!" she shot back.

"**Yes I do!** Do you need me?" (There it was—I DO—a marriage vow early on.)

Was it seconds or minutes that passed? I don't know. It seemed like all time had stopped. We were one! We lay there still, feeling our heartbeats as one rhythm, not two.

"**Yes, I DO**," Carol said. "I want to live and be with you, too, Joanie."

THAT REALLY WAS OUR MARRIAGE MOMENT!

OMG OMG OMG WOWIE!!!

She healed me in an instant and—unbeknownst to me—for the rest of my life. And I healed her, too, in ways that later rang true as devoted and dedicated beyond all things possible.

Fast forward **38 AMAZING** joyous, adventurous, trusting, loving, fun years with us a couple! An official couple in colorful pictures in our church directory, family portraits, hundreds of snapshots, digital photos, and videos.

Every image chronicled how we grew deeper in love by the day.

We missed each other when we were separated; we kissed day and night in our private home, car, and safe places. We held hands, snuggled on couches, slept soundly together on tiny twin mattresses too small for two grown ups, and made "Adventurous" our middle names. We loved the circumstances! We talked, we

Chapter 7 – I Do! I Do!

listened, we giggled and laughed at each other. We were connected by spirit. And we were profoundly in love—me, age 24, and Carol, 39 years young.

We were "a match made in heaven," as my mother said. This let me know immediately that Mom understood me, while affirming and celebrating me and Carol in a holy way. My mother's words filled me with tremendous joy and peace.

Carol and I believed with every ounce of our cells, and pulse of our hearts, that God had united us for His purposes. We learned to trust in our Lord—we, two women in love!

We were not always accepted in society, but that was improving. Our beautiful love, sex, and commitment were not and still are not approved by the Catholic Church today.

But so what! Despite the world's views, we were married! First in our hearts!

We did not label ourselves with friends or family as a united sexual lesbian couple, but most of them referred to us as a unit: "Carol and Joanie."

Yes, we were different from the norm, but it did not hold us back from our fun, positive attitudes and inner joys of peace and thankfulness. We sang, danced, hiked, and cooked scrumptious meals. We had multitudes of friends from **all** walks of life! We were great friends and had great friends.

We wondered, *Was marriage really the beginning and "end all" purpose of life?* This single societal question had been ingrained in all of us for centuries. To be a man and a woman (in love was optional, but hoped for), legally and officially married, it meant receiving perks such as: paying joint taxes; receiving Social Security benefits and even death benefits; getting lower car insurance rates; receiving joint medical benefits; and empowering only family members access to the hospital's Intensive Care Unit to make life and death decisions.

What about the huge topic of procreation to continue another generation of the family name and legacies of offspring who delight the hearts in those becoming a proud parent or grandparent? This was the way of life for the straight world.

But **not** the way of life for me and Carol, my sweetie. We will continue our family heritage with love stories, adventures, faith, hopes, and dreams for a better world. We believed we would make a difference for people everywhere. How, I didn't know, but God would make it happen through us. We so believed.

From the 1980s to the 2010s, we shared a married lifestyle for four decades. Those were some of the toughest times, yet it was being together that kept our smiles big and our uniqueness touching others.

After same-sex marriage became legal in the United States in 2015, Carol and I had many conversations about getting married. We wanted an official, sacramental Catholic Church wedding. However, the Catholic Church prohibited same-sex marriage. We petitioned the Pope to change this, but he did not.

So, we asked Father Bernie Lindley from St. Timothy's Episcopal Church to officiate our wedding. He had been a tremendous support for us while Carol was at Good Samaritan Care Center after her stroke in 2014.

On our wedding day on August 5th, 2020, Carol and I were overjoyed to finally feel recognized, allowed to marry, and celebrated in our home, with bright light from the drizzle of fog hugging us through our living room windows in Brookings, Oregon.

Father Bernie sanctified Carol and me in a sacramental blessing and legal marriage ceremony in our comfortable living room.

Our friends sat with beaming smiles, socially distanced thanks to the ongoing COVID pandemic, on the beige leather

Chapter 7 – I Do! I Do!

couch, the brown and gold squared recliner, and chairs circled around a vase of fresh flowers on the dining room table. Our witnesses were best friend Tim Guzik and Carol's sister, Sarah Tierheimer, our lifelong strong allies and advocates, while Father Bernie's wife Paige also attended the happy occasion.

Our wedding song, "I Feel You Everywhere" by Jan Philips, played loudly from our kitchen stereo from two-foot-tall speakers positioned on the credenza to carry the sound waves far and wide. The lyrics so powerfully symbolized our reliance and trust in each other and in Jesus, that it raised the hairs on our arms.

Carol and I knew that it was all Jesus and the Holy Spirit who had orchestrated the events for us to initially meet in a Catholic convent, become profoundly engrossed lovers, grow in maturity and unity, and become strong and fearless in our love while we wanted and needed each other to be complete. Yes, to bring out the best in each other, in turn to bring the best to the world, and to live a *Joyously Free* life! *Yahoo!!*

Today, this day, our original religious vows of chastity, poverty, and obedience transfigured into vows of sickness and health (as I was Carol's devoted caregiver for the last eight years of her life after the stroke), and until death do us part (she went to heaven on January 30, 2022). We meant, with vim and vigor, every word and prayer in our wedding script.

During our wedding ceremony, I sobbed with deep, deep joy, gently holding and rubbing her hand as Carol and I so eloquently and exuberantly proclaimed our marriage vows to each other!

It was so beautiful and endearing.

We loved that the wedding song CD and our stereo had been purchased 31 years earlier as an amenity in our new home. How cool! The funny thing was, that Carol had actually still been a nun when we had signed the paperwork to jointly purchase our house, and the old faithful stereo. The bottom line was:

Joyously Free

OUR MARRIAGE DAY dream came true!!

It was a 45-minute ceremony, yet our life was 39 years of sunsets, sunrises, and everyday beauty.

Alleluia for this AMAZING day, for this AMAZING life!!

Thank you, God! It was way bigger than us!

We believed that love always wins!

Our hopes, struggles, discernment, prayers, and petitions to Catholic leadership, including the Pope, would be answered in God's time.

The song, "Behold What Banner of Love," by The Maranatha Singers is a powerful expression of my thoughts and feelings.

So, have you ever been to a LGBTQ+ wedding ceremony?

We would have loved to have you at our wedding!!

Would you go if you were invited?

We would have invited you! Sure hope you would have said yes!

"Until death do us part"—*LGBTQ+ Funerals*

This is one of the most powerful lines in traditional wedding vows. So while we're on the topic of gay marriage, let's talk about LGBTQ+ funerals.

Have you ever been to a LGBTQ+ funeral or memorial ceremony service? Would you go if invited? Why?

So often, LGBTQ+ people die and that's it. They're dead and done with no closure, no celebration of life! It's like they are invisible.

Carol and I believed that life's greatest loves and achievements are to be celebrated and shared—including marriage and death.

What do you believe?

I can count on my fingers and toes the number of LGBTQ+ weddings I/we've attended. I/we've attended *far* more straight ones.

Our experience has been that LGBTQ+ weddings are exciting events that were never performed or celebrated in any denominational church or other religious building. Interesting, huh?

Chapter 7 – I Do! I Do!

Venues included beaches, homes, mountain/river lodges, parks, a bed and breakfast complex with catered food, and friends' homes. But not God's house in the form of a church, temple, synagogue, or mosque. *Ponder that one!*

Now think about this, Carol and I only attended four funerals for LGBTQ+ people. Yet we've had more LGBTQ+ people die than marry. *Ponder that one, too!*

One LGBTQ+ funeral was in a backyard with no biological family or mourning spouse present. Instead, Carol and I were among a group of 10 friends that we called family. We formed a circle by holding hands. Then our queer friends read poems, another read scripture, and some stood and cried. This "funeral" was a 15-minute final call that said, *Move on, forget.*

Two other LGBTQ+ funeral services were held in community hall buildings. They were both lively, meaningful, and attended by many, including LGBTQ+ people, allies, and parents. Carol and I were honored to spearhead, organize, and support widowed Bonnie. It was a joyous send-off and of course lots of hugs were shared. Bonnie felt loved and supported. At the third funeral in a local fire hall conference room, we hugged and consoled the family and friends of Linda, who had died.

The fourth LGBTQ+ funeral that we attended was in a Catholic Church where the siblings and family were **not** allowed to give a eulogy **in** the church building either before, during, or after the mass. *Crazy, disheartening and discriminatory!* in my mind. Instead, they were permitted to do so at the church reception hall 50 feet away.

So 75 of us—LGBTQ+ and straight people, people of color, and people wearing bright Sunday best clothing colors—packed that parish hall and poured on our love for the grieving and widowed T.

We created a joyous celebration of life by playing guitar, telling stories galore over an open mic, remembering hilarious

Joyously Free

memories, and enjoying so much food and laughter that our stomachs enlarged and our jaws ached for hours afterwards. That was special for the widowed husband T and all of their family.

Side note: "widow" and "widower" imply heterosexuality and are not inclusive. We need to reframe this concept. "Widowed" is a gender-neutral term.

I still wonder why the Catholic Church did not allow a eulogy from his beloved family "in the church building." The priest had barely even known the person who had died.

When Carol had one foot in heaven and one on earth before her death, she and I wrote our obituaries as well as what we wanted for our "life after death" celebrations. We designated Carol's mementos to be given to family and friends and me inserted into manilla envelopes and greeting cards. She and I did this as a way for Carol to say thank you to everyone for good times and to say, "See you in the next life."

Amazingly, this triggered more phone calls and sentimental cards that she devoured, held in her hands and on her chest, before she died. Everyone had an opportunity to say goodbye and thank her for being in their lives. The support from friends and family before her death was amazing. Carol was always thinking of others. I think it all added to the glory of salvation. Great for me, too!

Carol's celebration of life was at the local pizza restaurant—her favorite "out of the box" church—decorated with colorful tablecloths, fresh yellow daffodils, and a slide show of her brightly lived life. So many friends initiated help and baked homemade cookies, brownies, and sweet treats (Carol's favorites). They also helped create a memorial rose garden in her honor at our home, which enhanced the healing and celebration of her life.

As this book is published, we're approaching the four-year anniversary of our holy matrimony on August 5, 2020. The tears

Chapter 7 – I Do! I Do!

have been shed and every now and then my flood gates reopen. Carol is happily dancing in heaven and in my heart. Her spirit is with me. Just a few days ago, she surprised me and kissed me with two cheek pecks as the miraculous sun rays shined into my open car window. Yes, her unique, gentle, long kiss pressed on my upper cheekbone. This was her signature love act, all the way from heaven to earth. Really, it's not that far as one would think, because where there is love, it *is* heaven on earth!

I am once again blessed with a gift from the divine. A miracle!

So, are you ready to tie the knot? Are you daring enough to circle the globe or stand up with your family, your community or faith group as a single-hearted LGBTQ+ married couple? Do you support and encourage marriage equality? Do you want to dive deeper into exploring how LGBTQ+ people can be honored in death? Are you open to becoming *Joyously Free* in love, marriage, and death?

It's time for more discussion!

I'm in! Are You?

Joyously Free

I Only Have Enchanted Eyes for You

By Elizabeth

I had a traditional, hetero-monogamous marriage to a man, and my big, white wedding was one of the most glorious experiences of my life. However, after my fairytale wedding led to a nightmare divorce followed by dating disappointments, I became extremely disillusioned with the rigid relationship rules that society ingrains on our psyches from birth. I desire so much more than that, and I think many, many people do as well.

In fact, I believe that the majority of humans have some inkling, curiosity, or tendency to crave emotional, physical, sexual, and/or spiritual connection with individuals of the same sex. Ask my friends and family; I have been saying this for *years* based on my own experiences and observations.

So, I'm skeptical of statistics about the LGBTQ+ population, because they may be based on polls that require people to out themselves to strangers. For example, a Gallup poll in 2022 said that 7.1 percent of American adults identified as LGBT.[17]

And a report called, "We Are Here: Understanding the Size of the LGBTQ+ Community," said that 20 million American adults—almost eight percent of the adult population—could be gay, bisexual, lesbian, gay, or transgender. The report, compiled by the Human Rights Campaign Foundation (HRC), which analyzed results from the U.S. Census Bureau's Household Pulse Survey, also said that more than one percent of Americans identify as transgender, and that bisexual people are the largest segment—about four percent—amongst LGBTQ+ individuals.[18]

I believe that the numbers are much higher. And if we lived in a world where people did not risk getting *killed,* beaten,

Chapter 7 – I Do! I Do!

disowned, outcast, fired, rejected, ridiculed, and even arrested in some countries for living and loving outside society's puritanical boxes, and people had the freedom to explore their identities and sexuality in safe environments, then more would. Stigmas would disappear. And people would be happier. Imagine a world where we are free of the fear and risk around the beautiful gifts of romance, love, pleasure, companionship, and marriage!

So, as it pertains to same-sex marriage, I'm absolutely elated for people—straight or LGBTQ+—who find their forever person, make it official, and believe that they can sustain a blissful life together.

I encourage any- and everyone to marry the best *person* who can love, cherish, comfort, counsel, and pleasure them. I believe that love and sexuality are sacred and are more about soul connections and the mystique of attraction than about body parts and gender roles.

One of my favorite same-sex married couples—Daniel Perry Walkup (whose story is in this book) and his husband, Andrew Walkup—are one of the happiest, funnest couples I know. They epitomize #relationshipgoals, the hashtag on social media for couples who set the highest standard for what we can all strive to find in a romantic and/or life partner. Spend any time with these unique gentlemen, and you will find yourself smiling, laughing, and enjoying a unique experience that creates a happy memory.

It was a joy to edit Joanie's account of Daniel's and Andrew's wedding in *Nun Better*.

(I've never been to a gay wedding as a guest. Will someone please invite me to your wedding!? I promise to wear a pretty dress and enhance your festivities with a joyous spirit.)

Now let me share that I carry in my heart two profound, powerful things about love from lesbian couples who married.

Joyously Free

Both, coincidentally, involve Robin Roberts, the Emmy Award-winning anchor of ABC's Good Morning America. And both of these vignettes impressed my heart and soul with the hope that if I ever marry again, I can experience these two things that I witnessed—or I will not marry at all.

First, I am a quintessential romantic. I love the idea and feeling of whirlwind romance and love. Every week, I look forward to reading the "Love" section in The New York Times, which features stories and photos of couples (straight and LGBTQ+) who marry. I love reading about how they met, how they describe the magic spark that made them fall in love, and how they celebrated with a unique wedding. It is fascinating to think that we meet so many people in a lifetime, and only one or a few connect with us on such a deep, soul level that they become a lifetime love.

Unfortunately, I had become very cynical about whether the fiery-hot passion that blazes at the start of a relationship can endure for years or a lifetime.

However, I was tremendously inspired by the joy of a sacred union when Robin Roberts interviewed Emmy-nominated actress Niecy Nash-Betts and her wife, singer-songwriter Jessica "JB" Betts, in their first TV interview, shortly after their August 2020 wedding that was featured in *People* magazine.

First, when Robin Roberts asked Niecy Nash-Betts—who had previously married two men—if the wedding was her "coming out," the actress responded that her love for Jessica was not about being male or female. It was about her soul.

Then Robin Roberts asked Jessica how she knew she was in love with Niecy. Jessica responded that she knew she was in love when she lost all desire for anyone else, and that she just knew.[19]

That sentence, and her heartfelt delivery of it, gave me chills. It set the standard for what I want my person to feel and express.

Chapter 7 – I Do! I Do!

Oh, to believe that I could fall in love with someone who would say that and mean that and actually sustain that feeling to influence their behavior, for the rest of our lives—even when no one is looking—that single sentence has stayed in my heart and soul for four years now, and it stokes my hope that a truly loyal, exclusive love relationship with a soul mate is possible someday.

Ever since, I've followed Niecy and Jessica on Instagram and love watching them in media interviews. I'm awed by the joy and fun that they exude in photos and videos. Please watch their interview with Robin Roberts on YouTube.

#RelationshipGoals, for sure.

Now for the next breathtaking moment, also brought to us by Robin Roberts. It happened while I was watching a Good Morning America video on YouTube of Robin's own wedding to her longtime partner, Amber Laign.

As Robin was stating her vows to Amber, and as Amber recited her vows to Robin, I was awestruck by the intensity of love radiating from Robin's eyes as she gazed at Amber. I watched those few seconds of video, over and over, enchanted by the pure joy and adoration beaming from the proverbial windows to Robin's soul.[20]

It reminded me of the song by The Flamingos, "I Only Have Eyes for You."

Here again, this set the standard for extraordinary love that inspires someone to gaze at their partner, like that. And that their beloved's heart and soul would exude so much bliss, that they would reciprocate the same intensity and enchantment.

Joyously Free

Lesbian Love of a Lifetime: The Magic of Marriage

By Doris Beresford and Kathy Mullen

Here we were: two strong, independent, middle-aged women, following our own separate paths, and falling in love like two 20-year-olds.

Now—with one of us in our 70s and the other in her 90s—we continue to love life in a marriage that feels magical every day.

Literally.

Because Doris loves wearing eclectic costumes, including fairy costumes as the gentle touch of her magic wand on people's heads blesses them with joy and affirmation.

Meanwhile, Kathy flashes beaming smiles when Doris dons these costumes as a wizard on Halloween, a fall fairy in autumn, an elf for Christmas, a bunny for Easter, and many more.

We believe that falling in love is both an ageless and a universal experience.

When Kathy walked into my world, I soon became aware that she was the woman that I had been searching for.

It wasn't long before we moved into that incredible place called "falling in love" where all things seemed possible. Our space was filled with adventure, excitement, passion, tenderness, and delight.

Initially, most relationships are based on similar values, world views, heart-touching experiences, and humor. This is true for us; we are so in sync that when watching a movie, we can look at each other and burst into hysterical laughter, each knowing why the other thinks the scene is hilarious. Likewise, we celebrate each other's differences as well.

As our love blossomed and grew deeper, we built a

Chapter 7 – I Do! I Do!

foundation on mutual respect, support, admiration, understanding, and commitment.

When my mother could no longer live alone, we invited her into our world, and our duo became a trio. We had the privilege of knowing her, caring for her, and ushering her on her final journey.

I depend on Kathy's calmness, groundedness, and problem-solving skills. I have always known that she is my tether to the earth, and I have been able to help her get her feet off the ground.

In April 2005, we sealed our love with a commitment ceremony witnessed by family and friends. Hand in hand, we walked down the aisle dressed in matching tuxedos with white boutonnieres. It was a day filled with joy and delight. In our eyes, this was our wedding, but in 2008 we were able to legally become wife and wife.

Our life together has been filled with adventure and exploration. We have dipped our toes into the Arctic Ocean, walked across the equator, canoed the jungles of Ecuador, and stood on the easternmost point of the continent.

With Kathy at the wheel of our Ford pickup, we have driven our fifth wheel through British Columbia, Yukon, Canada, and Alaska. We have camped in deserts and redwood forests, on mountains, and along the Columbia River in Oregon.

We have also spent many hours and many miles following birds to their winter or summer destinations. During fall migration, we have witnessed thousands of snow geese descend to fields in the Central Valley of California and then swiftly and elegantly fly away. We've watched a robin build a nest in a tree in our backyard. We have seen the beautiful Green Jay along the Rio Grande and witnessed a Snowy Owl perched on a hillock in Newfoundland, eastern Canada. We also held Saw Whet Owls in our own hands as they were being banded, watched California

Joyously Free

Condors take flight, and observed birds of prey, from the common Red Hawk to the Peregrine Falcon, soar through the sky.

It has been an incredible journey!

In our home, there is a plaque that reads, "You will forever be my always."

This has been the mantra for our life together.

Kathy Mullen served in the U.S. Navy as a lieutenant commander for 11 years, then became a financial analyst for the city of Sacramento, California. She's 75 years old.

Doris Beresford returned to school at age 60 to complete her bachelor's degree and earned a master's degree in counseling. She's 91 years young!

A Pastor's Perspective: Spiritual Awakenings That Opened My World to LGBTQ+ Love

By Father Bernie Lindley

It was 1997 when I came back to St. Timothy's Episcopal Church in my hometown of Brookings, Oregon. I had been a bit spiritually adrift since leaving for college a dozen years earlier. As a child and a teenager, I had been an altar boy in that congregation.

I had been raised in the Church with a strong understanding of God's grace and how it applied to me and the rest of the world. But, during my 20s, I had put grace on the back burner—worldly ambitions had crept in and I turned lukewarm toward God.

When my spiritual reawakening started to happen after I turned 30, it took a bit for me to sort out who I was, because of cultural influences versus who I was in the context of the Gospel of Jesus Christ. This had a lot to do with my attitude toward other people—panhandlers, mentally ill folks, addicts, low-bottom alcoholics, and gays.

I guess I needed to feel superior to folks that I felt were beneath me. I suspect that is the root cause of racism, sexism, and all of the other "-isms." In our unconscious minds, I think people feel inadequate compared to the wealthy, powerful folks, so they console themselves by demeaning whomever they see as inferior.

Scapegoating comes into play as well. It is easier on the ego if perceived failures/shortcomings are the fault of "those people." In 1997, I still saw "those people" with contempt. But at the same time, the Holy Spirit was hounding me to see the world through the eyes of Jesus.

Joyously Free

The priest at St. Timothy's when I came back was Father Bill Smith. He had white, shaggy hair, wore tie-dye T-shirts, and usually wore big glasses. He was what I imagined the hippies from the San Francisco Bay Area of the 1960s all looked like when they hit retirement age. In fact, he had lived in the East Bay during those years. But, as his wife used to say, he was a crew-cut engineer back then, working for General Electric.

He had his own spiritual awakening in the early 1970s. That was when he started studying for the priesthood and his hair started to get shaggy. He became a church planter, starting three different congregations in different parts of California.

When I met Father Bill, I still had the idea that some folks chose to be gay out of some sort of perversion. I'm ashamed of that now. But at the time, I thought that there were two kinds of gay people: the ones who were born that way and the ones who were sexually abnormal. And I thought that the "abnormal" folks outnumbered the "honest" gays.

Of course, I was raised in a community where anyone who was deemed different was ridiculed. When I was in high school in the early 1980s, all of my gay peers were super closeted. I thought that I was a special kind of enlightened, because I knew that at least some people didn't choose to be gay.

I told Father Bill one day about my thoughts on the matter, that most gays were sex-crazed perverts. He was gentle in the way that he challenged me.

He said, "Why do you think that?" And, "What percentage of gays do you figure choose to be gay?"

Trying to articulate my ignorance out loud, I realized that I didn't know anything about what I thought I knew. It wasn't an instant awakening. But, Father Bill nudged me toward a better understanding of something that I smugly thought I knew. Looking back now, I'm embarrassed about that.

Chapter 7 – I Do! I Do!

In the summer of 2002, Father Bill asked me to come to his office. He didn't tell me why. I had that feeling of being summoned to the principal's office, wondering what I had done wrong.

"Have you ever considered becoming a priest?" Bill asked as soon as I sat down.

"I've thought about it," I said, "but I don't see how I can pick up and leave for seminary for three years at this point in my life. My kids are young. I've got a boat to run. It seems impossible."

"What if I told you we can find an alternate path toward ordination?" asked Bill.

Father Bill was true to his word. I studied with a group of aspiring deacons one weekend a month in a nearby town for three years and then finished my studies by spending a year at an accredited seminary on the East Coast. I was ordained to the priesthood in 2008 and became the vicar of my home parish the following month.

By the time I started toward ordination to the priesthood to follow in Father Bill's steps, I was more attuned to the reality of what my gay friends were going through.

When my wife, Paige, and I took our daughters to northern Virginia to attend seminary in 2006, we had new opportunities to increase our understanding. We had a church that we attended on Sundays out in Louden County that had several gay people as members.

One night, I was leading a table discussion at an introduction to Christianity class and a young guy named Andrew was talking about what it was like for him to be a gay man. He talked about what it was like to come out to his family and friends, how he was rejected by people he loved, and how much it hurt.

We were in a group discussion in a windowless church basement. It was winter and the room had a cold, gray feel. Andrew seemed to make himself small. He said, "Why would anyone choose to go through that much hurt?"

I knew what he was saying was true, but that solidified it for me—no one chooses to be gay, just like no one chooses to be straight.

There had been a gradual awakening to this reality in the Episcopal church over the years. In the 1970s the church had decided that being gay wasn't the issue. It was the sexual act that was sinful. So, celibate gays were okay. They could even be ordained, as long as they stayed celibate. That was a catch-22: sex outside of marriage was a sin, but gays couldn't marry, so they could never have sex.

The world within my church tradition got turned on its head when a gay priest named Gene Robinson was elected the bishop of the Episcopal Diocese of New Hampshire. Many congregations throughout The Episcopal Church decided to affiliate with other Anglican denominations as a protest against allowing a gay bishop. Disputes over church property rights became common. In 2007, one entire diocese in central California left The Episcopal Church and joined a denomination called the Anglican Church in North America.

Leaving a church, denomination, or faith tradition is easy. It is staying in relationship with people who have a different worldview, a different understanding of Scripture, that is hard.

Showing grace to a person who is different, however, is at the core of how I understand Christianity.

I worry about churches that are made up of people who all share the same opinions on issues, both secular and spiritual. I think that growth requires conversations and interactions with people who have had wide-ranging experiences and can gracefully challenge one another's unexamined assumptions.

In fact, I think that most people have beliefs that are

unexamined. I think a large number of Christians adhere to the views of their worshiping community because of some groupthink consensus. I think that is primarily where the Christian ban on homosexuality comes from: "We all believe it, because we have always believed it." That type of logic stifles the Holy Spirit's desire for spiritual growth in the Church.

When I examined the New Testament for teachings on homosexuality, I saw that Biblical translators had created theology through word choices. The biggest example of this has to do with the Greek word *"arsenokoitēs."* In the King James Translation, this word was translated as "abusers of themselves with mankind." Some more recent translations, such as the New International Version, have blatantly, through lazy scholarship, translated the word as "homosexual." There is plenty of debate around how to define this relatively obscure Greek word. But, in my way of thinking, the word does not describe consensual sex between a monogamous couple.

The real clincher for me doesn't come from translating St. Paul's Greek epistles into modern-day English. What makes the most sense to me is that people are simply born with a propensity to be gay. That being the case, it doesn't make sense that God would punish people for a biological attraction to the same gender over which they have no control. Consequently, in my mind, it isn't the Church's job to punish gays by denying them the sacrament of Holy Matrimony.

Fortunately for me, I belong to a faith tradition that agrees with my conclusions about human sexuality. The Episcopal Church has authorized liturgies for same-gender weddings, so that all people can receive the sacrament of Holy Matrimony.

I had been ordained for probably seven or eight years when I first offered to officiate at a same-gender wedding. I was at the local golf course doing a traditional wedding for a couple, and the photographer was a woman that I casually knew. While we were waiting for the bride and groom, we chatted about weddings and marriage.

She told me matter-of-fact that she could never get married because her potential spouse was her longtime girlfriend. Same-gender weddings were legal at that point, but it was more important to her that they were committed to one another than whether their relationship was legal. Her dad was a retired evangelical pastor. She had been raised with his understanding of Biblical sexuality that expressly forbids same-gender romance. It seemed to her that church and being gay were completely incompatible.

It was about three months later that she phoned me. She and her partner had talked it over and decided that they wanted the permanent commitment that comes from marriage. We excitedly made plans.

The wedding happened on the beach in a driftwood pile in front of a large, three-story hotel that had balconies for every room. The other bride and I met in the parking lot and walked through the sand, looking for a suitable gap in the driftwood. She looked back at the balconies and big windows of the hotel.

"All those people are watching out those windows," she said in a whisper, "wondering what those two women are doing down here."

There wasn't anyone paying attention to us that I could tell. She was experiencing a feeling that she was doing something wrong, something taboo. Decades of social conditioning had been ingrained in her. She felt vulnerable and judged as she prepared to celebrate her love for a woman who had been her soulmate for 25 years.

That moment of uncertainty passed, and the wedding

Chapter 7 – I Do! I Do!

was beautiful. There were only a dozen or so family and friends. It was an intimate and deeply moving service. They reaffirmed their love for each other, and I reassured them of God's blessing upon their relationship. We took pictures. Everyone was smiling.

I hardly told anyone about the wedding. I really wasn't worried that some of my parishioners would be offended. My real concern was how the other pastors in the community would ostracize me. There was a ministerial association in town that I didn't attend much, but I knew that I would be the topic of scandalous ridicule if they all knew.

I am just like everyone else—I don't enjoy being despised. I wasn't ashamed of doing the wedding; it was an honor and a privilege. I just didn't see any reason to give my acquaintances on the religious right a chance to throw metaphoric rocks through our stained-glass windows.

As time went on, I did four same-gender weddings. The first three weddings weren't blatantly sacramental. In other words, they weren't in a church in front of an altar. But, they were definitely in the context of the sacrament of Holy Matrimony. The fourth wedding was for a younger couple. It was bigger, more formal, with a large reception.

Eventually, I started talking about these weddings more openly. A few parish members quit the church when they found out.

I'm certainly not ashamed of doing same-gender weddings, but I am disappointed in myself for not being open about it. I've spent a lot of time being a closeted supporter of gay marriage.

Me, a hetero, middle-aged, white male of relative wealth, a person who is part of the social ruling class, was afraid and embarrassed to publicly support my gay friends because I didn't want to be hated by the Christian cool kids. That seems pretty pathetic when I consider what my gay friends have to live through.

The sad part is that I'm still reluctant to talk about it publicly.

Father, forgive me for not standing up for what I know to be true.

Father Bernie Lindley is an Episcopal Priest and co-pastor of St. Timothy's Episcopal Church in Brookings, Oregon.

Chapter 7 – I Do! I Do!

Tips for Gay Marriage

Know history! Gay marriage was legalized in June 2015, when the United States Supreme Court ruled that same-sex couples have a fundamental right to marry. (*Obergefell v. Hodges*, 576 U.S. 644 (2015).)

Follow your heart. Remember that love is love and love always wins.

Vote! Keep your voice being heard! Vote accordingly, so that this law does not get overturned.

Trust your feelings and thoughts. Being in a relationship makes you vulnerable. It's invigorating, but it can be scary. Kindred souls meet for a bigger purpose. When you meet your forever person, you'll know without a doubt.

Take action. Don't wait to express your love or intentions. Life is too short. Be bold and proclaim your marriage proposal by popping "the question" or by being the one who starts the discussion.

Communicate. Discuss and describe what marriage looks like for you and your sweetheart. Why do you want to be married? What does it mean, practically and romantically? Make sure it's mutual.

Discuss where you'll live. Will you move into one person's place or buy/rent an entirely new space? What is your long-term vision for where you'll live? Do you each want to retire in the same place?

Babies and children? Do you and your partner share a desire for children? If so, what does that look like?

Would you use a sperm donor or surrogate? Or adopt? If so, do you agree on how many children you'd like? Would one person stay home while the other works? Who will provide child care? In-laws or relatives? Members of your "found family"?

Make sure you share the same vision on whether to have children or not, before committing to a lifetime together. It's never smart to enter a relationship or marriage thinking you can "change" another person.

Money matters. First, how will you pay for the wedding and reception? And if you go on a honeymoon, what can you afford?

Next, how will you manage money together? Financial problems are one of the top reasons for divorce, and the LGBTQ+ divorce rate parallels that for the mainstream. Talking about money can be difficult. So now's the time to create a safe, honest space to discuss the financial realities of being married. How will you share finances? Do either of you have any debts or financial disclosures that would affect the marriage? How will you prepare for retirement together? Are you both willing to create a financial strategy that includes a budget and savings? Whose health benefits will you use?

If you're not confident or savvy with money, consult with a trusted financial advisor who can help you create a plan that makes life easier.

Share your deepest desires openly. Is your marriage about love, lust, and reliance? Do you want to be selfless and all-encompassing, taking their hand for everlasting life, until death do you part? Are you ready to commit to all of it: physical, mental, emotional, spiritual, and environmental?

Chapter 7 – I Do! I Do!

Lack of commitment and infidelity also rank among the top causes of divorce. So, talk about what commitment means to you, and why you're ready for it, and how you may respond to temptation. You can also discuss non-traditional marriages where both partners want to explore ENM—Ethical Non-Monogamy, polyamory, open relationships, throuples (that's three people who are committed to each other), commune-style living, and any alternative that you and your partner desire.

Are you both living *Joyously Free?* Chances are, if you've made it to the point of contemplating marriage, then you know you're compatible. However, are you both out? Or is one person playing it straight at work and/or with their parents, while living freely at home and in social circles? Are you OK with that? What would that mean in terms of accompanying your spouse to work functions?

Why are you getting married? Look at the whole picture and explore the pros and cons.

Your marriage may be inspired by many reasons that include: love, financial support, joint home-buying or joint insurance, tax benefits, citizenship, healing, promises, family values, children and child custody legalities, and cultural or medical reasons.

Be happy and healthy, first with yourself. When you are open and communicate, your intimacy grows like the night sky full of sparkling stars.

Religion matters. Explore whether you and your beloved share similar spiritual, religious, or cultural beliefs, and whether that matters for your future. For example, if one spouse is Muslim and fasting during Ramadan, and the other is Christian and wants to host an Easter feast, how will each of you simultaneously honor your partner and their religious holiday traditions? Is one person deeply spiritual while the other is atheist? How would this play out if you have children?

Ask your Higher Power for wisdom about marriage and love. What guidance are you receiving? Is your Higher Power giving you the green light to marry? Or is your intuition telling you not to rush or that this is not your forever person? Honor your intuition and the guidance you receive from your Higher Power. Trust that it's preparing you for the best possible outcome.

Know that all will be well.

Explore legalities and ceremonial options. What type of official union do you both want? Options include: a marriage or domestic partnership; and a service that is civic, religious, sacramental, or spiritual. Do you want your future spouse to sign a prenuptial agreement? You get to choose!

Make your big day an extravaganza by thinking gayly and out of the box. Your wedding day is the party of a lifetime, so make it spectacular! Research possibilities and have fun with planning the ceremony, the reception, and the honeymoon. Make every detail a unique reflection of you as a couple.

Do you want to select a date that has special significance for you both? Do you want to write your marriage vows, pick songs, and involve family members and friends? Do you prefer a private, personal, and meaningful commitment? Do you want to elope with a justice of the peace? Or do you envision a blow-out extravaganza? A destination wedding? How will you dress to express your gender identities?

Select an LGBTQ+ wedding planner who can share ideas that will make your big day feel like a tailor-made dream that reflects your tastes in food, music, and décor and sets the stage for a happy future.

Who will perform the event and where will it take place?

If your wedding is religion-based, does your temple, mosque, synagogue, or church celebrate same-sex marriage?

Do you want a friend to become ordained to perform the service? Or can you ask other married LGBTQ+ couples to recommend an officiant?

Make the invitation list. This is **your** celebration amongst people who love you just as you are and who are thrilled that you found your mate. You are not obligated to invite anyone who does not support who you are. If you want to test the waters with an estranged parent well in advance of the ceremony to explore whether healing can occur in time for them to attend your wedding in a spirit of happiness for you, then that's your choice.

Pay for the marriage license. This means visiting your local courthouse. Hopefully bigotry and prejudice do not taint this joyous task, and that you instead encounter people who are happy for you.

Stay on guard. Be proud and protective of your queer love relationship, for sour and hate-filled attitudes and discriminatory beliefs fester amongst family, friends, neighbors, and people who follow certain religious faiths and dogmas. Prejudicial perceptions might raise their ugly heads about same-sex marriages. You may need to leave your religion, your region, or your social circle. Your happiness is your top priority. It is not selfish. It is an act of self-love to spend your life with the person who fills you with peace and makes your soul sparkle. Protect that!

Live your queer life together in joy and peace. If your current location is stifling, consider relocating to a different city, state, or country. Do your research on the best places for LGBTQ+ people to live. Denmark, the first country in the world to legalize same-sex marriage in 1989, ranks as one of the best countries for LGBTQ+ people to live. In the United States, New York is the best state for LGBTQ+ people, according to OutLeadership.com.[21] What's the top gay-friendly city in America? *The Advocate* ranks San Francisco as number one.[22]

If you decide to move, reach out to friends or organizations in those areas for guidance on which neighborhoods are most accepting, and what areas to avoid. An LGBTQ+ real estate agent or queer-friendly property management company can also guide you to the best places to live in your new town.

Find your wedding venue. What venue do you envision for your wedding? It could be in your backyard, on a beach, in a park, at a restaurant or resort, and even on a cruise. The sky's the limit.

If you want your ceremony in your place of worship, then research churches, synagogues, temples, mosques, and faith communities that welcome LGBTQ+ couples. Meet with leaders to confirm that the place and its policies vibe with you as a couple and your vision for the wedding.

Remember to consider handicap accessibility that includes elevators, ramps, and bathrooms.

Keep it gender-neutral as you select your wedding party and plan the ceremony. Here's your chance to ditch convention and customize your ceremony as a

Joyously Free extravaganza. Who do you want in your wedding party?

You can make up your own terms or use gender-neutral ones such as "person of honor" instead of "best man" or "maid of honor." Rather than "bridesmaids" and "groomsmen," you can have "attendants." During announcements and toasts, you can replace "ladies and gentlemen" with "friends" or "folks."

Will someone "give you away"? Will you and your partner dress alike?

You don't have to include any person—even a blood relative—in your wedding party who is not 100 percent supportive of your same-sex union.

Invite friends and family. Here again, don't feel obligated to invite anyone just because they're a biological relative. It's your special day, and you have the right to only invite people who will support and celebrate your same-sex union. This can include your "found family," allies, advocates, your faith community, and friends in your LGBTQ+ tribe.

Display a symbol of your engagement, marriage, or love. This could be a ring, tattoo, photo, jewelry, framed love letter, or something else that's meaningful for both of you. You could even plant a tree.

"Love always wins!" Exclaim Joanie's favorite saying during your celebrations. Love is meant to be shared, honored, and lived. So follow your heart and don't listen to the naysayers. Celebrate your gift of love!
Congratulations!

Chapter 8
Religion: Follow Your Own Path to God and Spirituality
How to Heal Religious Hurts

By Elizabeth

Many religious leaders preach from their centuries-old, written doctrine that being LGBTQ+ is a sin or "deviant" behavior that is strictly prohibited.

Sadly, when LGBTQ+ people grow up in families that ascribe to these beliefs, this rhetoric can be extremely harmful. So much so, that LGBTQ+ and straight people alike may become agnostic, meaning they don't know if God exists, or atheist, which means they don't believe in God or a Higher Power.

That's why we're here to tell you that you are free to love God and receive God's love back unconditionally. You are beloved by the Creator, who made you just as you are.

God does not hate or punish or reject you. God loves you.

So please recognize that hateful messaging from religious leaders is manmade. These leaders and their institutions want to control people and wield power over them, to grow their flocks and amass strength in numbers, along with financial wealth and even political influence.

Even though our faith communities are supposed to create sanctuaries of peace, love, and acceptance, they can instead become hornets' nests that sting with painful words and poisonous experiences.

So, we need to follow God, not man-made religious rules that breed rage and rejection. You can heal your religious hurts, and our stories and tips can show you how. As can our next book, *Healing Religious Hurts: Stories and Tips to Find Love and Peace*, coming in October 2024 from Two Sisters Writing & Publishing® and available at TwoSistersWriting.com.

Don't Consume the MANufactured Rules; Go Organic with God

If you strive to nourish the temple that is your body with healthier foods, then you know that a plant-based, organic regimen is best. Fruits, vegetables, nuts, and beans, as well as fresh fish, meats, and poultry, come straight from Mother Nature.

On the contrary, manufactured foods such as packaged cookies, candy, soda pop, orange snack chips dusted with imitation cheese, processed meats, and fast food, are unhealthy and can lead to obesity, diabetes, high blood pressure, and even cancer. These foods are created in laboratories where food scientists calibrate the perfect blend of salt, fat, and sugar to create highly addictive flavors and textures that activate the human brain's pleasure centers as powerfully as cocaine and opioid drugs. The goal is to make the person keep eating, and keep buying, the fake food item.

On the contrary, when you follow "God's diet," you eat whole foods prepared by Mother Nature, enjoying the most powerful punch of nutrition and wellness.

You have to learn this for yourself, often after a battle with obesity or a serious health crisis related to an unhealthy diet. The food companies and fast food restaurants want to keep

Chapter 8 – Religion: Follow Your Own Path to God and Spirituality

people eating the delicious but potentially harmful fast food.

Similarly, we have to wake up to the reality that man-made religion wants to keep us hooked on its beliefs and fears, so we'll keep coming back to fill their places of worship and keep filling their golden coffers. Sometimes the sense of community and even spiritual upliftment that one experiences in the prayer, song, fellowship, and celebrations during religious services can be as addictive as foods that taste delicious but are actually harmful to our health. Why? Because they can trigger gnawing in a queer person's gut that the religion's doctrine is intolerant and toxic.

So which do you choose?

Religions whose rules can harm one's mental health with shame, rejection, and hate?

Or the pure love of God in its natural form that is ours for the taking to nourish our minds, bodies, and souls?

People Who Live in Glass Houses Shouldn't Throw Stones

Sometimes male religious leaders who shout the loudest to condemn what they call "the homosexual agenda" are engaging in sex with men behind closed doors.

Several high-profile scandals have demonstrated this profound hypocrisy.

For example, America's once-top evangelical pastor, Ted Haggard, who founded a mega-church and who publicly condemned same-sex marriage, sparked a scandal after admitting that he had paid a male prostitute for gay sex. And a young man from the church revealed an on-going, consensual relationship that was sexual. This story was told by HBO in 2009 in *The Trials of Ted Haggard*.[23]

Ousted from his church, he blamed his desire for having sex with men on being molested by a man when he was a boy. Then

Haggard opened another church, inviting LGBTQ+ people to join. All the while, he said he was heterosexual. Throughout the scandal, his wife stood at his side.[24]

His story is among many others about religious leaders who condemn gay people publicly but engage in same-sex relations behind closed doors. This is extremely hypocritical and emphasizes the old saying that people who live in glass houses shouldn't throw stones.

Chapter 8 – Religion: Follow Your Own Path to God and Spirituality

Pulpit Hate and Boxing

By Joanie

Carol and I were so hurt by church leaders and religious doctrine that we often didn't even have words to describe the constant, sharp attacks that blindsided us. We were two of millions who have personally felt this kind of pain.

Still, we found our solace and peace and even JOY by hanging onto each other and praying our hearts out. You might know those deep, emotional gut prayers, begging for a Higher Power to solve the problem.

How could this be happening? Why, Lord? Why are we hated for being us? What did we do to deserve this? When will it stop?

We realized that we were asking the wrong questions.

"Let go, let God," came to us in prayer through our personal relationship with our God, with a Higher Power. We realized we needed to surrender completely and accept His will.

It was OK to be angry and sad at the same time. It was and is OK to feel sorrow for those who call me names, for those who harshly and unkindly stared at us as we sat on our hard wooden church pew for the umpteenth time at a Saturday night mass.

It was the "pulpit hate"—spoken and preached with fervor by a diocesan Catholic priest and our pastor that hit our hearts the hardest but lasted the shortest.

From the pulpit, the priest told the congregation: "I was asked by a parishioner recently if it's OK to attend a gay marriage of a friend. No, it's not OK."

Carol and I were stunned by such a homophobic and stark, Catholic response. The local ministerial leader went on to explain that if you attended the gay wedding, you would be promoting and agreeing to something that goes against Catholic teachings.

Joyously Free

Not the answer we expected or wanted to hear, but this priest was exactly right on—unfortunately from our viewpoint—adamantly defending his Catholic doctrine. While we understood with our minds, our hearts felt he was missing the boat about how love is love and love is God. We so wished he had taken that angle during his homily.

Carol and I held our pinky fingers together, yet I really wanted to walk out the back door or give her a big fat kiss on the lips for all to see. With her calm finger-hold, I sensed her peace telling me, *Don't feed into his hate. Let us let Jesus guide our actions. Not centuries-old doctrines.*

We did not agree with this patriarchal, male chauvinist, high roller, black-and-white, legalistic-abiding fool. Sorry, Father, for calling you names.

Carol reminded me on our way home that this was what Jesus experienced in the company of his Jewish leaders. She said that we, too, would find the how, time, and place to open hearts. She was absolutely correct.

This particular moment was not the night or place to confront, disagree publicly, or be rude about it. We knew that our time would come, and that healing would come, but that night, the hairs were raised on my arms for quite awhile. Carol had already let go and let God.

We had two different ways of healing. I still love Carol for always teaching me new things.

Years later, someone asked Carol as she sat in her lime green-colored power chair: "How did you get this way?"

"I was a boxer," Carol retorted proudly, boldly, and emphatically.

I was so excited by her quick wit as she stymied the rude individual in his tracks. *Way to go, Carol!* My heart pounded as her smile beamed and she sped away in her chair, leaving him in the dust!

Chapter 8 – Religion: Follow Your Own Path to God and Spirituality

Imagine this . . . a voice booming through the smoke-filled, packed crowd in the dimly lit, enormous boxing arena.

"And in this corner is the dynamic duo, Carol and Joanie. The two strongest and fiercest women alive. Together they have conquered battles of church pulpit sermons where priestly eyes chastised them and an overpowering judgmental voice said, 'Don't ever go to your gay family member's wedding! Gays cannot marry and real Catholics go to mass ever Sunday!'"

Again, the boxing arena master of ceremonies' voice commands to the frantic crowd in a deep monotone:

"Here they are in their full glory of strength and perseverance. They are robust inside and out. Their endearing endurance is beyond human. They have trained night and day, feeding their minds, bodies, and souls from their prayer corners, adventures, and love. In constant gratitude, they express to others without fear, and the earth is shaken. They thrive on hope and pledge to never give in, give up, or quit! For themselves and for others!"

The announcer continues: "Here they are, folks, Joanie and Carol, right in front of your eyes. They rely solely on God almighty, just as David did when taking down Goliath."

Carol and Joanie shout in unison: "God put us together and we remain steadfast to our God. God's reasons are not ours, but we listen and we believe."

The crowd roars in agreement and the blow-horns circle the standing-room-only coliseum.

The announcer concludes: "These female champions held a positive mindset and their intuitive hearts delighted in prayer, hearing the ultimate responses from God."

This story reminds me of how God told us: "Follow me. Do as I do and more. Your love will grow immeasurably for the world to see! You are healed from all hurts because you are Mine and I am your God. I am always with you! Shalom! Peace be with you!"

Carol and I practiced forgiveness to release the negative emotions caused by hurtful situations.

Amen, Joanie.

P.S. — On December 18, 2023, Pope Francis announced in a landmark ruling that in the Universal Catholic Church, priests can *bless* same-sex couples, as long as they are not part of regular Church rituals or liturgies.

The window is open, yet the door is still closed. Let's keep HOPE alive.

More on this topic in our *Healing Religious Hurts* book. Stay tuned!

Chapter 8 – Religion: Follow Your Own Path to God and Spirituality

The Grandson of Mary and Joseph . . . and the Purple Sofa

By Daniel Perry Walkup

It seems so often that I hear accounts of people's negative experiences with their church or religion and their coming out stories.

While I easily understand this could be part of someone's journey, this would not be my story . . .

Like many, I grew up the product of great-grandparent and grandparent immigrants who moved from Europe during World War I for a better life in America. Immigrants rarely say, "the United States." It seems they always say, "America."

My grandparents moved here from Northern Spain, Portugal, the Azores, and Bavaria. After first settling in the San Francisco Bay Area, they began to homestead in the greater Santa Cruz and San Benito County farmlands on the Central Coast of California.

I grew up Catholic, very Catholic, Roman Catholic . . . so Catholic that my name is Daniel Joseph John . . . and my maternal grandparents' names were Mary and Joseph.

Our family was rich with culture and my family especially honored its Northern Spanish heritage after moving from Salamanca, Spain.

My grandmother, Mary Raphaela Horcajo Perry, was adamant that her grandchildren attended church.

Mary—known as "Mimi" to her grandchildren—made going to church an adventure! Even while attending a regular mass at Sacred Heart in Hollister, or at a rural hillside mass, at a small wooden church in Tres Pinos, or at my favorite masses at Mission San Juan Bautista . . . the largest of all the Catholic missions in California.

Joyously Free

At Mimi's insistence, I also served as an altar boy, and my favorite Sunday masses were at the Mission. Often the masses were in different languages—English, Spanish, and Latin. I am fairly certain that her secret dream was for me to become a priest.

I always found the priest and nuns that I assisted to be wonderful and warm. As an altar boy who did not speak Latin and did not always understand everything in Spanish, they would give me eye and hand signals during mass when it was time to carry out my duties, including ringing the bells.

Many in the church, including the priests and nuns, had tight bonds with my grandparents, as they had moved from the same areas of Europe that my grandparents' family had fled from. The priests and nuns in my life were family. We would sometimes have dinner together, work holiday events together, and come together for major celebrations that honored the families in the area . . . the Spanish Festival being the biggest of these events. I loved watching the interaction between my family, especially my grandparents, my great aunts and uncles, and the nuns and the priests of the mission and nearby churches.

Mimi made a point to explain religion and history. We would often walk the gardens after mass, discussing the various religious statues, their meanings, as well as the many blooming roses and succulents that are so common in this area. Many of the plants originated in Europe and those who immigrated went to great lengths to bring their beloved plants, flowers, and even grapevines with them to America, with cuttings tucked into their clothing and luggage.

While Mimi filled our minds with stories in English and Spanish of adventures, challenges, and our heritage, my grandfather Joseph—Papa to his grandchildren—would be in the park next to the Mission. There were barbecued meats, mostly beef and chicken, as well as farm-grown vegetables, beans, and

Chapter 8 – Religion: Follow Your Own Path to God and Spirituality

rice, on an open wood grill. The men of the valley, including Papa's father, his brother, and other immigrants all had such a strong bond that it was often difficult to tell who was a friend and who was family. They were often drinking wine, homemade wines called Portuguese Wine, which were often stronger than whiskey.

I loved everything about growing up Catholic . . . the people, the words, the languages, the history, the tradition, the music, the rituals . . . and especially the wrought-iron stands of flickering candles, detailed oil paintings, and gold embellishments everywhere. There were also the intricate wardrobes of those who attended mass. Parishioners in their Sunday best, older women in lace veils, nuns in their formal habits, and priests in their ornate robes.

As a young, middle school gay boy, I imagined this all to be what I now describe as an Indiana Jones movie . . . like living in an archaeological adventure! I often created my own stories as to how each artifact and each person had journeyed and eventually found their place in the mission.

I didn't come out until I was 26. Although I had quietly experimented in my teens and twenties, I publicly dated girls in high school and college. It wasn't that I didn't know that I was gay—my best friend was gay, and knew I was gay—but every time I broached the topic to those in openly gay environments, my Catholic religion was immediately debated or, even more, attacked. The words always sounded the same:

"Daniel, you can't be both Catholic or religious, and gay . . . you have to choose one or the other."

While I considered coming out after my senior year in high school, my best friend—my cousin Craig who was also gay—died tragically that year. I thought I could leave my heritage, my religion, and my family behind, if I had at least Craig there as my support mechanism. With his death, I retracted from life and

Joyously Free

quietly went through the motions from age 18 to 26, not sure if I could or would ever be me.

After school, I moved to Oregon when I was 24 and decided to make a new life for myself. With this distance from my family, and the Catholic Church, I decided I would come out ... but only after I had someone in my life who would love and support me. I had my first serious relationship ... six months long, but I didn't come out.

Even after nearly a decade of inner turmoil, I still couldn't come to terms of separating my religion from who I was as a person. Losing this aspect of myself seemed like losing everything that I loved and everything that made me ... well, me.

When I was 26 years old, I started working part-time at a furniture store and design center. This is where I met Carol and Joanie.

Even 30 years later, I can still clearly remember when Carol and Joanie walked into the store to buy a purple leather sofa. Technically the color was eggplant, but purple seems to create a more vibrant picture.

Carol and Joanie were simply joyous—bubbly to the point of effervescence.

Joanie seems to have a rainbow that always surrounds her ... then and now. Carol was spirited and decisive. They wanted to purchase a very nice piece of furniture, an Italian sofa, in purple leather ... well, eggplant.

I wrote up the sale, much to the uncertainty of the owner of the store, who specifically made me write on the invoice, "No Returns." He really didn't want to have to resell a purple leather sofa.

I instantly bonded with Carol and Joanie. They reminded me of some of my favorite nuns I had grown up with. To my surprise, after they made their purchase, they asked me if I had dinner plans. Not only did I not have dinner plans, but I also

Chapter 8 – Religion: Follow Your Own Path to God and Spirituality

barely had enough food for myself, so the thought of someone treating me to dinner was a huge luxury.

After I got off work, Carol and Joanie showed up at my sparsely furnished home with food they had picked up. We laughed and talked as if we had been lifelong friends. I was not surprised to learn that Carol and Joanie had been Catholic nuns. I shared my stories of growing up in the Catholic church, too. We all came out to each other without even coming out to each other. It was just natural and not something that I had experienced before.

I remember specifically when Carol and Joanie asked me who in my family knew I was gay.

"Well, no one, really," I replied.

"Why?" they asked.

I explained that I knew that coming out would also mean saying goodbye to my religion and, through tears, I told them, I just didn't know how I could do that.

Carol, always with the best combination of being kind and direct, asked me, "Couldn't you separate your spiritual beliefs from your religious beliefs and just continue on your journey?"

AND IT WAS THAT SIMPLE . . .

It was like a bolt of lightning. Here was my answer! I was never really my religion; I was a spiritual person . . . and I always would be.

Understanding that I could hold on to everything that made me my spiritual self, without necessarily holding onto everything in the Catholic doctrine, changed my life in an instant!

After this time with Carol and Joanie, my next relationship lasted 10 years.

My partner, Mathew Michael, and I attended the Catholic Church together at Holy Cross, in Santa Cruz, California. Now that I could fully be myself, we decided to return to my home in Santa Cruz.

Joyously Free

It was an amazing experience. Our priest was openly—but quietly—gay, and there was an awesome gay and lesbian support group at the church . . . in the 1990s! Family and friends accepted us with open arms, including Mimi and Papa, Mary and Joseph. I often joked that I think Mimi and Papa loved Matthew more than they loved me.

Carol and Joanie continued to be part of my life. When we moved to California, they visited our home. They were always there for guidance and fun! When my work brought a transfer to Sarasota, Florida, Carol and Joanie followed for more adventure! I will never forget our Jimmy Buffet Sunset Cruise in Sarasota Bay . . . and introducing Carol and Joanie to made-at-the-table white sangria at my favorite Colombian restaurant on Saint Armands Circle at Siesta Beach.

Although my relationship with Matthew lasted just 10 years, the journey was amazing. It was the first time I got to be me in my adult life. I look back at every moment of this time with a smile, gratefully and warmly.

Carol and Joanie continued to be part of my life and adventures. A decade later, after I met Andrew in 2015, I was ready to take another huge step . . . marriage!

As my father had passed away and my mother was in a care facility . . . there was only one choice as to who would stand up for me when Andrew and I took our vows . . . Carol and Joanie.

One of the biggest moments of my life, as I held back tears of joy, was when I asked Carol and Joanie to walk me down the aisle and they said "YES!" even before I could finish asking them.

It was a perfect ceremony with family and friends on the deck of a cabin, high up in the mountains of Oregon. Carol and Joanie were brightly dressed. The ceremony was spiritual, fun, full of music, friends, and family, with a backdrop of slowly swaying pine trees in the Cascade Mountains. I'll never forget

Chapter 8 – Religion: Follow Your Own Path to God and Spirituality

how Carol and Joanie tightly gripped my hands in theirs when they gave me away to Andrew.

It is now five years later. Carol passed more than a year ago. She gave me her beloved rainbow-painted rocking chair . . . one of her few treasures. I sit in it when I am seeking answers or when I forget my path. The rocking chair holds a place of honor in the 90-year-old farmhouse that Andrew and I have made a life in together with our two dogs and our two cats.

Joanie is more than a friend; after 30 years, she is as much my sister, as my own beloved sister. I love that we have had so many adventures together over the last 30 years, and I am excited as to what adventures lie ahead for me, Joanie, and Andrew. We know Carol is there, too . . . always watching, listening, and guiding from up above.

This was all written, on a very snowy day, up at the cabins where Andrew and I married. He is at work, and I am here with our two dogs, and our two cats, fully realizing how blessed I really am.

Daniel Perry Walkup is a well-known interior designer and Andrew Walkup is a critical cardiac nurse. They reside in Oregon with their two rescue dogs and two rescue cats.

Joyously Free

A Gay Man's Sister: The Hurt Never Seems to End

By Kennette Babb

I have three siblings—my oldest sister, followed by an eight-year gap before my next sister, me, and then my brother; we were born one year apart.

After 12 years of trying, my parents were hoping for a boy, and they figured I would be the last child. They named me after my dad, Kenneth. I am Kennette. Being the third girl in the family and my father's namesake, I was a tomboy. I was athletic.

Dad coached my sports teams and tried to get Gerald, my brother, involved in sports, but Gerald just wasn't sports minded. We girls teased, calling him Geraldine. He was interested in drama and English and was also into theater arts. My parents went to all his performances, but he and my mother had a special bond.

I think we always knew he was gay, but no one really knew for sure. He knew, though.

Our mother passed away at age 75 and our father lived 11 years longer until he passed at age 87. About a month later, Christmas 2006, we received Gerald's Christmas card with a picture of him and his partner. That was his announcement that he was gay and in a relationship! We later learned that they had been married since 2001.

On July 4, 2008, they legally married. This is historic for my brother Gerard and Eric, my brother-in-law, because on May 15, 2008, the California Supreme Court ruled that same-sex marriage was legal under the California Constitution. However, in November of 2008, same-sex marriages were suspended until they became legal again June 28, 2013.

Chapter 8 – Religion: Follow Your Own Path to God and Spirituality

Can you imagine a straight wedding being suspended?

My brother and Eric had a big wedding and a huge celebration hosted by his spouse's family. None of our side of the family was invited. I still feel this hurt.

Gerard said he would have invited me, but he thought I was out of state. It hurts to think that he didn't know I would have been there for him in a heartbeat, no matter where I was at the time.

The four of us were born, bred, and raised in the Catholic Church. We lived across the street from the Catholic Church. The three of us younger siblings went to Catholic school from first through eighth grade. The only reasons we didn't go to Catholic high school were because my parents couldn't afford it and we had no transportation to get there.

As adults, we were all active and practicing Catholics. My brother was an altar boy in his youth. He sang in the church choir as an adult. I was a youth minister for 12 years. My sisters were greeters, Eucharistic ministers, and catechists.

Understandably, my brother waited until both our parents were deceased before coming out. It would have been a huge disappointment to my mother and caused an enormous problem between the two of them. My father was a man of few words and let people live their lives. I suspect my brother was afraid of disappointing him, too, and that's why he waited to come out.

But my sisters' reactions: oh, wow! My oldest sister's first reaction was to say Gerard was going to hell. She was extremely uncomfortable around Gerard and his partner. She was so uncomfortable around them that she made *them* uncomfortable. It took a few years, but she has finally learned to be more accepting and less judgmental. We did quite a bit of reminding to "judge not lest ye be judged." This part of my family has grown closer together in the years since my brothers' coming out.

But my other sister, well, she has never accepted Gerard's lifestyle. To this day, she does not talk to him and has completely disassociated herself from him. It's as if he doesn't exist. The rest of the family is not able to talk about him in front of her. We never get together for family gatherings. We have a huge rift in our family. We can never be as one.

When our nephew married in 2016, my sister and brother both attended the wedding. It was the first time since my dad's death 10 years earlier that the four of us had been together. When we arrived at the wedding site, my brother went to give her a hug and she physically pushed him away.

My brother was hurt, and we were shocked. I had asked the photographer for a picture of the four of us together. My sister only agreed to be in the picture on the condition that she did not have to stand next to Gerard. For a weekend that should have been filled with joy and happiness, it was devastating. A huge cloud hung over the entire weekend.

In 2017, this same sister married in the Catholic Church and our brother was not invited to her wedding. The rest of us were present.

The hurts never seem to end. In February 2020, we three sisters, along with her husband, my nephew, and his daughter, went on a week-long vacation at the beach. My brother-in-law had such a good time, he suggested that we all return to the beach that summer to celebrate June birthdays for himself, me, my nephew, and my brother.

I immediately agreed and said I would make sure to invite Gerard and his partner. My thinking was that this would be an excellent opportunity for a family reconciliation of sorts. Unfortunately, all conversation immediately ended. Needless to say, that vacation never happened.

In February 2022, I needed major surgery. I would need to have someone available to take care of me for several weeks

Chapter 8 – Religion: Follow Your Own Path to God and Spirituality

after the procedure. My oldest sister flew out to be with me for six weeks. Gerard and my brother-in-law also drove out to care for me for a week. But my sister and her husband, who originally said they would also come to assist, eventually bowed out. I suspect after they realized they might run into my brother during the transition between caregivers, they decided to not come.

I am no biblical scholar or authority on the Catholic faith. I am aware of what the Bible says about homosexuality. But I have come to question a church where all are not welcome. I believe we are all sinners. I believe in a loving God. I believe Jesus preached love, compassion, and forgiveness. I also believe that only God is the ultimate judge.

I've been a practicing member of the Roman Catholic Church for all of my 69 years. Certainly, I don't agree with all of its policies and concepts. I've always said I make a better Christian than a Catholic.

But these same church policies, held to an extreme by some of my family members, are creating a huge problem in my family. We no longer love each other. We no longer accept each other. We don't show understanding and compassion for each other. This extremism is tearing my family apart. And it is all done in the name of Jesus Christ and the Roman Catholic Church. Can this truly be what God wants of us? I don't think so.

So how exactly do I deal with all these conflicts? Dealing with the stress of my surgery as well as the conflicts in my family has been difficult. I was becoming depressed. Playing pickleball is a passion of mine, but the physical exercise was only doing so much to make me feel better. Going to church has always been a comfort and a release for me. But I wasn't finding happiness there anymore. I was staying home a lot. Reading helped. Saying the rosary helped some. Being with friends also helped.

In the last few months, I have begun attending an Episcopal church, a place where all are welcome. I discovered just last week that I was beginning to find more happiness in my life since I started attending there.

Also, over the course of these past 17 years, my brother and I have become even closer. We are able to talk about our family difficulties. Talking really seems to help. And while I try to keep the lines of communication open between me and my other sister, we are definitely drifting further and further apart. While this saddens me, sometimes I think it is for the best.

Kennette Babb is a retired educator. She is an active member of St. Timothy's Episcopal Church in Brookings, Oregon, plays pickleball, and is an avid LGBTQ+ supporter.

Chapter 8 – Religion: Follow Your Own Path to God and Spirituality

A Married Male Couple Hiding the Truth for Their Baby Godson's Baptism

By Derek

It's a shame how society treats minorities of any creed, color, or gender. We are all human! What is worse is when a non-profit organization (which really is a for-profit organization with all the riches they have) does it and hides behind their own morals to justify their "rules and regulations," when in fact their own followers break some of these rules!

Who am I talking about?

The Catholic Church, of course, and more specifically, the ones in Mexico.

As a gay man, I have been out and proud since I was 24. I have never denied or lied about my sexuality. I do not flaunt it, but I also don't lie about it if asked.

I am happily married to a man, or to be more specific, a "hot-blooded" Mexican man. Married for the last 10 years, we have been together for 19 years!

His family has accepted me as their own and I am honored! They don't see us as anything but loving individuals!

I love the Mexican culture and its heritage. So much so that I have gone out of my way to research it and embrace it and teach it to our nieces (who are my husband's brother's kids—they are American but have this Mexican heritage that they need to know).

Things like "Día De Muertos" (aka Day of the Dead Celebration) and things like knowing how the Mayan and Spanish (from Spain) cultures have contributed to a rich tapestry that is the country of Mexico. And that gives them their unique history that I hope they are proud of, because I am!

Joyously Free

I was very excited when the next child to be born was that of my husband's sister, who lives in Mexico. This is his only sister, and as you can imagine, the family was overjoyed to hear that she was expecting! Her son, whom we all call "Rafalito" (meaning "little Rafael" or "junior") is a term we Mexican families use to honor the grandfather who died (whose name was Rafale). He never got to hold his grandchild—he was taken by a heart attack—but his grandchild will always hold his namesake and hence our family heritage goes on.

Finally, the day arrived when my sister-in-law asked me and my husband if we would accept the honor of being Rafalito's "Padrinos" (Godparents) and of course, without even thinking about it, we said YES! What an honor that will be.

Oddly, I was raised Catholic myself, but no longer follow the religion (nor any other organized religion, for that matter). Do not get me wrong, I don't judge those who are religious; I respect all beliefs! As for my husband and a lot of Mexicans in general, they claim to be religious and/or Catholic, but they really only follow the religion when it benefits them (like attending Christmas masses or a baptism). But again, I don't judge. To each his own!

So why write all these good things? Where is the bad part? That is the next part of this tale.

My husband and I have been asked to lie! And we have been asked to lie to a priest in a church! I seem to recall that lying was not allowed per the 10 Commandments, so I asked my family: "Why do I have to lie?"

Only for them to explain to me that the churches in Mexico do not believe same-sex couples should have the right to be godparents (or even parents for that matter).

REALLY!?

How dare they stand and judge me when the Catholic

Chapter 8 – Religion: Follow Your Own Path to God and Spirituality

Church has had so many issues with priests abusing children and so many of them abusing children of the same sex!

What a dilemma.

Do I "turn the other cheek" (that's a Bible phrase, right?) and lie in order to be my nephew's godfather?

Or do I stand tall and tell the church to get over it?

Sadly, I have had to lie because they don't care! This is a situation where my hands are tied, and I have no choice. My husband and I, in the church's eyes, are simply two uncles who are NOT married and have been chosen by the mother to be godparents.

The priest will never know who we really are to this child. Which seems odd, because all we are wanting to do is protect this child should something happen to his mother (which is the role of a Padrino/godparent). I do not understand why the church can't get over themselves and understand this. Get with the times!

At the end of the day, I will stand in a church and in front of a priest and in front of all my family and lie. But if God does exist, He will know it's not a lie. And the family knows it's not a lie.

Does that mean I won? That if the deity these people all believe in knows I am doing the right thing, and He judges me, that it doesn't matter that the priest we stand in front of isn't given the chance to judge me?

What a double-edged sword! What a "two-faced" way to go about things. What a naïve and straight-out foolish and stupid thing it really is, because at the end of the day, my husband and I and our family get exactly what we want out of it . . . even if we go to hell!

The church should practice what it preaches and be open to all and let God judge us instead of some priest or some organized religion's rules.

Joyously Free

I am human; I feel like everyone else and bleed like everyone else. I'm just attracted to hot Latin men! Sue me!

So, I will stand in a church and in front of a priest and know the whole time that this show—this spectacle—is simply for a piece of paper that says little Rafalito is "clean" in God's eyes and that should anything happen, God forbid (neat how God keeps coming onto this story that way) to my sister-in-law, Rafalito will be well taken care. He will be taught to love all and NOT JUDGE ANYONE and NOT TO LIE . . . unless it's for a good reason!

Wow . . . am I confused!

Chapter 8 – Religion: Follow Your Own Path to God and Spirituality

Questions About a Gay Man Officiating a Straight Wedding

By Skylar Windham

Inky wings of apricot, peach, and tangerine flutter above an orchard in the Rogue Valley of Southern Oregon. Through ivy-laden arbors framing aisles of clover, the monarch butterflies follow a train of Alençon lace, finally alighting upon a linen shoulder in waiting.

The ceremony has begun.

Today it is a secular ritual, or a ceremony of unholy matrimony. Such simultaneous irreverence and deference are ironic. The bride makes her way to the altar and the crowd of cousins and colleagues sits down, while the violins glide to a whispering hum. At the top step of the altar stands the ordained, the bride's brother: me.

I am unholy in the traditional sense, in that I am a man who sleeps with men. It hadn't occurred to me that this detail should prohibit my participation in the wedding, or be considered at all, until it was brought to my attention afterward.

More than a few people in my queer circle expressed their disapproval at my involvement. One questioned, "Why would you subject yourself to that? Why would you play such a servile role in the name of a privilege that has been denied to people like you for so long?"

Another shared, "I chose not to attend a friend's wedding, because I refuse to be the only minority there."

It was almost as if a jury of my peers had found me guilty of a crime. By their logic, I had become complicit in my own oppression, and somehow theirs.

My reality differs from these slanted accusations. When my youngest sister asked if I would ordain her wedding, I didn't

Joyously Free

interpret the question as a decision to be made, or even an invitation to be accepted or denied; I was simply touched that I was given an opportunity to be part of their celebration of love. Had it felt like a decision, the outcome would have been the same, because a union of love is never about the witness of the bond.

My ordination of my sister's wedding was not a political statement, although if it had been, I would say we have a duty to show up wholeheartedly in every space we can, in every space we have earned. Yet it was not political; it was an act of love. Mothers crying at the first dance, aunts disregarding their assigned seats at reception, one of the groom's old college buddies sneakily taking more than his fair share (one cupcake at a time); love present in all of its iterations.

To take something beautiful and reduce it to ammunition is to deny ourselves the opportunity to experience joy. There is a time and a place for defense; love is for always and everywhere.

Skylar Windham is a psychotherapist and sailor. Learn more about him at HeadwindsCounseling.com.

Chapter 8 – Religion: Follow Your Own Path to God and Spirituality

TIPS for Experiencing God & Spirituality on Your Own Terms

You're connected! Know that you have direct access to God, Spirit, Universe, your Higher Self, angels, ancestors, or other names that you prefer to describe your Higher Power.

Prayer and meditation are the best way to enjoy two-way communication with this Higher Power. Call out to it in your mind, whisper, or talk out loud. Express your deepest, most private concerns, fears, dreams, and sadness. Let go and share—or yell!—everything and anything. You will be heard.

Then, be quiet, calm, and centered. Listen. Answers will come in time and in many forms, including: feelings, experiences in nature; signs and symbols that only you understand; synchronicities and serendipitous moments; people; song lyrics; scripture; art; dancing; readings; and silence.

The Universe speaks through symbols, such as a rainbow showing up in the sky at the same moment that you were feeling anxious about something. That's a heavenly sign that your prayers have been heard.

Build a personal relationship with your Higher Power, which is with you around the clock for your entire life. You have constant and immediate access at all times. Let that unique relationship be as profound as the ones you enjoy with your lover, dear friends, and family. Believe that God/

your Higher Power wants you to be happy, so be joy-filled and trust that anything is possible.

Do things every day that fortify this connection. Listen to songs with spiritual messages that make you feel happy. Don't listen to music with depressing lyrics. Surround yourself with people who share your quest for spiritual peace and comfort. Avoid those who do the opposite. Make time daily for quiet reflection, meditation, prayer, or another activity that makes you feel close to the Creator.

Count your blessings. Gratitude deepens your connection to your Higher Power. Think about all the people, experiences, and things that you're thankful for. Also give thanks for the many things we take for granted, such as food in our stomachs, fresh air to breathe, clean water to drink, hot water to bathe in, a safe place to sleep, the ability to hear, see, walk, and talk, and anything else you can think of.

Dwell on blessings that have already occurred as a reminder that things can work out for the better when you believe that they will. Be grateful for being made the way you are as an LGBTQ+ person, parent, ally or advocate.

Believe in miracles. This is when the divine does something extraordinary and inexplicable. Divine ways are not always our ways. And sometimes when things don't work out the way we want, it's because God has a much bigger plan or reason, which cannot be explained at the moment, but later becomes evident. When this happens, you just know that forces greater than yourself are conspiring to bring you the best possible outcome.

Trust, believe, and have faith! The more you trust

Chapter 8 – Religion: Follow Your Own Path to God and Spirituality

in the unbelievable, with an unselfish yet open heart, asking, "Please God, Your will be done," it will be granted to you with great peace, joy, and surprise. You can create your own phrase.

This mindset helps you believe that everything happens for a reason and in divine timing. One example can be the loss of a romantic relationship. Rejection is God's protection, so consider this a blessing to spare you from problems that might have evolved if the relationship had continued. Or know that the divine has removed this person to clear space in your life for your true love to appear and become your happily ever after partner.

Be totally honest with yourself. Find your true beautiful self in prayer, in reflection, and in forgiveness. Forgiving yourself is a powerful act of releasing anything that makes you feel regret, guilt, or other self-imposed emotions. You are made in a divine image for a magical, profound purpose. Releasing the heavy-duty emotions that are baggage from the past can help you live *Joyously Free*.

Listen to your intuition. This is your inner voice, and it speaks your queer truth. Listen to it. Trust it. Follow it. Your inner gay voice sings and resonates love. Your intuition is the voice of God.

Find a faith community that celebrates you for who you are. You'll know it when you find it. When you walk in, you'll feel perfect peace and knowing, and you'll feel embraced with love and acceptance by the people there. Trust this feeling.

If you can't find a spiritual sanctuary in your area, consider starting your own. You could begin small, in your home or backyard, in a private room at an LGBTQ+

restaurant or café, in a garden, or at another special venue. You don't even need a person with religious credentials; you can create and lead the type of service that fulfills you, knowing that it will help others as well. Include music, poetry, candles, incense, celebratory decorations, and even the opportunity for everyone to talk. Then enjoy a potluck meal together.

Just like you're free to express your unique LGBTQ+ identity, you have the power to imagine how you want to worship, as well as when, where, and with whom, in ways that satisfy your soul.

Remember, religion and spirituality are bigger than a church, synagogue, mosque, temple, religious institution, bigotry, prejudice, and hatred. Love is love.

Be open to whatever God and the Universe are putting in your heart.

Chapter 9

I've Got That JOY JOY JOY!

How to Create Your Joyously Free Life

Fall in Love with the New You

By Elizabeth

Being *Joyously Free* starts with YOU!

It's not about someone else coming into your life to give you the joy and freedom you're seeking. It's not about finding another person who "completes" you. You are whole and complete. You are enough. And it's your birthright to maximize your infinite potential, personally and professionally.

All you need to do is give yourself permission to step into the life of your dreams, hopefully inspired by the tips in this book.

Joy is an inside job. It sparks in your heart and soul, and starts in your mind with a decision that:

Now is my time. I will not go another minute in this life feeling anything less than thrilled to be me, just as I am!

If you've suffered criticism, rejection, shame, guilt, or even trauma from people who don't approve of you as an LGBTQ+ person, then it's time to heal and release that. It's time to undo the damage and leave it in the past.

It's time to fall in love with yourself as the New You who is *Joyously Free*.

Joyously Free

But first, if you've had any mental health challenges around this with anxiety, depression, body dysmorphia, self-hatred, self-harm, self-medicating with alcohol or drugs, and/or suicidal ideation, please allow a professional therapist to help you.

Meanwhile, it's time to love yourself like never before.

Please read *You Can Heal Your Life* by Louise Hay. This amazing book is a *New York Times* best-seller that has sold more than 50 million copies worldwide. You can also listen to Louise Hay's videos on YouTube. She is the queen of self-love and shares her messages with a soothing voice and peaceful aura. Her affirming words can help reprogram your inner voice with words to speak more kindly to yourself. It's especially calming to listen to her videos while falling asleep.

Next, **decide that you deserve love**, first from yourself, then from others, even if you've never felt it the way you dream about receiving it. Know that someone and/or people out there in the world are aching to find you and shower you with this love. At the same time, you can reciprocate that love back to them to create an infinite flow of affection, kind words, and acts of appreciation that cultivate emotional security and a "home, sweet home" feeling that you can enjoy with another person and/or people.

Start small. What do you already love about yourself? It can be as simple as your hair, your hands, your talent for painting, your gift of counseling friends through dilemmas, or your ability to wake up every morning on time without an alarm clock. Dwell on the positives about yourself, and look for one new thing every day.

Do mirror work. Look in the mirror, into your own eyes. Feel whatever feelings this evokes and let them pass. Then say, "I accept you just as you are."

Advance to saying, "I like you just as you are."

Next, tell yourself, "I love you just as you are."

Chapter 9 – I've Got That Joy Joy Joy!

Then, "I deserve to be happy and healthy and live a great life, on my terms." If you can smile at yourself, do it.

Know that your self-love will magnetize you to attract people who love you. We attract what we are because our emotions emit a vibrational frequency. The highest frequencies are joy, peace, and love, so when you activate those feelings inside yourself, it sends a signal through the universe to attract people who are emitting the same frequency.

Know that you were born on this earth for a reason, and that your challenges have been lessons to prepare you for the next and best phases of your life.

Work with a "Coming Out Coach." These are trained professionals who can guide you through the process of coming out. Some offer private as well as group coaching, along with workshops and retreats. Which options are best for you?

You can find coming out coaches through online searches and on social media. Read reviews and get referrals, then interview coaches to find the best match.

Get inspiration from social media and podcasts. Watch videos, read posts, and listen to podcasts about people who share their coming out stories, along with insights and experiences that showcase and celebrate their particular identity. This can help you learn about different labels, and the unique culture around each.

If you're looking for love, many couples share their lives online to help you find your person or people and give you a peek into their relationships. Find the best folks by searching online for websites, podcasts, and social media personalities who align with you. You could even comment and/or Direct Message them with your questions.

You can also search online for "Top LGBTQ Influencers" and follow those whose messaging inspires you.

Joyously Free

Use your imagination. When you worry and envision worst case scenarios, you're using your imagination. What you're thinking and envisioning is not real. It has not happened, and you don't want it to. Plus, it only makes you feel worse.

The alternative is to focus your imagination on best case scenarios. Your thoughts are the first step toward manifesting experiences, things, and people in your life. With them, you are mentally building images that can and do come true. So, use "creative visualization" to create pictures and mini filmstrips in your mind of what you want your best life to look and feel like. No matter what's happening in the present moment, keep those images alive in your mind, knowing that someday they can become your present reality.

Celebrate the gift of now. The past is over. The future is not here yet. All we have is this moment, right now, so stay in "the present," because it's a gift.

Don't look back; the past can weigh you down. Imagine packing all the things from your past into boxes that you seal up and try to carry around all day today and into tomorrow. You would be exhausted and too weighed down and strained to achieve anything but the heavy, burdensome lifting and carrying.

Now imagine shipping those boxes off to a storage facility called "I don't need this anymore." You'll feel so light and free. You can do this mentally, by declaring to yourself in your mind, out loud, and in your journal, that, "I hereby release _____ from my mind and heart so I'm free to soar into my best self and life right now." A professional counselor can help you with this process.

Your past pain and struggles led you to where you are now, so view those boxes with grace and gratitude for preparing you for the gift of today.

Express yourself, baby! When you're ready, it's so fun to express yourself by the way you dress, talk, and cultivate

Chapter 9 - I've Got That Joy Joy Joy!

environments that reflect who you are.

Do you want your appearance and style to shOUT to the world that you're here and happy and ready to explore all life's glorious possibilities?

Then **dress like it!** And adorn your body as a celebration of your uniqueness. Now's the time to experiment with clothing styles and colors to showcase your personality. If you're into all black, go for it. If you love sparkling with crystals or jewelry from your pierced ears to your toe rings, then go for it. If you want to wear clothes splashed with rainbows and hearts and peace signs, do it!

Hair and makeup? You can be as dramatic and colorful or as basic as you'd like.

Tattoos? Design your own that shOUT your truth and/or display symbols that have powerful meanings for you.

Piercings? You may like the aesthetic of piercings, but did you know that they can activate energy centers in your body that empower your authenticity? You can learn more by watching my interview with Chari Weatherford—a ceremonial piercer with 24 years of experience and founder of Ritual Evolution—on The Goddess Power Show with Elizabeth Ann Atkins® on YouTube.

If you're not ready to shOUT it to the world, you can express yourself in private ways that have powerful meaning for you. For example, you could have a tattoo that declares your truth on skin that is usually covered by clothing. You could also wear a ring, a bracelet, or other piece of jewelry that is a gift to yourself or from a special person, that symbolizes who you really are.

Make your environment reflect you. Decorate your bedroom, bathroom, office, entire home—interior and exterior, garden or patio or yard, and even your car. Display flags, rainbows, photographs, posters, blinking lights, images of celebrity role models, and anything that expresses who you are.

Talk your truth! Joanie uses words like "Shazam!" and "Wowie!" and "Yippee!" to express her joy in conversation, text messages, emails, and social media posts. I often exclaim, "Beautiful!" and "Awesome!" and "Phenomenal!" and "Yeah, baby!" and "I love it!"

So, which words make you feel happy and excited when you say them? If none come to mind, then find some! As you go about your day, listen for song lyrics, movie lines, sayings on social media, and live conversations. Do you hear any words or phrases that resonate with how you'd like to express yourself? Sprinkle these happy words into all your communications. They make you feel better and they uplift others as well.

Give your inner critic a happier script. How do you speak to yourself? Did you know that words have the power to create your reality? It's so easy to dwell on the negative.

So, now's the time to do a self-audit of how you speak about yourself, your life, and your future. If you find yourself speaking negativity over yourself and your life, make a conscious effort to spin your expressions into positive words to help manifest a better reality. For example, if you say: "I hate my life. I feel so stuck. Things will never change."

Practice saying, "I'm doing things every day to make positive changes to create a life that I love."

Go wild with this! You don't have to tell anyone what you're thinking as you transform your mental chatter into self-talk that helps you become *Joyously Free*.

Move your body like you mean business. Walk and gesture in ways that show the true you. Gay men are masters at expressing themselves with body language. Drag queens finesse their walk and talk in ways that are mesmerizing.

I love watching #masclesbiansoftiktok videos because each person has a unique way of flexing their masculinity—with

Chapter 9 – I've Got That Joy Joy Joy!

facial expressions, hand gestures, posture, and swagger. Not to mention their hairstyles, clothing, and jewelry.

So, what's the best body language for your authentic self to shine?

It's time to fall in love with the New You!

How Carol and I Created a *Joyously Free* Life

By Joanie

Creating joy came naturally for me and Carol. We inherited positive DNA from our happy families. And we did our best by thinking happy thoughts and keeping our words positive, hope-filled, and encouraging.

Elizabeth mentioned how she loves videos by spiritual leader Louise L. Hay, author of *You Can Heal Your Life.*

With its rainbow-splashed cover, this was the very first book that I saw sitting by Sister Carol's rocking chair in her convent bedroom in Lewiston, Idaho, more than 42 years ago. Carol and I would take turns and read it aloud together. Now it's displayed on my kitchen bookshelf, and when I caress the book cover, I can still feel Carol's presence and the touch of her soft hand, right here, right now!

Throughout our life together, we catapulted through the insanely stereotypical heterosexual societal norms and the church's hierarchical male leadership, some with chauvinistic attitudes. We saw that the cup of life and love was not half empty, but it was a deep ocean full of positive "what if's." There was always a new world coming!

"How did you and Carol live such a joyous life?"

Oh, this question has been asked many times by friends, family, coworkers, and community people during our 40 years as a loving, committed, same-sex couple.

The answer is . . . drum roll . . . we were our best selves and we brought out the best in each other with Jesus' help!

Plain and simple, that was how we did it! There's the answer that everyone, especially *Nun Better* readers, want to know.

Chapter 9 – I've Got That Joy Joy Joy!

Imagine if you are super happy with yourself and then you meet a soulmate who transforms your life and their life, exponentially bearing fruit, by sharing and doing life together. That was us!

Sharing experiences—sad or glad—grabbed a hold of our hearts and souls. This happened when watching a sunrise, breathing the same fresh air, and seeing a rosebud bundled tight, but knowing it will open and spread its petals to become vibrant and fragrant. We committed ourselves to sharing, serving, and loving without costs, regrets, or fears.

All the while, we asked a lot of "what if" questions that boiled down to:

What if you are the best you?

What if I am the best me?

What if together, we make the best us?

What if we have God do the rest?

So the next step was to trust and have faith in something bigger than us. There you go, 40 years of AMAZING love.

Life is full of ups and downs and all arounds. Carol and I did not go slowly over life's speed bumps, but instead hydroplaned fast and furious over them. Together, hand in hand, eye to eye, we fed each other abundant love!

We chose to dance in our secretive, safe space of bedrooms, behind convent doors for a few years, and in every room in our own home thereafter. Two songs that express this joy are "New World Coming" and "Make Your Own Kind of Music" by Mama Cass Elliot.

Carol and I chose to sing while we strummed guitars in prayer together in churches and in our living room prayer corners. We played catch with flying frisbees in windstorms, blasted tennis balls accidentally over fences, and laughed when landing the three-inch-long "catch of the day" fish on Lake Quinault.

Forgetting to secure the rope on crab pots led to joyous forgiveness. We boasted with hysteria as we decided to change the rules in the middle of a serious competitive card game with friends and we threw air kisses here, there, and everywhere.

We shared passionate kisses while standing or sitting cuddled on redwood decks under the bright full moon and blinking stars.

Life was alive and kicking and we were in the middle of it. We *were* it!

The funnest part of all this was a lifetime of courtship. Married couples would share with us that they really "worked at" their relationship. We were a different kind of couple, I guess. It was a privilege and pleasure to just hang out together. We saw something that affirmed this at The Disney Store in Anaheim, California. It sells sweatshirts printed with the words, "I love you. I love you. I love you. I love you." Hanging next to it, is the response on another sweatshirt, which reads, "I know. I know. I know. I know." Oh, what a feeling of bliss! That was us!

We didn't work at it; we listened, we spoke up, we were honest and faithful, and we were kind. We thought of the other before ourselves most of the time. We enJOYed life!

How Did This Joy Begin?

Imagine several Catholic nuns covered in long black and white penguin gowns with striking black shoes, with only their faces visible, striding into the local tavern like they owned the place.

The women radiated joy and captured attention like the Hollywood movie star John Wayne did in old westerns when he entered a cowboy saloon.

Beer drinkers, pool players, bar-sitting loggers, and couples dancing to oldies but goodies on the jukebox turned to stare, squint, and even frown as these women entered the local hotspot,

Chapter 9 – I've Got That Joy Joy Joy!

the Hideaway Tavern, on a cold, dark night in Lewiston, Idaho.

Onlookers enjoyed their burgers and fries as the staff greeted the women with nods and grins as the unusual bunch filled a long table.

Leading them was Sister Carol, a Catholic-vowed young woman at heart who had invited these convent sisters to splurge and dine out. It was the early 1980s, and this motley crew was shattering the stereotypes of nuns.

At age 23, I was elated to be among these young, middle-aged and elderly women, each dressed in unique fashions that conveyed our individualism, commitment, and sexual identity. Some of us wore black skirts that hung just below the knee and white buttoned blouses with sharp black blazer jackets. Several sisters, who had nice-looking legs with beige nylons and black pumps, walked tall and proud across the sawdust-covered floor.

Carol, others, and I wore navy blue, black, or green casual pants with zippered coats. I wore a sporty hooded sweatshirt under my coat. Carol looked so cute with her signature purple wool hat.

As the spinning vinyl 45 records continued to play, I enjoyed the exciting dialogue between Sister Carol, the leader of our club—the congregation of the Catholic religious Sisters of St. Joseph—and the packed house of people who greeted her:

"Hi, Sister Carol, good to see you!"

"How are you, Sister Carol?"

She responded with enthusiasm: "We are great! How about you? How's so and so?" She was absolutely radiant, caring, and kind. Her aura beamed around her.

That night was my first of many joyous adventures that Carol and I would experience at a tavern bar. We connected eye to eye, sitting at opposite ends of the long wooden table loaded with plastic cups of soda pop and water.

Heart to heart, Carol and I bobbed our heads as all of us shared stories, laughed, and celebrated my night out. Yes, the Lord was already in the midst of a great plan for me and Carol! What a joyous night. I remember it like it's happening now. The inner joy we shared was wordless, but the attraction—though secret at the time—was strong and clear.

Bug Station Fun

Six years later, Carol and I were traveling in our 15-year-old, four-door economy car as we drove through Oregon to California, heading south on Interstate 5. We were going to visit Elaine, Carol's sister who later became my sister-in-law, along with their teenagers—niece Carrie and nephew Will—in Paradise, California.

On this gorgeous, warm, sunny day, Carol wore sunglasses while driving and chatting up a storm. I loved it when she, the less extroverted of us, got on a nonstop talking roll.

She guided our car towards the green light lane for a California agricultural inspection—or a "bug station" as locals call it—where an inspector would ask us a few questions about what plants or fruit we had with us. This was to prevent exotic invasive species from spreading and to monitor plant quarantine regulations.

This familiar occurrence was no biggie. In fact, I did it every day, traveling on Coastal Highway 101 from our Oregon home to my work across the state line in California. We were pros at passing through the inspection bug station. We knew the do's and don'ts.

This time, Carol slowed the car, but did not completely stop, as required. She pushed the button to lower her window and speak to the attendant, smiled, and without a break in her conversation with me, she told the worker, "No fruit today!"

Chapter 9 – I've Got That Joy Joy Joy!

Then she accelerated to 65 mph, heading south on the highway.

I burst into laughter as I looked backward at the inspection employee. He had his hands on his hips, elbows protruding wide with a most surprised, quizzical expression. He looked upset and shocked, and then he shook his head from side to side and flashed a huge smile.

"Carol, did you hear what he asked?"

"Yes," she said. "'Do you have any fruit?' I told him no fruit."

Laughing, I said, "No, he didn't, sweetie. He asked you, 'How are you today?'"

I was laughing my head off! Hysterical, about ready to pee my pants. And you said, "No fruit!"

Carol laughed from her belly. "Really, Joanie?"

"Yes, really, sweetie! He was overly perplexed with you as you sped off. He had his hands on his hips and then the funniest expression on his face. You made his day, Carol!!" We laughed and laughed and laughed for miles and even years later.

Laughter and love definitely go together!

When was the last time you had a deep belly laugh?

I'm sure that this young employee went home sharing or told his work colleagues about these two crazy ladies! Maybe it is on a training video?

Former Nuns Pole Dancing in New York City

Fast forward 20 years to when Carol and I took a vacation back East. Yes, we were still creating memories, with every day full of new surprises and "God moments" that popped up and delighted us.

Oh the joy I witnessed as Carol twirled around in a complete circle while hanging onto the subway pole on the New York City express train. As it lurched forward, she hung on with such grace and style. This was her one and only pole dance!

Joyously Free

Those seated on the early morning commuter subway were stunned by her fun, frolic dance show. Oh golly, such spontaneous joy erupted on her face and everyone else's too.

"We are tourists," I said.

"We know!" passengers exclaimed in a chorus.

We all laughed and they even offered us seats after her grand performance.

"How did we get into this?" we often asked in the midst of strange situations. "And how are we going to get out of it?"

Joyfully, that's how!

After our subway ride, we visited the breathtaking architecture of St. Patrick's Cathedral in New York City, which takes up an entire city block. It was our first visit to this Catholic church, and we had been out of the convent for more than 15 years and still loved our Catholic faith.

We arrived late for mass, but just in time for holy communion. We dashed up the center aisle toward the altar to receive Jesus in host and body form. The eucharistic minister eyed our every stride and waited patiently for us to hurry up the 300-foot, marble-floored aisle.

During the long walk, we noticed several strange stares and glares from those already served, fed, and seated, waiting for mass to end. I thought, *Oh well, give them peace, Lord.*

We were obviously tourists. Carol's bright floral dress swooshed as I followed behind her, wearing shorts, a T-shirt and tennis shoes, with a red backpack bouncing on my shoulders.

After receiving Jesus in the sacrament of Eucharist, we quickly found a seat in a hard pew between large white columns, then plunked our butts down to catch our breath. I looked up in awe at the highest cathedral ceiling I'd ever seen in an American church. I was also mesmerized by the gorgeous, colorful stained-glass windows in Jesus' home.

Chapter 9 – I've Got That Joy Joy Joy!

I thanked our Lord for this day and for being inside both of us, from head to toe.

"Jesus," I prayed, "take care of Carol, bless everyone here, and thank you for this vacation."

When the mass ended with the final blessing to go in peace, we discovered a side chapel shrine where we lit a candle for our loved ones, family, and friends. Quietly and tenderly, we interlocked our pinkie fingers. Our deep love for each other felt like it was a spectrum of colored sun rays shooting forth, ricocheting light off the huge, rose-stained glass window, and reflecting off the ornate majesty all around.

This holy, loving moment occurred as we were surrounded by statues of St. Joseph, St. Patrick, and St. Frances X Cabrini, the patron for immigrants. Oh, the guardian angels were there, too.

As we peacefully exited the church, I spotted a holy water fount and a spigot, which I used to fill the plastic bottle that was in the side pocket of my backpack. Ahhh, I guzzled the water.

Of course, messy Joanie, I accidentally spilled it down the front of my white, New York tourist t-shirt that had a big red heart in the center. I became a wet T-shirt woman, in the house of God, with a see-through view exposing my plump breasts and nipples. Carol was goo-goo eyed, smiling and giggling while staring at my sexiness.

I unscrewed the cap of the empty water bottle and placed it under the holy water spigot, filling it to the very top saying:

"Knock, knock!"

"Who's there?" Carol responded.

"John!"

"Who?"

"John the Baptist," I said, sprinkling water from my fingertips onto her face. She was totally surprised, winking, and wiping

Joyously Free

her hands over her gorgeous green eyes. We laughed loudly and uncontrollably!

As we turned to walk out of the cathedral's huge, heavy bronze front doors that are propped open for safety—laughing and casually naturally holding hands—we caught the attention of others.

We were being watched! Oh, now what? Is it our lesbian hand hold? My wet T-shirt? The holy water droplets still gracing Carol's soft Egyptian face? Or the plastic water bottle filled with blessed water carefully being held in my hand?

We were so happy and our smiles beamed. Time seemed to slow and speed up all at once. We stood and watched with amazement as others began filling their water containers from the "holy water" faucet, too! What a hoot! Total jubilance!

"Rejoice in the Lord, always," came humming out of Carol's and my lips. How fun!

Yes, joy and laughter are for sharing and they are so wonderfully contagious!

Make your own kind of music! That's how we created our joy!

It's time to be your true Self. Can't wait to meet you!!

Lesbian for a Lifetime:
Peace and Power, Living *Joyously Free!*

By Eve DeRusha

I have been aware of my gayness for six decades, beginning at age 19. I'm now 84.

I hope for a perfect future, but always remember that in the imperfect past, every experience prepares us for our present life.

Looking back, I was very ignorant of my sexuality until college. So I decided to research the history of homosexuality in the library at Wayne State University in Detroit, Michigan, where I was born in 1939, then raised.

I had a wonderful, kind, sweet mother who made life work well for me and my two older brothers, while my dad was in the U.S. Army during World War II.

After the war, when Dad came home, he was a changed man (I was told). He was an alcoholic. When I was about eight years old during the late 1940s, Mom kicked him out of the house and invited her mother to live with us. Mom got a job at a local dime store and was on her feet all day for the wage of 50 cents per hour.

We rented an old house and had the entire attic to ourselves, while the other building residents shared a one-room apartment. I went to public schools. I was a good student—a handful for weak teachers, but an angel with the more experienced teachers.

Looking back, I was seeking more attention than my mother could supply. Even negative attention is attention.

I think I had a crush on my female teacher in third grade. I told my mom that I was not attracted to men and never would be. She just nodded and we never brought up the subject again!

Joyously Free

On a Saturday afternoon in 1959, when I was 20 years old, I ran into a boy I had met in grade school. Robert R. had moved away, but we had reconnected in high school. I recall him acting very girlish, while I was the boyish kid, called a tomboy then. The *gaydar* was working for both of us. He told me about a café in downtown Detroit called the Hub Grill that catered to gays in the evenings and on weekends. This was news to me and I was very interested in checking it out.

Robert also told me about a gay bar in Toledo, Ohio, about an hour south of Detroit. He told me I'd be able to drink because, unlike Michigan with its legal drinking age of 21, the drinking age in Ohio was only 18.

I drove my mom's car with a few gals I'd met at the Hub. At last, I could find my people! When we got there, we drank "nearbeer," which had a 3.2 percent alcohol content.

At one point in the restroom, I was cornered by a short, dark-haired, thick-eyeglasses-wearing gal who said she had met a gorgeous woman there.

I foolishly asked, "Who? Where?"

She assured me that it was me, and she sealed it with my first gay kiss. YIKES!

"I'm Brad," she said. "Who are you? Where do you live and work?"

I foolishly told her that I worked at Wayne State.

By then, my group was ready to leave, so we headed back to Detroit.

I forgot about Brad, but a couple of weeks later, she had tracked me down. She wanted to know when I could visit Toledo again. We wrote letters back and forth. Long story short: I learned that when I met Brad, she had been on a two-day pass from the local mental hospital. I had hoped to meet a sweet gal and enjoy a relationship, but Brad was not available for that.

Chapter 9 – I've Got That Joy Joy Joy!

As my adventures continued, one night I saw a good-looking "queen" strutting down the street with a drunk straight guy in hot pursuit—until she lifted her dress and showed "his jewels." The drunk ran away in horror down the street. We stood there and cracked up. It was hysterically funny! Oh wow!

My crew and I started frequenting The Scenic regularly. Once when we were there, and I was with a gal I really liked, a big fight broke out. The huge, horseshoe-shaped bar was packed. Someone threw a bottle and it smashed the mirrored wall behind the bar. My friend Donna, who was deaf, was sitting across from me with her back to the bar.

Broken glass flew everywhere! Knowing Donna couldn't hear anything, I pulled her under the table with me. She gave me a very frightened look, and we crawled to the exit door.

Outside, we found the rest of my friends. We knew the police would be coming, so we made it to mom's car, pointed it north, and that was my last time in Toledo. It scared the hell out of me!

As I grew older and wiser, I met more and more gay people, while hanging out at the Hub Grill and trying to get into gay bars before I was 21. I moved to East Lansing, Michigan, and finished my Bachelor of Arts there.

I have had many "girlfriends with benefits" over the years and I recall several with great love and affection! One gal, Barb, was 14 years older than me. Barb was a school counselor in a Detroit suburb. While living with her, I earned my Master of Arts degree in Educational Guidance and Counseling.

All the while, I was "undercover," because I was getting trained to work with kids and I was "Queer." The anti-gay stigma in school systems still exists today in 2024 and is totally ridiculous.

Years later, after ending a 40-year relationship with my lover Sybil Grace, I was with a gal 17 years younger than me. That did not end well. Live and learn!

Now I have "taken vows" to remain happily single. Today it's just me and my dog and a whole slew of gay and straight friends.

One of my brothers was gay and lost his life to AIDS in 1988! He was a contractor, and the doctor said he would lose his arms and legs. He died the next day at age 55. I was mad at him for years and still am for being stupid, not using rubbers (condoms), getting AIDS, and dying so young. It deeply hurts and I cry telling this, because at the time, I couldn't do anything about it; AIDS was a death sentence. We were scared for each other. I wasn't ready for him to die in both a physically painful way and in a hateful, societal, ugly way. More than 100,000 people died of AIDS in the United States during the 1980s; the epidemic was personal to me.

Meanwhile, my oldest brother had married young and lasted 65 years in a straight marriage. So, in my family, two of us were queer and one straight.

What can you do to find your peace and power to live *Joyously Free?*

First, I highly recommend that you read Joanie's fabulous book, *Nun Better: An AMAZING Love Story*. Also, find an online support group such as PFLAG (Parents, Families and Friends of Lesbians and Gays) online. It's especially helpful to hear from parents who have learned that their child is a "HOMO SEX U ALL." These parents can share their stories and tips about how to deal with what they view as a terrible catastrophe.

Finding your peace and power to live *Joyously Free* is the best gift you can give yourself. It's your job to figure out what that looks and feels like for you.

If you're struggling, do not give up!

Do not kill yourself, because being gay is not your fault!

In my opinion, **you and I were born this way.** We didn't ask for it. Life is what it is; gayness is not catching and believe me

Chapter 9 – I've Got That Joy Joy Joy!

when I say it's a process that many people go through all over the world.

Here are my tips:

- Join a support group.

- Fight the bullies. This doesn't mean physically fight, unless you're defending yourself. Get help from appropriate authorities that include school officials and the police.

- Take care of your health.

- Give life a chance.

- Get a good education!

- Even if you have a rough start, **don't give up!**

- Find your peace, power, and joy!

Joyously Free

A Tearful Moment Unites Two LGBTQ+ Souls as Joy Takes Flight

By Jeffrey Church

Life, much like an airport, is a bustling panorama of experiences and emotions. Amidst the chaos and hurried footsteps, there are moments that transcend the ordinary, and remind us that a simple gesture of kindness can help ease a turbulent moment in someone's life.

On October 14, 2022, I finished packing for a work conference, kissed my husband goodbye, and made my way to the Oakland International Airport to catch a quick flight to Las Vegas.

As I make my way to the gate, I decide to sit at the outer row looking towards the small café by the gate. As part of my travel routine, I set up my air pods, got my Southwest drink coupons ready, and texted my hubby and momma that I made it safely to the airport (yes, I'm a huge momma's boy).

I have ample time before boarding and decide to watch some *Golden Girls* (the episode when the girls end up in jail and Sophia gets to see Burt Reynolds instead) to pass the time.

A few minutes pass when I notice at the corner of my eye a woman struggling with her bag, a cup of coffee, and a random piece of paper that falls from one of her pockets. I know how clumsy and prone to dropping things I am, so I get up and make my way across the walkway to pick up the paper and offer to help. Her eyes light up, and her voice, full of sincere appreciation, gives me the sweetest "Thank you!" I have heard in some time.

I help bring her items over to where I'm sitting, get her settled in, introduce myself, and ask if she needs anything else. She seems less flustered; I can tell she's rattled and running on fumes, so before I even let her respond with her name, I ask:

"Do you want a hug?"

Chapter 9 – I've Got That Joy Joy Joy!

Her eyes water, her arms open and we give each other a big bear hug that lasts a good minute.

I rub her back to comfort her as we hug, and can feel a sense of relief, gratitude, and love radiating from her. I start crying, too, thinking about how she's around my mom's age, feeling the same joy that emanates from my *Mommita Chula* (beautiful mom).

We both let go from the hug, wipe the tears from our eyes, and she tells me her name: Joanie Lindenmeyer.

After the waterworks wash away any and all barriers, we start learning about each other's past adventures, present travels, and future destinations.

She starts off by telling me she's from Brookings, Oregon, traveling to Tucson, Arizona. She says the day started at dawn with a debacle of flight issues from Crescent City, California, as she made her way to Oakland International Airport for a final leg of her flight. That alone would make any reasonable person want to curl up in a ball and cry.

"What's waiting for you in Tucson?" I ask.

She shares that she's going to visit her friends. I look into her eyes, and although she's smiling with true joy in her voice, her eyes water again.

I hold her hand.

"Tell me why you're tearing up," I say.

Still smiling, she says, "My partner of 40 years, Carol, just passed away in January, and I'm visiting our friends for the first time since she went to heaven."

My heart sinks, my eyes well up, and I go in for another hug. I'm crying again, now thinking about my husband, Glenn. We were lucky to meet when I was 20 and fortunate to start our love at an early age. Now in our thirties, the thought of losing one another had never really crossed my mind. Until now. I let Joanie know about my husband and she smiles, letting me know

Joyously Free

how beautiful it is to see me so in love with him.

This moment makes me feel joy, true joy, in so many ways. Joy in that I could give a little kindness to a stranger and help them feel secure. Joy that God, or any higher being, could bring two people together and let them share a moment of love and compassion. Joy in that two queer people could gravitate towards each other and celebrate their love for their partners.

Joanie and I board the plane to Vegas together and spend the flight sharing stories of love. How her love of God led her to the Catholic sisterhood, which led her to find love with her partner Carol, while in the congregation. How my mom's unconditional love, even as a devout Catholic, never wavered, even when I came out. And how that love allowed me to open my heart and find my husband, Glenn.

Joanie's story is amazing, and as we near our descent, she lets me know that she's going to publish it in a book called *Nun Better: an Amazing Love Story*. She shows me a mockup of the cover.

When we arrive in Vegas, we share goodbye hugs, take a few selfies to commemorate our new friendship, exchange numbers, and part ways.

Joanie and Carol's love story is now a best seller, and as we come to the final chapter of her second book, I can say that I am blessed to have not only met her, but had the privilege to be part of her new journey ahead.

Joy takes flight when you open your heart. It lifts you and those around you.

Thank you, Joanie, for reminding me that we are all put on this earth to share joy with each other.

Jeffrey Church is CEO & President of Visit Berkeley. He lives in Berkeley, California, with his husband of 11 years, Glenn Ramit. Everyone is a little Berkeley! Learn more at VisitBerkeley.com.

Chapter 9 – I've Got That Joy Joy Joy!

Tips to Create Your *Joyously Free* Life

Be gentle with yourself. Know that you are evolving and will experience a range of emotions, good and bad. It's OK to feel lost, confused, and scared. The journey *is* the destination because we as human beings are constantly evolving. Change is the only constant in life. This applies to one's age, job/career, seasons, relationships, hair color, and so many factors. Likewise, a person's LGBTQ+ identity can ebb and flow with self-discovery. Throughout this, make self-care a top priority.

Seek role models. These can be people you know or those you watch online. Follow folks on social media who express your gender identity. Glean courage and confidence from them as they boldly declare who they are and provide glimpses into their thoughts, lives, and relationships.

You can also read books by LGBTQ+ authors and follow bloggers who do the same. Their stories will underscore the fact that you're not alone, that there are people out there just like you, and that you can find a safe, affirming community where you're free to be authentically you.

Listen to podcasts. Search online for podcasts about the particular aspect of queer identity that resonates with you and listen away. Podcasts enable you to glean insights from people who are out and talking about it for all to hear. Many LGBTQ+ podcasts focus on specific topics, such as dating, sex, friendships, celebrities, wellness, family issues, and holidays. Find your favorites and fill your ears with this affirmation.

Know that you are enough. Compare-itis is a real problem in our digital world because we're inundated with images that can make us feel lacking in comparison to the picture-perfect people we see online. Counter this by declaring, "I am enough!" Look in the mirror and say it with love and compassion for yourself.

And while you may long for your LGBTQ+ soul mate or partner or spouse, know that another person does not "complete" you or serve as "your other half." You are whole and complete just as you are. Another person can add and multiply value in your life and enhance the beautiful wholeness that you already are in mind, body, and soul.

Take care of yourself. We feel best when we honor our bodies with healthy food, exercise, sufficient sleep, hydration, and relaxation techniques. All of the above are excellent elixirs that can help ease the intense emotions of your LGBTQ+ journey. You are what you eat, and research shows that a junk food diet—especially when combined with a sedentary lifestyle and stress—has a detrimental effect on our mental health.

If you engage in excessive smoking or drinking, and want to make a change, consider fun activities that you can do instead, such as roller skating, joining a club, or creating a blog, a YouTube channel, or a Pinterest board that shares your LGBTQ+ journey or another topic.

A healthy lifestyle cultivates the best brain chemistry and physical stamina for processing emotions, making good decisions, and creating a life you love.

Chapter 9 – I've Got That Joy Joy Joy!

We want you to step into every moment of your life exclaiming, "I've got that JOY, JOY, JOY! Because I'm *Joyously Free!*"

Chapter 10
Have Fun!

Rituals That Help You Live *Joyously Free*

Celebrating Yourself with Daily Rituals

By Elizabeth

What simple things can you do every day to celebrate that you are *Joyously Free*?

What can you do daily to lavish yourself with love and approval?

Here's your chance to create some new routines that are fun, relaxing, and affirming.

These rituals—which are actions that you repeat in a ceremonial way—can be anything that makes YOU feel great, whether they directly relate to being LGBTQ+ or not. These activities help you feel happy, peaceful, courageous, and confident. They're all about self-care and self-love. And you can do them in private or with a partner and friends, or even in public.

One ritual could be to start every morning by blasting a song that celebrates who you are, like "Born This Way" by Lady Gaga or "I Kissed a Girl" by Katy Perry or "Y.M.C.A." by The Village People or one of the long list of other awesome songs.

You could even make up your own "happy dance" that you do in the mirror, twirl, smile, and blow a kiss to yourself, knowing that you'll make this the best day possible.

Joyously Free

As a parent, relative, ally or advocate, you can create rituals that empower your role as someone who loves and supports LGBTQ+ youth and adults.

Your rituals can be super simple and happen in a split-second. For example, every time I walk past my dresser, I glimpse a pair of beautiful rainbow earrings hanging from my jewelry tree. The earrings were hand-made in Guatemala with bright-colored beads that hang about five inches long. I purchased the earrings at a festival with beloved friends.

This ritual, which happens in a blink, is powerful because it symbolically affirms me as *Joyously Free*. The beautiful colors make me happy and excited to wear these big, bold earrings at Motor City Pride 2024 and elsewhere while autographing this book. And I feel proud to display the message that rainbows convey to any- and everyone who sees me as an LGBTQ+ ally.

Your rituals are all about nourishing and empowering yourself in every way. Here are some examples for you to custom-design your own daily actions to celebrate your identity and your life.

Coffee & Journaling. Every morning when I wake up, I look forward to my coffee. It's been waiting for me all night; before bedtime, I grind the beans, put the black powder in my French Press, add boiling spring water, and let the java brew overnight.

Then in the morning, I heat one cup and prepare a pretty saucer with a napkin under the matching cup, which I fill while inhaling the aromatic brew.

I carry it to my desk, where I add organic half and half, loving the swirls of cream that transform the black liquid to a butterscotch hue. I delight in the sight and smell of the creamy, steamy cup so much that I use a spoon—a big, golden spoon!—to savor the first tastes as if it's soup.

Meanwhile, I journal on my laptop. I write the time, the date, and how I slept, then I express gratitude for all that is good in

Chapter 10 – Have Fun!

my life. I write what's on my mind and heart—personally and professionally, the outcomes I want for the day, and how I'm striving to manifest my most grandiose dreams into reality.

If I'm facing any difficulties or challenges, I write, "Thank you God that (insert issue) is resolved in ways that are bigger and better than I could ever imagine."

I also write: "I trust the divine orchestration of my life to maximize my power to (insert goal)."

All while savoring my coffee, often picking up the warm cup and loving the feeling of the hot ceramic under all eight of my fingers and two thumbs as I hold the cup close to my nose to inhale the java scent. Then I slowly sip it, enjoying the feeling of the hot liquid in my mouth, down my throat, and in my empty stomach.

After savoring the very last drop, I don't want another cup. I am happy and satisfied and know that this morning caffeine is my limit.

So, what does this have to do with living *Joyously Free?*

Everything. This ritual revs me up to do whatever I damn well please that day, however I want to do it.

My coffee and journaling rituals are a celebration of being free to be **me** and live in ways that keep me peaceful and happy. I *loooooove* doing this on my own time, exactly as I want. It's nobody else's decision how I make the coffee, how strong or weak it is, what kind of cream to use, or how I consume it in total peace and solitude. This small freedom sets the stage for independence in everything that I do.

My coffee ritual is a small symbol for the big picture of my life. It declares: this is what I want, how I want it—regarding my coffee, and the way I live and love.

Do you see how one simple ritual can help you flex your power in other areas of your life? The more you flex your Me Muscles, the stronger you get in living on your unique terms.

Yes, I've enjoyed magic moments over morning coffee with a lover, or when they serve coffee to me in their home or on vacation. That's all delightful.

But the rest of the time, this ritual of self-care and self-love sets the stage for a day and a life that I script, orchestrate, and enjoy to reflect what Elizabeth wants to experience.

All while the caffeine jolt and confidence nourish my soul to spend the morning in my genius zone, writing with clarity, focus, and stamina. That is bliss!

This epitomizes GoddessLife that you can learn how to cultivate in my next book, *The Biss Tribe: Activating Your Goddess Power*, available at TwoSistersWriting.com.

How does this self-love coffee ritual have anything to do with gender identity and sexual orientation? When I do me, my way, and maximize my happiness on every level, this activates my power, self-esteem, self-worth, and belief in myself to be and do any- and everything I desire in every other aspect of life, including how and with whom I enjoy love, romance, passion, and pleasure.

So, what can **you** do every day to create and cultivate a ritual that affirms who you are and what you love? It could be anything, such as: taking a morning jog, doing yoga, lighting a candle, listening to an affirming song, or covering yourself with your favorite scented bubbling body soap in the shower. Write some ideas here:

_____

_____

_____

_____

_____

Chapter 10 – Have Fun!

Make Mealtime a Celebration.

Eating alone? Nourish yourself in grand style!

Your body is the beautiful vessel that enables you to experience this life. Treat it with love by filling it with your favorite foods in a spirit of joy.

Set a pretty table for yourself. Don't answer phone calls, texts, or emails. Block all distractions. As you eat, savor the sight, taste, and texture of every bite. Inhale the aromas and enjoy that moment. Admire the delicious foods arranged on your plate. Feel happy that it's the perfect temperature, cooked to your preferences (well done, raw, mushy, firm, you decide!) Season it as much as you love. Douse it with olive oil, hot sauce, or your condiment of choice, with no prying eyes or opinionated voices around to question or criticize how you enjoy your meal.

Feel gratitude for the blessing and bounty of having and enjoying your favorite foods, prepared your way. Express your gratitude out loud. Do not rush. Savor the sensory extravaganza of every bite.

You can enhance this experience even more with "tantric eating." Tantric simply means the merging of spiritual and physical, so when you add a spiritual dimension to eating, you enhance the pleasure of taste and texture while literally nourishing your soul.

Exercise & Eat Healthy

Big changes can be stressful, even if they're positive. You are what you eat, your mind is the machine powering your life, and your body is the vessel that enables you to live this great adventure.

We can power our journeys by optimizing the chemical balances in our minds and maximizing the strength and stamina of our bodies. Studies show that junk food is detrimental to brain chemistry and therefore a person's mental health, making someone more prone to anxiety, depression, and mood swings.

I'm here to testify that back when I was caught in the hell of sugar addiction, I was moody, depressed, anxious, and miserable with self-loathing. The slightest thing could trigger a tearfest.

Sugar is toxic, so except for very infrequent indulgences of flourless chocolate cake on my birthday and Christmas, I eat a very low-carb, plant-based diet with lots of healthy protein. When tempted with cravings for chocolate or sweets, I'm stopped by the memory of how bad I used to feel, and how great I feel now—better than ever!—and that removes the temptation.

Likewise, my desire to maintain a fit body that gives me mental and physical stamina to write books, host my podcast, be a motivational speaker, and run our publishing company, is powerful inspiration to make daily exercise a non-negotiable priority.

So, very importantly, as you embark on your *Joyously Free* journey, you want to be your absolute best as you venture out to socialize and celebrate in your LGBTQ+ community. How exciting to feel your most phenomenal at PRIDE festivities, festivals, and other events!

This isn't about being skinny or super fit or fitting into society's impossible standards of beauty. Regardless of your size or shape, a healthy lifestyle will feed your body positivity and confidence, knowing that you're being your best and presenting your best YOU to the world.

Your health is your wealth, so let's all be as rich as possible and share our joyous, creative treasures with each other!

Make Pleasure a Top Priority

Did you know that physical pleasure has many benefits beyond just feeling good? Having an orgasm floods the human body with feel-good hormones, including dopamine and

Chapter 10 – Have Fun!

endorphins, which can ease pain, relieve stress, help you sleep better, and boost your mood.[25]

Orgasms also strengthen your immune system, make your skin glow and hair grow, and strengthen your pelvic floor.[26]

And when you orgasm with a partner, the intense pleasure and hormone surges help you bond.

Enjoying physical pleasures—whether solo or with consenting adults—is a beautiful gift that enhances your well-being and adds extra sparkle to being *Joyously Free*.

Manifest with a *Joyously Free* Vision Board

A vision board is a collage of pictures and words that showcase dreams that you want to make real.

So how does a vision board work? You put it where you will see it frequently throughout the day, and if you have a digital one, you can display it as the wallpaper on your phone or the screensaver on your computer or tablet.

Make it a daily ritual to look at each image on your vision board, read the words, and imagine that everything on the board is already real.

This keeps the dream alive and active in your conscious thoughts, which activates something in the universe to bring your dreams to life in magical and miraculous ways.

If you are the parent or relative of an LGBTQ+ youth, you can create vision boards together to showcase the best outcomes for your young person to thrive. As an ally or advocate, you can also make a vision board that displays the change you're working to make happen.

So how do you make a vision board? Find photos on the Internet, in magazines, and even from your personal collection on your phone . . . and create a colorful mosaic on your vision board to represent everything that you want.

You can glue the images and words onto a posterboard, or you can create a digital vision board with images from the Internet, using a free graphic design website such as Canva.com. You can also use colorful pens, crayons, or even paint and stickers to decorate your vision board with your name, rainbows, your favorite flag(s), your picture, and anything else you like.

To begin, head back to what you wrote in Chapter 1 about your vision for your *Joyously Free* self, life, and work/career. Then gather images and words that illustrate what you want. A vision board puts your ideas into pictures, which is a powerful step toward manifesting your dreams.

If you want to attract and marry your life partner, paste a photo of a happy LGBTQ+ couple in wedding attire, celebrating amongst friends and family in a locale that resonates with you, such as a beach or mountaintop or the backyard of your dream home.

If you want to become an activist, include photos of yourself and/or others at parades, pickets, and even congressional hearings. If you want to unite and heal fractured friendships and family relationships, include photos of you with those individuals during happier times. Write or paste cut-out words that give you hope, such as love, peace, harmony, forgiveness, freedom, acceptance, celebration, and gratitude.

Create a Joyously Free "Altar"

Imagine how affirming it could be to designate a spot where you display your vision board along with anything else that boosts your Pride.

You could create a sacred space on a table, dresser top, fireplace mantle, cabinet top, corner (preferably not a *closet*), yard/patio/garden area—you name it!—where you can display photos, your vision board, candles, mementos, crystals, flag(s), rainbows, your ID badge from Pride festivals or events like The

Chapter 10 – Have Fun!

Dinah, your summer dream home on Fire Island, the building you want to buy as your town's first gay bar or house for homeless trans teens where you provide mental health and medical services, an LGBTQ+ community center, or whatever your soul is calling you to do as a *Joyously Free* person who wants to guide others into a safe, healthy, affirming life.

Create a Peace Place in Your Home

Similar to an altar, your Peace Place can be the special spot where you go to detox, decompress, release, and heal from the stress of the day, especially anything pertaining to anxiety or pain around being LGBTQ+. You can decorate and furnish a corner, a room, a bench in a garden, a balcony, your bathroom, a treehouse, or even your whole house!

Joanie has a prayer corner and a rose garden. My peace places include the soft, animal-print rug in my living room where I love to pray, do yoga, and meditate surrounded by my green vine plants whose leaves appear to dance around me.

Create a ritual where you go to your Peace Place to cleanse your mind, body, and spirit of any angst and anxiety. Meditate. Say prayers. Journal. Take a bubble bath. Recite mantras.

Curate this experience for what soothes your soul. If you love pink, make it pink! If you love black, make it black! Plants and flowers can also help you feel happy. If you love soft fabrics, fill your Peace Place with fuzzy pillows, plush blankets, feather boas, velvet . . . even drape colorful sheer fabrics from the ceiling for an exotic feel or womb-like space.

Train Your Brain with Affirmations.

Train your inner voice to be gentle, kind, and loving. Program it to affirm that you are perfect and whole just as you are. Use affirmations that you think, say aloud, and write, such as, "I deserve to live and love *Joyously Free* as the best ME with my BEST LIFE, all day, every day!"

As a parent, relative, ally, or advocate, you can create and use mantras that help you with a specific situation. Examples:

"Every day I'm helping my child with love, support, patience, and grace."

"I love (person's name) unconditionally and will do everything in my power to help them."

"As an ally/advocate, I know I am making a difference in changing and even saving lives."

Please create your own affirmations. Think and recite them often. They force your brain to shift out of worry and anxiety and into the action of speaking, which your ears hear, and your mind receives. This helps retrain your brain to focus on all that's best for you.

Begin New Traditions with Your "Found Family"

Holidays, birthdays, weddings, and funerals can be a very lonely time for LGBTQ+ people whose families no longer include them in gatherings.

This is a time to create your "found family"—the people you meet along your LGBTQ+ journey who love you as you are. Brainstorm ways that you as a group can create new traditions for holiday meals, such as a potluck feast that rotates at each other's homes every year.

Come up with special nicknames and mottos. Write a toast that you give each other at weddings. And for funerals, perhaps you can all sing a song or have a tribute for the person who passed.

Have fun and give the kind of love that you want to receive, and you will.

If you're a relative, ally, or advocate, ask how you can participate and/or support "found family" celebrations for an LGBTQ+ person.

Chapter 10 – Have Fun!

Joanie's Rituals:
The Beach, the Garden, and the Community

Daily rituals fill me with peace and happiness, and they help me cope with grief, hate, and conflict. Perhaps they can inspire you to create your own rituals that make your soul sing.

Enjoy Mother Nature on the beach. I love taking daily walks on the beach along the Pacific Coast in Southern Oregon where I live. Every sensation is delightful, including the sunshine on my shoulders, and the winds grazing my purple shirt. I take long, strong strides, raising my walking stick up then down as if directing a university marching band while singing aloud. I savor the moments of hearing crashing waves, tasting salty air sprays, and feeling that my life is totally worth living. I enjoy child-like fun, feeling honest to the core with zero regrets.

This ritual for self-care and solitude is all about being *Joyously Free* from the inside OUT.

Enjoy Mother Nature in the garden. When you marvel at Mother Nature's majesty, you'll feel happy and forget whatever else might be on your mind. Stay in the moment and treat yourself to a mental reprieve.

You can do this by focusing on the details of nature. Have you ever looked closely at how delicate and precious a flower petal is? Take time to focus on a flower's magnificent color. Touch its textures. Smell it. These simple joys can boost your mood.

I do this daily in the memorial garden outside the home where I shared a lifetime of love with Carol before she went to heaven in 2022. Friends donated 55 rose bushes along with their time to create this floral paradise where I sit on a bench and enjoy total peace while reflecting on life's blessings.

During the summer months, I give away robust bouquets of roses that adorn neighbors' living rooms, church altars, business offices, teleconference Zooms, and residential care facilities. This ritual enables me to put smiles on people's faces.

Cultivate Community. Carol and I loved our ritual of spontaneously inviting friends over to feast and play cards. We were happy to clean and decorate the house, shop for food, and prepare scrumptious meals. As our LGBTQ+ and straight friends and family gathered, we talked about everything but labels, sexual identity, or orientation. Instead, we lit people up with yummy homemade desserts **first**, followed by fresh green salads, and meat or seafood that was perfectly cooked and seasoned with spices and herbs. We served them as kings and queens, and our happy attitudes shined brighter than the full moon. Such grand times!

We hosted two annual events: our Easter/Springtime picnic and parade, and the Christmas/Winter Solstice bash.

At our winter gatherings, Carol made veggie and hamburger soups with fresh-baked bread. Laughter, joy, and hugs warmed hearts as neighbors who barely knew each other sparkled brighter than our Christmas tree lights. This was a festive scene that was more straight than queer and no one cared, for it was a "whatever you are" occasion.

The ritual of cultivating community in our home provided a safe space for people to relax and enjoy life. How can you bring people together to celebrate being *Joyously Free?*

We wish you
the courage to live
Joyously Free!!

About the Authors + Contact Info

Elizabeth Ann Atkins

*E*lizabeth's life mission is to cultivate human harmony through the written and spoken word, and through daily interactions with people.

This mission was born when she was one day old and her father baptized her in the hospital room, asking God to make her a "Princess of Peace." As a one-year-old, she helped unite a divided family, opening the door for loving unity for generations.

Elizabeth's desire to create a happier world springs from a trailblazing union of colorblind love and courage, thanks to her mother, an African American and Italian role model, and her father, a former Roman Catholic priest who was English, French, and Cherokee.

To amplify messages of peace and inclusion, Elizabeth and her sister, Catherine Greenspan, co-founded Two Sisters Writing & Publishing® in 2016, publishing their own fiction and non-fiction books that celebrate colorblind love and empowered self-identity.

They have since published nearly 50 books, mostly against-the-odds success stories by diverse authors from across America. Learn more at TwoSistersWriting.com.

Elizabeth's education laid the foundation for her career as an author, journalist, speaker, and publisher. She earned a Bachelor of Arts degree as an English Literature major at the University of Michigan, where she began her journalism career as a reporter and editor at the campus newspaper, *The Michigan Daily*.

Then she earned a Master of Science degree from the Columbia University Graduate School of Journalism in New York City, where she focused on broadcast news and international reporting. During that time, she had a part-time job as a copy clerk at *The New York Times,* which published a portion of her master's thesis about mixed-race people.

Elizabeth is an inspirational speaker.

On diversity, she rouses ovations by performing her autobiographical poem, "White Chocolate," then invites audiences to explore their perceptions about race and identity. They walk away with a new understanding to never judge a book by its cover.

Elizabeth has spoken at Columbia University, the University of Michigan, GM's World Diversity Day, Gannett, Beaumont Health, 100 Black Men, the NAACP, national conferences, and many other venues.

As a wellness speaker, Elizabeth shares her long struggle with food and fat, and the depression and suicidal ideation that it triggered, and how she triumphed over that with faith and fitness. She talks about how she lost 100 pounds after childbirth (without drugs or surgery) and celebrated her transformation on *The Oprah Winfrey Show.*

Now a certified fitness trainer through ISSA, Elizabeth coaches others on how to achieve a mindset shift as the first step to transforming one's body and life. Learn more on the Wellness page at TheGoddessPowerShow.com.

Deeply spiritual, Elizabeth shares her experiences, perspectives, and tools for high vibe living in her best-selling memoir, *God's Answer Is Know: Lessons From a Spiritual Life.* She shares how meditation has helped her heal and awaken her most authentic self and serve as a spiritual teacher for others.

As an Intuitive Practitioner certified by Lori Lipten's Sacred Balance Academy in Bloomfield Hills, Michigan, Elizabeth teaches meditation and energy clearing.

Her next book, *The Biss Tribe: Activating Your Goddess Power,* aims to empower people with the tools that Elizabeth uses every day to look and feel her best, connect with Spirit, manifest blessings, and achieve a creative flow state in her creative genius zone.

Elizabeth's Goddess mission was born during terrible moments of verbal abuse after her divorce. Spirit infused her with the peace and power of God energy to cultivate strength to persevere through difficulties.

She created and hosts The Goddess Power Show with Elizabeth Ann Atkins®. The podcast aims to explore sometimes taboo topics that help people live bigger, better, and bolder and manifest their wildest desires. You can watch interviews on the YouTube channel for The Goddess Power Show with Elizabeth Ann Atkins®. And you can listen to episodes on Apple Podcasts, Spotify, iHeart radio, and wherever you listen to podcasts. TheGoddessPowerShow.com provides links to all of the above.

Elizabeth also co-hosts an Emmy-nominated TV show about mental health.

She has written and published nearly 50 books—fiction and nonfiction, published by major New York publishing houses as well as by Two Sisters Writing & Publishing®. Her bestselling books include *White Chocolate*, *Dark Secret*, and *Twilight* with Billy Dee Williams. Her memoir is *God's Answer Is Know: Lessons From a Spiritual Life*. She writes erotic fiction under the pen name, Sasha Maxwell, and her novels include *Husbands, Incorporated*, *Eleven Men*, and *Eleven Women*.

As America's Book Coach, Elizabeth guides aspiring writers along the sometimes-treacherous terrain of writing, publishing, and promoting a book. Learn more about her "6 Months to Best Selling Book Success" group coaching program at TwoSistersWriting.com.

Elizabeth has taught writing at Wayne State University, Oakland University, Wayne County Community College District, and at national conferences.

As an actress, she plays a major role in the feature-length film, *Anything Is Possible*, nominated for "Best Foreign Film" by the Nollywood and African Film Critics Association.

And she plays a 1950s journalist in the international shipwreck drama, *The Andrea Doria: Are The Passengers Saved?* The award-winning film is in Italian with English subtitles.

Elizabeth composed an original screenplay, *Redemption*, a gritty drama about a Detroit gangster and a writer.

Elizabeth has been a guest on *Oprah, Montel, NPR, Good Morning America Sunday, The CBS Evening News, Black Entertainment Television (BET), The NBC Nightly News, The Today Show,* and many national and local TV programs.

Her work has been published in *The New York Times, The San Diego Tribune, Essence, Ebony, HOUR Detroit, BLAC Detroit,* and many publications. Her *Detroit News* articles on race were nominated for the Pulitzer Prize, and she wrote a biography for the Presidential Medal of Freedom tribute for Rosa Parks.

Elizabeth runs, cycles, lifts weights, does yoga, journals, travels, reveres nature, and meditates to cultivate a joyous and peaceful mind, body and spirit.

You can contact Elizabeth at TwoSistersWriting.com.

Please subscribe to the YouTube channels for Two Sisters Writing & Publishing® and The Goddess Power Show with Elizabeth Ann Atkins®. You can also follow her on Instagram @elizabethannatkins.

About the Authors

Joanie Lindenmeyer

Joanie Lindenmeyer is 66 years young, a former Sister of St. Joseph of Carondelet Catholic nun who is now an Episcopalian with St. Timothy's.

Joanie serves on the church vestry and in the local community in many ways that include speaking about and promoting LGBTQ+ inclusion.

She was a public high school physical education and health teacher and sports coach for 25 years. Prior to that, she taught religion and youth ministry for four years in Catholic schools.

Joanie enjoys playing pickleball, watching sports, traveling, fishing, gardening, playing guitar, listening to music, walking and hiking, baking treats, and hanging out with family and friends.

She has worked at two nonprofits and a county department of health in areas of community health, addictions, teen pregnancy, sexuality, child abuse prevention, HIV/AIDS prevention, STI testing and counseling, and wellness.

A San Diego State University graduate, she was a member of the university volleyball team and has a California teaching credential.

Her dedication shines for people of all ages, making their lives brighter, happier, and healthier.

For 40 years, she was committed to her one and only lifetime lover and spouse, Carol Tierheimer. In 2022, she became widowed and is embarking on new adventures as a single LGBTQ+ woman.

In March of 2023, she wrote a best-selling memoir, *Nun Better: An AMAZING Love Story* by Joanie Lindenmeyer with Carol Tierheimer.

You can find her book trailer, events calendar, and links to the weekly podcast that she does with Elizabeth Ann Atkins on the Two Sisters Writing & Publishing® YouTube channel at

Joyously Free

TwoSistersWriting.com. There you can order *Nun Better* and *Joyously Free;* the books are also available wherever books are sold online.

Joanie's next book, *Healing Religious Hurts: Stories & Tips to Find Love & Peace,* co-authored with Elizabeth Ann Atkins, is available for pre-order at TwoSistersWriting.com and will be published in October 2024.

Joanie is extremely grateful for her dear friends and family and the opportunities to meet new friends. Her mantra is, "Every day is a new day, never been lived before."

She has lived in Brookings, Oregon, for 33 years. Carol's memorial rose garden awaits you to come take a seat and enjoy the tremendous peace and beauty of this colorful, fragrant sanctuary.

Filled with joy and hope, Joanie believes that Jesus is her best friend and that "Love always wins!"

You can contact Joanie on Facebook @JoanieLindenmeyer.

And she invites you to follow her on TikTok @JoanieLindenmeyer.

Check out her author page at TwoSistersWriting.com to learn when and where Joanie will be speaking and doing book signings across America. She'd love to meet you in person!

LGBTQ+ Resources

Congratulations, readers, for wanting resources that can support and encourage you. The best resources are people: family, friends, faith community members, colleagues, LGBTQ+ individuals and couples, Allies, and Advocates.

Next, the Internet is a treasure trove of information, as are organizations that you can find online and connect with in-person chapters and events.

Pride events are great places to learn as you explore booths, discover new resources, and meet people from organizations, all in an environment that affirms and supports LGBTQ+ people, Parents, Allies, and Advocates.

On the next page are reputable websites, books, and movies to empower your journey to become *Joyously Free*.

QSpirit	LGBTQIA2S+ Christian resources	https://qspirit.net/
GLAAD	GLAAD tackles tough issues to shape the narrative and provoke dialogue that leads to cultural change.	www.GLAAD.org
PFLAG	Resources for Parents & Families of Lesbian and Gay	www.PFLAG.org
Human Rights Campaign	HRC supports LGBTQ equality through legal action, political awareness, and advocacy for business and employment inclusion.	www.hrc.org
988 Suicide Hotline	988 Lifeline provides 24/7, free and confidential support for people in distress, prevention and crisis resources and best practices for professionals in the United States.	By phone: 988 https://988lifeline.org/
Genders and Sexuality Alliance Network	GSA is a middle and high school-based club that are student-run organizations that unite LGBTQ+ and allied youth to build community and organize around issues impacting them in their schools and communities.	www.gsanetwork.org
Lambda Legal	Legal help for LGBTQ+ people and those living with HIV. They defend and expand protections for transgender and non-binary people.	www.LambdaLegal.org
The Trevor Project	The Trevor Project is the leading suicide prevention, crisis intervention, and resources for LGBTQ young people.	www.trevorproject.org
SOGIE Center	The National Center for Youth with Diverse Sexual Orientation, Gender Identity & Expression (The National SOGIE Center) provides trainings, resources, and information.	www.SOGIECenter.org

Endnotes

[1] "Let's Get It Right: Using Correct Pronouns and Names," Anti-Defamation League, accessed April 15, 2024, https://www.adl.org/resources/tools-and-strategies/lets-get-it-right-using-correct-pronouns-and-names?gad_source=1&gclid=CjwKCAjwwr6wBhBcEiwAfMEQsORUZcUwqIO45WExpRwLVAOfMZGXsDcfv5-x_LezRHCTW3YQ_VWJJBoCxZkQAvD_BwE&gclsrc=aw.ds.

[2] "I Am Jazz' Star Jazz Jennings Gets Candid About Her Journey," The New York Times, accessed April 15, 2024, https://www.nytimes.com/2020/01/30/arts/television/i-am-jazz-jennings.html#:~:text=Finally%20undergoing%20bottom%20surgery%20has,I%20felt%20on%20the%20inside.

[3] GLAAD, "About," accessed April 15, 2024, https://glaad.org/about/

[4] "Suicidality Among Transgender Youth: Elucidating the Role of Interpersonal Risk Factors," by Austin, Craig, D'Souza, McInroy, National Library of Medicine, April 2020, accessed April 15, 2024, https://pubmed.ncbi.nlm.nih.gov/32345113/.

[5] "Suicidality Among Transgender Youth: Elucidating the Role of Interpersonal Risk Factors," by Austin, Craig, D'Souza, McInroy, National Library of Medicine, April 2020, accessed April 15, 2024, https://pubmed.ncbi.nlm.nih.gov/32345113/.

[6] "List of U.S. jurisdictions banning conversion therapy," Wikipedia, accessed April 15, 2024, https://en.wikipedia.org/wiki/List_of_U.S._jurisdictions_banning_conversion_therapy

[7] "Legality of conversion therapy," Wikipedia, accessed April 15, 2024, https://en.wikipedia.org/wiki/Legality_of_conversion_therapy

[8] "Conversion therapy," Wikipedia, accessed April 15, 2024, https://en.wikipedia.org/wiki/Conversion_therapy

[9] "Glossary of Terms," Human Rights Campaign, accessed April 15, 2024, https://www.hrc.org/resources/glossary-of-terms?utm_source=ads_ms_HRC_20240306-HRC-AW-GS-Natl-GlossaryRP_GlossaryKeywords_a001-dynamic-rst_b:all%20lgbt%20terms&gad_source=1&gclid=CjwKCAjwnv-vBhBdEiwABCYQA3gVAePqgQJWEtZlS68z7wfPBRS6etUhjvLUNzYN_7zurzRlEC_eQhoCJL0QAvD_BwE

[10] Google dictionary, "advocate," accessed April 15, 2024, https://www.google.com/search?q=advocate+definition&oq=advoca&gs_lcrp=EgZjaHJvbWUqDggAEEUYJxg7GIAEGIoFMg4IABBFGCcYOxiABBiKBTIQCAEQLhjHARixAxjRAxiABDIGCAIQRRg5MgwIAxAAGEMYgAQYigUyDQgEEAAYkgMYgAQYigUyBggFEEUYPDIGCAYQRRg8MgYIBxBFGDyoAgCwAgA&sourceid=chrome&ie=UTF-8

[11] "LGBTQ Heritage Theme Study," National Park Service, accessed April 15, 2024, https://www.nps.gov/subjects/tellingallamericansstories/lgbtqthemestudy.htm

[12] "Glossary of Terms: LGBTQ," GLAAD, accessed April 15, 2024, https://glaad.org/reference/terms

[13] GLAAD, "About," accessed April 15, 2024, https://glaad.org/about/

[14] GLAAD, "About," accessed April 15, 2024, https://glaad.org/about/

[15] "Free Mom Hugs, About Us," accessed April 15, 2024, https://freemomhugs.

org/index.cfm?fuseaction=page.viewpage&pageid=545

16 Google dictionary, "system," accessed April 15, 2024, https://www.google.com/search?q=system+definition&oq=system+definit&gs_lcrp=EgZjaH-JvbWUqCggAEAAYsQMYgAQyCggAEAAYsQMYgAQyBwgBEAAYgAQyBgg-CEEUYOTIHCAMQABiABDIHCAQQABiABDIHCAUQABiABDIHCAYQABiAB-DIHCAcQABiABDIHCAgQABiABDIHCAkQABiABKgCALACAA&sourceid=-chrome&ie=UTF-8

17 "LGBT demographics of the United States," Wikipedia, accessed April 15, 2024, https://en.wikipedia.org/wiki/LGBT_demographics_of_the_United_States#:~:text=Studies%20from%20several%20nations%2C%20including,adult%20population%20identifying%20as%20LGBT.

18 "We are here: LGBTQ+ adult population in United States reaches at least 20 million, according to human rights campaign foundation report," Human Rights Campaign, accessed April 15, 2024, https://www.hrc.org/press-releases/we-are-here-lgbtq-adult-population-in-united-states-reaches-at-least-20-million-according-to-human-rights-campaign-foundation-report

19 "Niecy Nash and Jessica Betts open up about their surprise wedding/GMA," accessed April 15, 2024, https://youtu.be/B4lKbF_b6KA?si=Of6-Xds-BqSw6Cyh4

20 "Inside Robin Roberts and Amber Laign's wedding day/GMA," accessed April 15, 2024, https://youtu.be/b6QFrR16CZc?si=i_wCSS8RlIaDwnbQ

21 "The best and worst states for LGBTQ+ equality," OutLeadership.com, accessed April 15, 2024, https://outleadership.com/news/the-best-and-worst-states-for-lgbtq-equality/

22 "Here are the 15 most LGBTQ-friendly cities in the U.S.," The Advocate, accessed April 15, 2024, https://www.advocate.com/news/gay-friendly-cities-2023#rebelltitem7

23 "Ted Haggard," Wikipedia, accessed April 15, 2024, https://en.wikipedia.org/wiki/Ted_Haggard#:~:text=On%20January%2023%2C%202009%2C%20less,-consensual%20sexual%20relationship%20%5Bthat%5D%20went

24 "Ted Haggard, mega-church founder felled by sex scandal, returns to pulpit," The Guardian, June 6, 2010, accessed April 15, 2024, https://www.theguardian.com/world/2010/jun/06/us-gay-scandal-pastor-church

25 "7 Benefits of Orgasm," Health.com, accessed April 15, 2024, https://www.health.com/sex/benefits-of-orgasm

26 "13 Benefits of Orgasms," Glamour, accessed April 15, 2024, https://www.glamour.com/story/6-super-surprising-health-bene

Printed in the USA
CPSIA information can be obtained
at www.ICGtesting.com
LVHW021400110724
785127LV00001B/18